Queer Thriving in Catholic Education

Sean Whittle · Seán Henry
Editors

Queer Thriving in Catholic Education

Going Beyond the Pastoral Paradigm for LGBTQ+ Inclusion

Editors
Sean Whittle
St Mary's University Twickenham London
Twickenham, UK

Seán Henry
Edge Hill University
Ormskirk, UK

ISBN 978-981-97-0322-7   ISBN 978-981-97-0323-4 (eBook)
https://doi.org/10.1007/978-981-97-0323-4

© The Editor(s) (if applicable) and The Author(s), under exclusive license to Springer Nature Singapore Pte Ltd. 2024

This work is subject to copyright. All rights are solely and exclusively licensed by the Publisher, whether the whole or part of the material is concerned, specifically the rights of translation, reprinting, reuse of illustrations, recitation, broadcasting, reproduction on microfilms or in any other physical way, and transmission or information storage and retrieval, electronic adaptation, computer software, or by similar or dissimilar methodology now known or hereafter developed.
The use of general descriptive names, registered names, trademarks, service marks, etc. in this publication does not imply, even in the absence of a specific statement, that such names are exempt from the relevant protective laws and regulations and therefore free for general use.
The publisher, the authors and the editors are safe to assume that the advice and information in this book are believed to be true and accurate at the date of publication. Neither the publisher nor the authors or the editors give a warranty, expressed or implied, with respect to the material contained herein or for any errors or omissions that may have been made. The publisher remains neutral with regard to jurisdictional claims in published maps and institutional affiliations.

This Springer imprint is published by the registered company Springer Nature Singapore Pte Ltd.
The registered company address is: 152 Beach Road, #21-01/04 Gateway East, Singapore 189721, Singapore

Paper in this product is recyclable.

Preface

It is a real pleasure to be able to present this edited collection of chapters that explores LGBTQ+ inclusion in Catholic education. This volume is the enduring legacy of a conference on Catholic education and LGBTQ+ inclusion held at the *Mater Dei Centre for Catholic Education* at Dublin City University, in February 2022. This conference was the first ever to be exclusively devoted to exploring the relationship between Catholic education and LGBTQ+ issues. As the conference organizers Sean Whittle and Seán Henry are extremely grateful to the Director, Dr. Cora O'Farrell, who provided so much to make the conference such a success.

The conference was marked by a spirit of genuine dialogue and real pleasure that at long last some serious academic attention is being given to the relationship between Catholic education and LGBTQ+ inclusion. In order to keep the spirit of this first conference burning it became obvious that we should draw many of the papers together and develop them into a collection of edited chapters.

This edited volume is an enduring legacy of the NfRCE, which sponsored the conference at DCU. It embodies high-quality studies and research about Catholic education in relation to LGBTQ+ inclusion. In addition, this volume demonstrates what has become one of the key principles of the NfRCE. This is our ability to bring established researchers into dialogue with the emerging academics and researchers cultivating the field of Catholic education studies.

This volume is no exception. We would like to thank all of the contributors to this volume for their dedicated work in converting their very good conference papers into high-quality chapters for this volume. They made the task of editing this volume a pleasurable and straightforward process.

We would also like to convey my thanks to Grace Liyan Ma and the rest of the team at Springer for all the practical help and support with ensuring this volume is published.

As joint editors, it has been a pleasure to work with each other in bringing this volume to fruition. In addition to thanking each other, there a few personal words of thanks we need to declare.

Sean Whittle: As always my deepest thanks are reserved for my wife, Bernie Whittle. Her constant love and unwavering support have allowed me to find the time to bring this volume to completion. It is only through having Bernie's constant love and support that I have been able to bring this volume and my work for the NfRCE to fruition. Thank you so much for this and for all you do for me.

Seán Henry: I would like to thank Sean Whittle, who first invited me to co-chair the conference that has led to this volume. A special word of thanks goes to my brother, Kenneth, who has always encouraged me to be brave in my scholarship, and to Joseph Rynhart, whose love and support means so much. Thanks also to Sharon Todd, Tom Walsh, Angela Rickard, Audrey Doyle, Sinéad Matson, and Juliette Bertoldo, all of whom have been allies to my work from its early beginnings.

Twickenham, UK
Ormskirk, UK

Sean Whittle
Seán Henry

Praise for *Queer Thriving in Catholic Education*

"This is an important and timely book which needs to be read by all interested in a Catholic vision of education. Whittle and Henry are to be congratulated for opening up a space for a challenging conversation which they do in a manner that is thoughtful, generous, and deeply respectful of the diverse positions and contexts people come from.

The book hinges around Seán Henry's scholarly introduction to the concept of queering Catholic education. This will be new for many readers but Henry guides us through this in a nuanced and invitational way. Though on the edges of Catholic discourse, the queering of theology and education offers a rich source for a vocabulary sensitive to the values of inclusion.

The central tenet of the book is its argument that a truly inclusive Catholic education provides a space for LGBTQ+ people to thrive. In the call to move beyond the pastoral paradigm the contributors to this volume affirm that people are not in need of pastoral care on the basis of sexuality or gender.

The dissonances between some of the perspectives are part of the essential feature of the volume. What unites these perspectives, however, is a commitment to challenging the binary set up between LGBTQ+ and Catholic identities. In opening up a conversation about the alienating effect of such binary stances, this book moves the discourse somewhat nearer the possibility of ensuring that Catholic education is genuine in its commitment to genuinely supporting each person to thrive in all their complexity.

I really enjoyed reading this book and value the hospitable space created by Whittle and Henry to reflect on human sexuality and gender identity as integral to human and religious identity. My own understanding has been challenged, deepened, and sometimes upended by the insights I have encountered in this volume."

—Sandra Cullen *is Associate Professor of Religious Education and Head of the School of Human Development at the Institute of Education, Dublin City University*

"This is a book that aims to open up an honest and sincere discussion and dialogue about an authentic form of inclusion for LGBTQ+ children and young people in

Catholic schools. At the beginning of the book, there is a rich synthesis of theological and philosophical ideas about the position of LGBTQ+ children and young people in the Catholic church and in Catholic schools. This synthesis is written by Seán Henry, and he explores some fundamental issues, going beyond the pastoral paradigm for the inclusion of LGBTQ+ children and young people towards queer thriving in Catholic schools. His carefully constructed arguments act as a conceptual direction and stimulus for many of the subsequent chapters. Some prominent themes emerge from the different chapters including some close examinations of the scope of Christian anthropology and scrutiny of the mission of the Catholic school, rooted in the example of Jesus Christ, to include all children and young people such that they can thrive. Many of the chapters focus on Catholic schools or Catholic education in Ireland though many of the key ideas can be applied to Catholic schools in other contexts. For example, a number of the chapters include a discussion of the application of the Relationships and Sexuality Education (RSE) programme in Ireland. In particular, they focus on the content and delivery of the programme. These discussions raise issues that are pertinent for other programmes of RSE in different contexts. Some of the chapters focus on fieldwork and provide some valuable insights from parents, teachers, and pupils. The authors are aware that some readers may find the ideas contained in the book to be very challenging and counter to their personal and/or religious beliefs. This book is characterised by a high level of sensitivity for children and young people who identify as LGBTQ+ but also sensitivity towards Church leaders, parents, and teachers who may find this topic uncomfortable and unsettling. The authors are very careful to avoid claiming any moral high ground. Instead, this is a book that contains very thoughtful and nuanced contributions that seek to prompt the reader (whatever the viewpoint of the reader) into some form of engagement with the prominent themes in a constructive manner. This is an excellent and thought-provoking introduction to the inclusion for LGBTQ+ children and young people in Catholic schools and a book that deserves a wide readership."

—Stephen McKinney *is Professor of Education at the University of Glasgow*

Contents

1 Introduction 1
  Sean Whittle and Seán Henry

2 Laying the Groundwork: Sexualities, Genders,
  and the Catholic Church 9
  Seán Henry

Part I Catholic Schools as Places of Queer Thriving

3 Queer Thriving in Catholic Education: The Role of Queer
  Theologies 21
  Seán Henry

4 A Call to Reimagine Catholic Education and
  Schooling—A Response to Dr. Seán Henry 35
  Cora O'Farrell

5 Encounters with LGBTQ+ Lives in Catholic Schools:
  A Fragile Hermeneutical Space?—A Response to Dr. Seán
  Henry 41
  David Kennedy

6 Towards a Theory of Queer Thriving in Catholic
  Education—A Response to Dr. Seán Henry 49
  Sean Whittle

Part II Research in Relation to Catholic Education and LGBT+ Matters

7 Relationships and Sexuality Education (RSE) in Catholic Post
  Primary Schools in Ireland: LGBT+ *Matters* in a Church
  that is Learning to Love 57
  Vivek da Silva

| 8 | On the Journey to Authentic Inclusion: One School's Experience of Empowering Student Voice to Mobilise Positive Change | 71 |

Gillian Sullivan

| 9 | Relationships and Sexuality Education in Catholic Schools in Northern Ireland | 85 |

Sean Whittle

| 10 | A Transgender Perspective on Concerns About TGNB Young People in Catholic Schools | 99 |

Claire Jenkins

| 11 | What Can the Adult Religious Education and Faith Development Project (AREFD) Tell Us About the Research Agenda in Catholic Education in Relation to LGBTQI+ matters? | 113 |

Bernadette Sweetman

| 12 | Faith-Sensitive RSE and Catholic Schooling: An Educational Goods Approach | 123 |

Ruth Wareham

| 13 | Conclusion: Queer Thriving in Catholic Education: Progressing the Research Agenda | 147 |

Seán Henry

Index 153

Editors and Contributors

About the Editors

Dr. Sean Whittle is a Senior Lecturer in Catholic Education at St Mary's University, Twickenham, and a Research Associate with Professor Gerald Grace. Alongside these academic roles, he works as a secondary school RE teacher at Gumley House FCJ Catholic School in West London. His book, *A Theory of Catholic Education* (Bloomsbury 2014), presents a robust philosophy of Catholic education that draws fruitfully on the theology of Karl Rahner. He has edited five books on Catholic Education (*Vatican II and New Thinking about Catholic Education 2016; Researching Catholic Education 2018; Religious Education in Catholic schools in the UK and Ireland 2018; Irish and British Reflections on Catholic Education 2021*, and (jointly with Dr. Gareth Byrne) *Catholic Education: A life long journey (2021)*. Further volumes on Leadership in Catholic Schools and another on Guiding Research into Catholic Education Studies are in preparation for release in 2024. Since 2016, Sean Whittle has been collaborating with other academics working in the field of Catholic education in order to create the *Network for Researchers in Catholic Education* (NfRCE).

He has also been engaged in a range of research projects (including a Post-Doctoral Research Fellow at Brunel University on a Religious Literacy project, Researching RSE in Catholic schools in Northern Ireland, and a research project of a Catholic Multi-Academy Trust in Birmingham). Prior to that, he was a visiting Research Fellow at Heythrop College. He continues to serve as the secretary for the NfRCE and is also Chair of the academic association AULRE.

Dr. Seán Henry is a Lecturer in Education at Edge Hill University. Prior to this, he worked as a Postdoctoral Researcher at the Research Centre on Inclusive and Equitable Cultures, Technological University Dublin (2021–2022), and as an Assistant Lecturer in Philosophy of Education at Maynooth University (2019–2021). He currently has a monograph in development entitled *Queer Thriving in Religious Schools*, which offers a queer theory of Jewish, Christian, and Muslim education, and is also in the process of co-editing a special issue on gender and adult education for the journal *Studies in the Education of Adults*. He has published around issues of sexuality, gender, religion, and education in several international, peer-reviewed journals including *Journal of Philosophy of Education*, *Sex Education*, *Educational Theory Ethics and Education*, and *Cambridge Journal of Education*. He currently sits on the advisory board for the International Network of Philosophers of Education, as well as the editorial board for *Ethics and Education*. Throughout his career so far, he has contributed to a range of funded research projects. These include projects on: building equitable policy responses to the COVID-19 pandemic; crafting resources for responding educationally to so-called radicalization and extremism in schools; and designing materials for integrating social justice concerns into higher education teaching. In addition to his research on religion, gender, and sexuality, He has started research on the queer pedagogical potential of comedy, and on theories of embodiment and intersectionality more broadly. Before starting his academic career, he qualified as a teacher of religious education and English.

Contributors

Vivek da Silva Dublin City University, Dublin, Ireland

Seán Henry Edge Hill University, Ormskirk, UK

Claire Jenkins The Margaret Beaufort Institute of Theology, Cambridge University, Cambridge, UK

David Kennedy DCU, Institute of Education, Dublin, Ireland

Cora O'Farrell Dublin City University (Mater Dei Centre for Catholic Education), Dublin, Ireland

Gillian Sullivan Dublin City University, Dublin, Ireland

Bernadette Sweetman Mater Dei Centre for Catholic Education (MDCCE), Dublin, Ireland

Ruth Wareham University of Birmingham, Birmingham, UK

Sean Whittle St Mary's University, Twickenham, UK

Chapter 1
Introduction

Sean Whittle and Seán Henry

This is an edited collection of chapters that explores LGBTQ+ inclusion in Catholic education. Although the field of Catholic Education Studies has grown exponentially over the past two decades, until recently little if any attention has been published specifically about the place of LGBTQ+ students (and teachers) in the context of Catholic education. This volume will offer readers the opportunity to go beyond an oppositional approach to LGBTQ+ inclusion in Catholic education, providing the chance to rethink the relationship between Catholic education and LGBTQ+ inclusion with greater imagination and sensitivity.

In terms of context, research outside Catholic education has pointed to long-standing tensions at the interface between Catholic education and LGBTQ+ inclusion. For instance, Grace and Wells (2005) have written about the exclusion of a gay student's boyfriend from a Catholic school prom in Canada with the following assessment: *Catholic schooling is marked by perpetual power plays inextricably linked to cultural technologies like heterosexism and tradition and by codes of obedience demanding acculturation to Catholicised ways of being, acting and expressing oneself in the world* (2005, p. 260). This is resonant with Tonya Callaghan's assertion that the creation of 'safe spaces' for LGBTQ+ students is 'difficult to achieve' in Catholic education owing to the 'panoptic power of Catholic doctrine', a power that 'forms the basis of curricular and policy decisions taken in [Catholic] schools' (2016, 271–272).

Love and Tosolt (2013) offer similar insights on the experiences of lesbian, bisexual and trans students in girls' Catholic high schools in the United States. Love

---

S. Whittle (✉)
St. Mary's University, Twickenham, UK
e-mail: sean.whittle@stmarys.ac.uk

S. Henry
Edge Hill University, Ormskirk, UK
e-mail: Sean.Henry@edgehill.ac.uk

© The Author(s), under exclusive license to Springer Nature Singapore Pte Ltd. 2024
S. Whittle and S. Henry (eds.), *Queer Thriving in Catholic Education*,
https://doi.org/10.1007/978-981-97-0323-4_1

and Tosolt argue that there exists 'an overwhelming and stifling climate of heteronormativity in all-girls' Catholic schools' (2013, p. 202). What they draw attention to is akin to Bailey's observations (2017), who doubts whether anti-homophobic and –transphobic bullying policies can be enacted in Catholic school contexts in Ireland owing to what she sees to be their inevitable investment in the 'moral socialisation' of children into Catholicism. She writes of how tackling homophobic and transphobic bullying in Catholic schools 'will inevitably be hindered by the largely denominational nature of Ireland's education system and, therefore, policies which do not adhere to the Catholic ethos will, quite possibly, be appropriated by Catholicism and neutralized within its parameters' (2017, 33). Similar points are made by Neary (2013) and Fahie (2016), both of whom have pointed to the role Catholic school ethos has played in alienating LGBTQ+ teachers in Catholic educational settings in Ireland.

This research context notwithstanding, it would be inaccurate to assume that all Catholic schools are inevitably monocultural places of exclusion and alienation for LGBTQ+ staff and students. Indeed, according to the Catholic Education Service, Catholic schools in England and Wales are the most ethnically diverse schools in the country. In this sense, rather than existing as the exclusive preserve of children from Catholic families, some of these schools are becoming increasingly diverse learning communities. Furthermore, research on Catholic education has slowly begun to craft a more affirming agenda with respect to LGBTQ+ inclusion. Huchting and Fisher (2019), for example, recently edited a special issue on the relationship between Catholic education and LGBTQ+ inclusion in the context of the *Journal of Catholic Education*. Within this, Herriot and Callaghan (2019) wrote of the potential to embed trans inclusive policies in Canadian Catholic schools, and Hughes devised recommendations for LGBTQ+ inclusion in the context of Catholic higher education.

Furthermore, McDonough (2016) has offered a general theory of dissent for Catholic education that he applies to justify the establishment of gay-straight alliances in diverse Catholic school settings.

Across this limited pool of literature, it is often in terms of pastoral support that LGBTQ+ inclusion is framed. Of course, appeals to this pastoral paradigm are understandable given the biblical and doctrinal context of the Church: it allows Catholic school personnel to curate a space of acceptance, inclusion and love without entering into debates and justifications around so-called 'thorny' issues. For many Catholics in Catholic education, this pastoral approach has found further support in the tenor of recent comments by Pope Francis, who famously posed the question 'Who am I to judge?' in response to the realities of gay men in the priesthood. For advocates of Catholic education, certainly in Ireland and the UK, the combined effect of high levels of pastoral care, a tacit avoidance of doctrinal condemnations of homosexuality, and an overall change in tone on the part of the Pontiff has meant that Catholic education has had the potential, now more than ever, to become explicitly inclusive for LGBTQ+ students and staff. At the crux of this shift, then, the question of whether the pastoral approach to LGBTQ+ inclusion is the best strategy for Catholic education to engage in arises, and it is in response to this that this volume arises.

In thinking about this question, what quickly emerges for us is that this pastoral paradigm triggers two difficulties. First, it deflects attention away from addressing or challenging any of the inherent weaknesses and theological problems with framing being gay or lesbian as an *abomination in the eyes of God*. In effect, in providing students with pastoral care (the support, help, affirmation and encouragement to be 'true to themselves') it nearly always involves a decision to dismiss the thorny doctrines as somehow not relevant in *this* Catholic school. Second, it perpetuates the tendency to align being gay, bi, or trans as a deficit or more needy position to be in, when compared to other students. The pastoral care structures in a school often act like a safety-net, set in place to support those students who need extra provision (from learning support or counselling or behaviour management to emotional support whilst dealing with grief). If being LGBTQ+ is routinely framed in this way in a Catholic school setting, it sends out a subtle but powerful signal that being LGBTQ+ is an extra 'burden' or difficulty that (sadly) some young people are saddled with as they grow up. The concern here is eloquently depicted as the 'victim trope' that typically gets applied to members of the LGBTQ+ community. Thus, as 'victims' of homophobia, gay people have to assert their rights and be prepared to navigate life in a defensive way. However, this sort of default position is stifling. It also unfairly subverts the huge social and legal strides that have taken place across Irish and British society over the past five decades. Indeed a key thrust of LGBTQ+ pride is to declare that there is nothing to be ashamed of or lacking with being LGBTQ+. There is nothing deficit about a human being identifing as LGBTQ+. If this is recognised, then it might indeed be the time for us to find ways of going beyond the pastoral paradigm adopted in Catholic schools.

It is incumbent on Catholic educators to help the members of their schools who are LGBTQ+ to be able to thrive as they receive their Catholic education, so it is with the view to offering and extending an account of queer thriving that this volume proceeds. This involves depicting an account of Catholic education that positively draws on queer theology in order to adopt a more theologically expansive account of human sexuality and gender. Part-and-parcel of this is embracing the complex realities of human sexuality and gender as something much more like a spectrum than an entrenched binary. Such work also entails situating the task of LGBTQ+ inclusion in Catholic education within another register, a register that refuses to kowtow to institutional homophobia and transphobia, and delights instead in the capacity of LGBTQ+ lives to signal other, thriving, ways of living in the Church and in the world.

This volume seeks to address five central themes. First, is it possible for Catholic education to sit in harmony with the concerns of LGBTQ+ inclusive education? Second, what does it mean to 'queer' education at all? Third, how does this sit in relation to Catholic perspectives on the purposes of Catholic education? Fourth, how might Catholic schools move beyond a 'pastoral' approach to LGBTQ+ students? And fifth, what does the evidence from research in Catholic schools indicate? To what extent are they places of inclusion, hospitality and welcome for LGBTQ+ young people? What more needs to be done?

The Structure of This Volume

The purpose of the first chapter is to offer an overview how the Catholic Church has broadly understood and responded to the realities of sexual and gender diversities from a theological perspective. Seán Henry surveys in particular the 'marital morality' that has characterised the Church's theological approach to sexual ethics, before moving to the specific implications of this for how the Church has understood (and continues to understand) same-sex sexual acts. From here, the chapter summarises some of the key theological elements informing the Church's understanding and response to gender diversities in particular, before reflecting on the implications of these perspectives vis-à-vis the Church's views on education. The chapter concludes with some notes on how this context lays the groundwork for cultivating queer thriving in Catholic education.

The first section of this volume consists of two parts. The first being an eloquently argued appeal for queer thriving in Catholic education by Seán Henry. This is followed by a second part which consists of three shorter responses to the arguments and analysis offered by Dr. Henry.

In this pivotal chapter the concept of 'queer thriving' in relation to Catholic education is carefully developed. It is argued that rather than beginning from discourses of vulnerability, trauma, or suicidality that typically characterise engagements across LGBTQ+ and religious concerns, the analysis begins from the assumption that LGBTQ+ lives are not 'problems' or 'issues' to be accommodated, tolerated, or 'saved' by Catholic education, but are instead sites of infinite potential from which Catholic education can gain insight and inspiration. The argument here is structured around making the case for two potential contributions queer theologies can bring to Catholic education. First, queer theologies can offer Catholic education a theological resource that remedies overly disembodied approaches to questions of sexuality, gender, and education. Second, Queer theologies can offer Catholic education alternative, more expansive, understandings of LGBTQ+ and religious subjectivities that foreground the agency of LGBTQ+ people. The final part of the chapter reflects on three commitments which are needed in order to enact a queer approach to Catholic education. The opening part of this chapter clears the ground by clarifying the concepts of queer, queer-theologies, queer agency, and embodiment.

In the first response Cora O'Farrell reflects on the call to re-imagine Catholic education and schooling. This response to Dr. Henry's chapter takes a measured whilst positive assessment of what is being advocated in relation 'queering Catholic education'. It is recognised that the stance taken by Dr. Henry is a deeply challenging one for Catholic Education. It is explained that there is growing awareness of the need to support and nurture young people who are LGBTQ+, both in Catholic schools and more widely in the life of the Catholic Church.

However, no change to official Church teaching is taking place. It is this context which makes the challenging invitation to re-imagine Catholic education and schooling through the filter of queer theology both challenging and intriguing.

It is concluded that the disruptive quality of Henry's argument is a welcome partner for ongoing changes in approaches to Catholic education.

The second response, from David Kennedy focuses on the notion of Queer-Thriving. This response explores the central place that hermeneutics has in underpinning the stance taken by Henry. Some reservations are raised over the stance which Biesta takes, which is important because this provides much of the supporting conceptual architecture that Henry deploys.

However, allowing for these reservations over hermeneutics, the remainder of the response draws out the positive insights pieced together around the notion of Queer Thriving.

The third response to Dr. Henry's chapter, offered by Sean Whittle, draws out the positive potential in aligning Catholic education with the theme of 'queer thriving'. It is explained that a positive response can be given to Henry's argument precisely because it allows movement beyond the pastoral care paradigm. This is because in shifting the starting point (from where LGBQT+ lives are problems or issues to be 'dealt' with) it allows Catholic schools to begin by framing the inclusion of LGBQT+ students in more positive terms. Part of this response is to speculate what the idea of queer thriving might mean in practical terms for Catholic schools. One practical challenge would be to reframe school policy statements in relation to LGBQT+ students, and one way of doing this is briefly outlined.

In the next section of the volume, the focus shifts to a presentation of the current research being undertaken in relation to LGBQT+ issues. In Chap. 6 Vivek De Silva presents a sustained discussion of the needs of older school students (secondary or post-primary) to have a coherent and nurturing RSE programme. In the changing socio-cultural landscape of contemporary Ireland there is a need for Catholic schools to offer a rich and supportive RSE programme. This involves drawing on the insights of scripture and a theology of inclusion. This will allow Catholic schools to be a place of hospitality and welcome to all, capable of supporting students who are at ease with their sexuality.

In Chap. 7 Gillian Sullivan focuses on Relationships and Sexuality Education (RSE) in Catholic Post Primary Schools in Ireland, in order to offer a snapshot into one Catholic post-primary school and how through the use of the Lundy Model of Participation, students and staff are able to plan and facilitate activities and celebrations of its diverse religious, cultural and LGBTQI+ community. It highlights that when the agenda moves beyond tokenism to purposeful listening, then the school community can flourish for the good of all its members. This work, which helps people to no longer feel oppressed or imprisoned by a culture of fear or exclusion, is affirmed by Christ's own understanding of his mission as summed up in John 10:10. This chapter explores the role of Student Voice in a Catholic post-primary school in enabling students to flourish and be their true selves. It argues that allowing for and listening to Student Voice is integral to the true identity of Catholic schooling, which includes the identity formation of the students who attend them, in all of their diversity: ability, culture, race, religion and sexual orientation.

Keeping the focus on student experience, Chap. 8, composed by Sean Whittle, offers a summary of research findings from an investigation of Relationship and Sex

Education in seven Catholic schools in Northern Ireland. Evidence was collected in the autumn of 2019, in order to form the basis of a scoping report assessing the current practice and state of *Relationship and Sex Education* (RSE) in Catholic schools in Northern Ireland. This chapter describes the six central themes identified in the report. The empirical research findings summarised in this chapter indicate that in the schools sampled, the RSE is effectively meeting the needs of students and their parents. The schools are successfully navigating the need to provide high quality RSE with a balanced presentation of official Church teaching on aspects of sexuality and sexual ethics. A firmly pastoral approach is taken in order to ensure that these Catholic schools are safe spaces for all students. In terms of LGBTQ+ students there was positive evidence of supportive pastoral care structures and respectful and affirmative relationships amongst students.

In contrast Chap. 9 raises potential concerns and reservations in relation to Trans Gender non-binary (TGNB) young people and their experiences in Catholic schools. This chapter, by Claire Jenkins, offers a transgender perspective. Jenkins draws attention to the changing context of schooling in relation to TGNB students through recollecting some personal conversations. In this chapter three research questions are considered. The final part of the chapter offers a personal reflection on the notion of queer thriving.

In Chap. 10 Bernadette Sweetman considers what can the Adult Religious Education and Faith Development project (AREFD) tell us about the research agenda in Catholic education in relation to LGBTQI+ matters? The Adult Religious Education and Faith Development project (AREFD) commenced in October 2018 at the *Mater Dei* Centre with the aim of identifying the current landscape of religious education and faith development for adults in Ireland. Over the course of the last three years, two key data collection phases took place. The first was an online survey publicised nationwide and open to all adults in Ireland over 18. The second phase of data collection were consultations with a total of 22 people (some individual interviews and some focus groups) who have been involved in AREFD in Ireland in a variety of contexts for an established period of time. The overall brief given to participants was to articulate what their understanding of religious education and faith development; what experience (if any) they had of same as an adult; what areas would they like to see developed in AREFD and suggestions on how this might be achieved. The specific issue of LGBTQ+ in relation to AREFD was not expressly addressed by the research team during the study. Nonetheless, some LGBTQ+-related insights were offered by the participants. The context in which they occur and to some extent the absence of certain elements of this topic may prompt purposeful and guided conversation as to the research agenda of Catholic education for adults in relation to LGBTQ+ issues. This chapter provides a commentary on the data and suggests some avenues for research.

In Chap. 11 Ruth Wareham brings an 'outsider' perspective to bare on the discussions in this volume. This chapter argues that when it comes to Relationship and Sex Education (RSE), there is a need to be a reconfiguration from being *faith-orientated* to be being *faith-sensitive*. For Catholic education RSE can legitimately be sensitive to insights and beliefs drawn from Catholic belief, but it cannot be orientated to handing these on as the true or definitive way of teaching RSE. It is explained that there are complex issues at stake because Catholic education is primarily justified in terms of parental rights. This means there is an inherent risk of always giving primacy to the rights of the parents over above the child. Using and 'educational goods approach' it is argued that when it comes to RSE (at least for state funded Catholic schools) there is no justification for using this part of the curriculum to privilege and promote Catholic belief about sex and relationships.

The final contribution to this volume is a concluding chapter by Seán Henry. In it, Henry brings together different strands from across the volume to posit some preliminary suggestions for future research on queer thriving in Catholic education. In particular, he emphasises the importance of pursuing research on queer thriving that challenges, without ignoring, the tensions that exist between normative and non-normative accounts of queer praxis. Building on this, he suggests the need for future research in Catholic education to attend to the complexities of educational encounters that lie in excess of binary logics around sexualities and genders, and turns to queer and trans pedagogical theories as frameworks for engagement in this respect. Finally, Henry offers some thoughts on the need for future research on queer thriving in Catholic education to reflect more closely on the field's relationship to Catholic theology itself, as well as on the role interfaith dialogue can have in cultivating the conditions for queer thriving in Catholic educational settings.

This volume will provide readers with the opportunity to consider the range of complex issues that arise when reflecting on the relationship between Catholic education and LGBTQ+ inclusion. This book will stimulate wide ranging appeal for anyone who has an interest in Catholic education, both its advocates as well as its critics.

References

Bailey, S. (2017). From invisibility to visibility: A policy archaeology of the introduction of anti-transphobic and anti-homophobic bullying guidelines into the Irish primary education system. *Irish Educational Studies, 36*(1), 25–42.

Callaghan, T. (2016). Young, queer, and Catholic: Youth resistance to homophobia in Catholic schools. *Journal of LGBT Youth, 13*(3), 270–287.

Fahie, D. (2016). 'Spectacularly exposed and vulnerable'—How Irish equality legislation subverted the personal and professional security of lesbian, gay and bisexual teachers. *Sexualities, 19*(4), 393–411.

Grace, A. P., & Wells, K. (2005). The Marc Hall Prom predicament: Queer individual rights v. institutional church rights in Canadian public education. *Canadian Journal of Education/Revue canadienne de l'éducation, 28*(3), 237–270.

Herriot, L., & Callaghan, T. D. (2019). Possibilities trans-affirming policy potential: A case study of a Canadian Catholic school. *Journal of Catholic Education, 22*(3), 57–83.

Huchting, K., & Fisher, E. (2019). Introduction to the special issue: The challenges and opportunities of including the LGBTQ community in Catholic education. *Journal of Catholic Education, 22*(3), 1–13.

Love, B. L., & Tosolt, B. (2013). Go underground or in your face: Queer students' negotiation of all-girls Catholic schools. *Journal of LGBT Youth, 10*(3), 186–207.

McDonough, G. (2016). Cultivating identities: The Catholic school as diverse ecclesial space. *Philosophical Inquiry in Education, 23*(2), 160–177.

Neary, A. (2013). Lesbian and gay teachers' experiences of 'coming out' in Irish schools. *British Journal of Sociology of Education, 34*(4), 583–602.

Dr. Sean Whittle is a Senior Lecturer in Catholic Education at St. Mary's University, Twickenham, and a Research Associate with Professor Gerald Grace. Alongside these academic roles he works as a secondary school RE teacher at Gumley House FCJ Catholic School in West London. His book, *A Theory of Catholic Education* (Bloomsbury 2014), presents a robust philosophy of Catholic education that draws fruitfully on the theology of Karl Rahner. He has edited five books on Catholic Education (*Vatican II and New Thinking about Catholic Education 2016; Researching Catholic Education 2018; Religious Education in Catholic schools in the UK and Ireland 2018; Irish and British Reflections on Catholic Education 2021, and (jointly with Dr. Gareth Byrne) Catholic Education: A life long journey (2021)*). Further volumes on Leadership in Catholic Schools and another on Guiding Research into Catholic Education Studies are in preparation for release in 2024. Since 2016 Sean Whittle has been collaborating with other academics working in the field of Catholic Education in order to create the *Network for Researchers in Catholic Education* (NfRCE).

He has also been engaged in a range of research projects (including a Post-Doctoral Research Fellow at Brunel University on a Religious Literacy project, Researching RSE in Catholic schools in Northern Ireland, and a research project of a Catholic Multi-Academy Trust in Birmingham). Prior to that he was a visiting Research Fellow at Heythrop College. Sean Whittle continues to serves as the secretary for the NfRCE and is also Chair of the academic association AULRE.

Dr. Seán Henry is a Lecturer in Education at Edge Hill University. Prior to this, Seán worked as a Postdoctoral Researcher at the Research Centre on Inclusive and Equitable Cultures, Technological University Dublin (2021–2022), and as an Assistant Lecturer in Philosophy of Education at Maynooth University (2019–2021). He currently has a monograph in development entitled *Queer Thriving in Religious Schools*, which offers a queer theory of Jewish, Christian, and Muslim education, and is also in the process of co-editing a special issue on gender and adult education for the journal *Studies in the Education of Adults*. He has published around issues of sexuality, gender, religion, and education in several international, peer-reviewed journals including *Journal of Philosophy of Education, Sex Education, Educational Theory, Ethics and Education*, and *Cambridge Journal of Education*. He currently sits on the advisory board for the International Network of Philosophers of Education, as well as the editorial board for *Ethics and Education*. Throughout his career so far, Seán has contributed to a range of funded research projects. These include projects on: building equitable policy responses to the Covid-19 pandemic; crafting resources for responding educationally to so-called radicalisation and extremism in schools; and designing materials for integrating social justice concerns into higher education teaching. In addition to his research on religion, gender, and sexuality, Seán has started research on the queer pedagogical potential of comedy, and on theories of embodiment and intersectionality more broadly. Before starting his academic career, Seán qualified as a teacher of Religious Education and English.

Chapter 2
Laying the Groundwork: Sexualities, Genders, and the Catholic Church

Seán Henry

Introduction

'Who am I to judge?' So said Pope Francis in his now famous response to journalists on the question of homosexual priests in the Catholic Church. These, and similar comments made by the Pontiff, have been hailed as signalling a potential change in the Church's attitudes towards people of diverse genders and sexualities in recent years. Perhaps emblematic of this, the Synodal Assembly, focused on reform of the Catholic Church, adopted a paper in Frankfurt in March 2023 calling for the blessing of same-sex couples in the German Catholic Church by 2026. This passed overwhelmingly, with 176 of the 202 synodal members voting in favour. In April 2020, Pope Francis similarly approved a Vatican donation to a group of trans sex workers in Italy, and in 2022 the Pontiff met with a group of trans people who had taken shelter at the Blessed Immaculate Virgin community in Rome during the coronavirus pandemic.

At the same time, however, there have been no substantial shifts in Church teachings pertaining to sexual and gender diversities. The Congregation for Catholic Education (2019) recently characterised trans-inclusive educational programmes as posing an 'educational crisis' for Catholic education. Pope Francis has similarly likened the effects of so-called 'gender ideology' to the blurring of differences between men and women. Institutional heteronormativity and cisnormativity persist, with the Catholic Church continuing to privilege heterosexual and cisgender identities in how it understands and responds to the realities of gender and sexual diversities. In this context, to what extent is cultivating queer thriving in Catholic education viable? Does the historical and ongoing nature of the Church's violence towards people of diverse sexualities and genders render the task of queer thriving in Catholic education

S. Henry (✉)
Edge Hill University, Ormskirk, UK
e-mail: Sean.Henry@edgehill.ac.uk

© The Author(s), under exclusive license to Springer Nature Singapore Pte Ltd. 2024
S. Whittle and S. Henry (eds.), *Queer Thriving in Catholic Education*,
https://doi.org/10.1007/978-981-97-0323-4_2

obsolete? Or are there resources in the historical and contemporary context of the Church that can 'lay the groundwork' for such a task?

With these questions in mind, the purpose of this chapter is to provide a limited overview of how the institutional Church has broadly understood and responded to the realities of sexual and gender diversities from a theological perspective. It surveys in particular the 'marital morality' that has characterised the Church's theological approach to sexual ethics, before moving to the specific implications of this for how the Church has understood (and continues to understand) same-sex sexual acts. From here, the chapter summarises some of the key theological elements informing the Church's understanding and response to gender diversities in particular, before reflecting on the implications of these perspectives vis-à-vis the Church's views on education. The chapter concludes with some notes on what this context offers for cultivating queer thriving in Catholic education.

Catholic Perspectives on Diverse Sexualities and Genders

In contemporary Catholic thought, sexual expression is understood (at least by the Magisterium, the teaching authority of the Church) as morally good when it takes place in the context of marriage, and is open to the possibility of new life through procreation. The primacy of what Salzman and Lawler term 'marital' morality has been affirmed by the Church in its various encyclicals and decrees across the latter half of the twentieth century (2012, p. 7).

For instance, in 1975 the Congregation for the Doctrine of the Faith (CDF) asserted that, to be moral, 'any human genital act whatsoever may be placed only within the framework of marriage'. Here, moral sexual expression is confined to the institution of marriage, which, for the Magisterium, is a necessarily heterosexual institution owing to the obligations that the institution brings in terms of having and raising children by so-called 'natural' means. Indeed, as Pope Paul VI affirms in his 1968 encyclical *Humanae vitae*, in marriage 'each and every marriage act must remain open to the transmission of life'. Of course, the Church's position on the 'ends' or purposes of marriage is not framed exclusively in terms of a procreative model.

Indeed, in *Gaudium et spes* (1965) marriage is described by Pope Paul VI as a 'communion of love', an 'intimate partnership of conjugal life and love'. In spite of this, however, we nonetheless encounter a prioritisation of the procreative model in the Pope's description of such communion as being that which is 'ordained for the procreation and education of children', who are considered by the Pope to be the 'ultimate crown' of married life.

The institutional Church's belief in the inseparability of marital unity and procreation in evaluating the moral goodness of a sexual act has been central in establishing the incongruence between conventional Catholic perspectives on sexual ethics and homosexual sexual acts. The CDF's *Persona humana* (1975), as well as the *Catechism of the Catholic Church* (1992), both condemn homosexual acts as 'intrinsically disordered' and gravely immoral. The Magisterium (1975) does so on the basis of each of the following: first, the teaching of scripture, in which homosexual acts are 'condemned as a serious depravity and even presented as the sad consequence of rejecting God'; second, 'the constant teaching of the Magisterium'; and third, 'the moral sense of the Christian people'.

First, the teaching of scripture. The biblical tradition has been appealed to consistently by the institutional Church as a key resource in passing judgement on the moral status of homosexuality. The Congregation for the Doctrine of the Faith (1986), for instance, turns to the Bible in its condemnation of same-sex relations, rhetorically affirming that 'there is ... a clear consistency within the sacred scriptures for judging the moral issue of homosexual behaviour'. The biblical texts upon which the Congregation grounds its argument include classic biblical passages such as Genesis 19:1-11, Leviticus 18:22 and 20:13, Romans 1:26-27, 1 Corinthians 6:9, and 1 Timothy 1:10. Crucially, the Congregation's assessment of these passages is used to frame the conviction that 'It is only in the marital relationship that the use of the sexual faculty can be morally good.' The biblical tradition upon which the Congregation draws is seen here as resonant with the emphasis upon marital morality found in the likes of *Humanae vitae, Gaudium et spes,* and *Persona humana.*

Of course, it would be inaccurate to suggest that the Catholic tradition has been devoid of contestation in terms of the biblical position on homosexuality. Indeed theologians like Jordan (2000) have argued that the biblical texts upon which the Church grounds its arguments around homosexuality can rarely be interpreted in a literalistic way, and must instead be understood in conversation with the contexts (both historical and contemporary) in which they have been written, read, rewritten, and reread. The Pontificaial Biblical Commission's, 1994 document *The Interpretation of the Bible in the Church* takes a similar view with respect to the more general point around historicity and scriptural interpretation, insisting that scripture 'inasmuch as it is "the Word of God in human language" has been composed by human authors in all its various parts and in all the sources that lie behind them. Because of this, its proper understanding not only admits the use of [the historical critical] method but actually requires it.' We will return to the implications of this historical approach to scripture later in laying the groundwork for queering Catholic education.

Second, the 'constant teaching' of the Magisterium. As we have seen, the Magisterium's influence has been strong in shaping the ethical perspectives on homosexuality elaborated upon thus far. The CDF's response to the possibility of marriage rights for same-sex couples, for example, brings to the fore the Magisterium's perspective on the 'intrinsically disordered' nature of homosexual acts. The CDF (2003) argues that such acts are 'contrary to the natural law' owing to the fact that 'they close the sexual act to the gift of life' and 'do not proceed from a genuine' complementarity between the sexes. For the Church, a sexual relationship is morally good when it gives expression to, and enhances, the complementarity between the spouses in the context of marriage. The term 'complementarity' appeared only relatively recently in Magisterial sexual teaching, with its roots in Pope John Paul II's fourth apostolic exhortation *Familiaris Consortio* (1981). Salzman and Lawler offer a useful discussion of a key feature of complementarity characterising their reading of the Magisterium's theology of the body that emerged from this exhortation: 'biological' complementarity (2012, 64).

For Salzman and Lawler, biological complementarity has as its foundation a 'heterogenital' understanding of sexual relations: sexual activity is morally permissible and mutually enriching for both partners insofar as the activity involves the use of physically functioning male and female sexual organs. The use of 'functioning' sexual organs is important from the Magisterium's perspective as it attests to the physical 'two-in-oneness' of heterosexual intercourse, embodying the unitive 'communion' of which Pope Paul VI was supportive. Of course, every heterogenital act carried out by a heterosexual couple is not necessarily exhibitive of biological complementarity in a reproductive sense. Indeed, as Moore notes in the case of infertile heterosexual couples: 'vaginal intercourse which we know to be sterile is a different type of act from vaginal intercourse which, as far as we know, might result in conception' (2001, 162). To such concerns, Magisterial teaching would respond by arguing that heterogenital complementarity, in its unitive and biological *symbolism*, sacramentally gives expression to the reproductive complementarity of heterosexual intercourse. In doing so, heterogenital complementarity grants sexual relations between heterosexuals moral and sacramental weight, even in contexts 'for serious reasons and observing moral precepts' that a heterosexual cannot, or chooses not to, reproduce. To put it crudely, the absence of male and female sexual organs in homosexual acts between two persons renders such acts sinful, as they fail to embody the heterogenital and reproductive complementarity that gives marital sexual intercourse its unitive and biological value.

Lastly, the CDF (1975) appeals to the 'moral sense of the Christian people' in defending its opposition to homosexual relations. The Congregation argues that the Church's opposition to homosexual acts is justifiable in that it resonates with the general sentiments and judgements of the wider Christian community, what Pope John Paul II (1981) refers to as the '*sensus fidei*'. In recent years, however, this appeal to the *sensus fidei* has been complicated by a growing disconnect between the Church and the attitudes of many lay Catholics. General sociological studies carried out by Hoge et al. (2001), Hornsby-Smith (1991) and Fulton (2000), for example, have all suggested that a majority of Catholics in various Western contexts disagree with the Magisterium's position on many matters of sexual ethics and personal conscience, including its perspectives on homosexuality. Other more recent critics like Flanagan (2015), have argued that LGBTQ+ Catholics calling for more inclusive responses on the part of the institutional Church also exist as constituent parts of the *sensus fidei*. Again, the significance of this in laying the groundwork for queering Catholic education will be returned to later.

The institutional Church's ongoing resistance to trans inclusive approaches to gender diversity has its roots in a theological anthropology drawn from the creation narratives of Genesis, where it reads: 'God created man in his own image […] male and female he created them.' (Genesis 1:27). This anthropology begins from an understanding of creation tied to the fundamental biological differences between men and women, differences (from the Church's perspective) that discourses of trans inclusion and gender diversity by definition 'erase'. From a theological perspective, such differences are anthropologically significant in signalling the capacities of human beings to participate in the creative nature of God's design as part of what it means to be human. This design, as Pope John Paul II (1981) notes 'has assigned as a task to man his body, his masculinity and femininity; and in that masculinity and femininity he, in a way, assigned to him as a task his humanity, the dignity of the person, and also the clear sign of the interpersonal communion in which man fulfils himself through the authentic gift of himself.' Put differently, reaffirming the metaphysical basis of sexual difference is important for the Church in safeguarding the heterogenital, marital morality referred to above. Indeed, as the Congregation for Catholic Education notes: 'There is a need to reaffirm the metaphysical roots of sexual difference as an anthropological refutation of attempts to negate the male-female duality of human nature, from which the family is generated' (2019, 19). On this meaning, discourses of trans inclusion and gender diversity are positioned by the Church as erasing the basis of the family itself, as well as creating the idea of the human person as an abstraction who 'chooses for himself what his nature is to be' (2019, 9).

Given the contribution of the Congregation for Catholic Education to these discussions, clearly the Church's views on diverse sexualities and genders have had a direct effect on the Church's views on the provision of Catholic education. It is to this that I now turn.

Catholic Education and Diverse Sexualities and Genders

In 1983, the Congregation for Catholic Education offered a statement on sex education in Catholic contexts entitled *Educational Guidance in Human Love: Outlines for Sex Education.* In it, the Congregation offers an educational philosophy for sex education inspired by a perspective on sexual ethics in line with the procreative-union model of marriage espoused by the institutional Church: 'Sexual intercourse, ordained towards procreation, is the maximum expression on the physical level of the communion of love of the married'. In this document, a Catholic perspective on sex education is one that endorses an exclusively heterosexual and procreative view of sexual relations in the context of marriage. This perspective has been reiterated more recently in the Irish context by the Irish Catholic Bishops' Conference, who write of how 'The values of love and life are seen most fully in the context of marriage and the family', and that any educational activity that seeks to address issues relating to relationships and sexuality should aim to speak to such values (2014, p. 5).

Both documents frame sex education in terms that exclude alternatives to the heterosexual and procreative marital model of sexual relations. *Educational Guidance in Human Love* (1983), for instance, is noteworthy in its treatment of homosexuality as follows: 'Homosexuality, which impedes the person's acquisition of sexual maturity, whether from the individual point of view, or the inter-personal, is a problem which must be faced in all objectivity by the pupil and the educator when the case presents itself.' Here, the Congregation frames homosexuality as a 'problem', and elsewhere in the document as a 'contracted habit', a 'disorder', an 'obsessive impulse' that families and teachers must respond to by taking account of 'the elements of judgement proposed by the ecclesiastical Magisterium'. The more recent contribution by the Irish Catholic Bishops' Conference offers an educational philosophy in the context of schooling much in line with the exclusiveness of the Congregation's, albeit expressed in a less inflammatory register: 'The Catholic school, in the formulation of its policy, should reflect Catholic moral teaching on sexual matters. Even more fundamentally, it needs to be specific in excluding approaches which are inconsistent with the very foundations and formulations of Catholic moral thought' (2014, 9).

The Congregation for Catholic Education's (2019) more recent document *Male and Female He Created Them: Towards a Path of Dialogue on the Question of Gender Theory in Education* adopts, in certain respects, a more pastorally sensitive tone to these questions, insofar as it emphasises the importance of dialogue and listening in reflecting on the realities of gender diversities in education. In this spirit, it outlines certain points of agreement between the Church and those who the Church identifies as 'writing on gender theory' (2019, 9). These points of agreement include an appreciation for educational programmes that 'combat all expressions of unjust discrimination', as well as programmes that emphasise 'the need to educate children and young people to respect every person in their particularity and difference, so that no one should suffer bullying, violence, insults, or unjust discrimination based on their specific characteristics (such as special needs, race, religion, sexual tendencies, etc.)' (2019, 9–10). In this latter respect, the Congregation notes that such commitment involves 'educating for active and responsible citizenship, which is marked by the ability to welcome all legitimate expressions of human personhood with respect' (2019, 10).

At the same time, however, the Congregation is clear in its critique of educational programmes that are inclusive of gender diversities. As referenced earlier, it accuses such programmes (and 'gender theory' more generally) of eliding the biological differences between men and women, reducing people to abstractions devoid of connection to their material lives.

The Congregation writes of how so-called 'gender ideology' 'inspires educational programmes and legislative trends that promote ideas of personal identity and affective intimacy that make a radical break with the actual *biological difference* between male and female' (2019, 12). This is expanded in the Congregation's emphasis on the importance of safeguarding biological difference on the basis of its role in creation and the family unit: 'It is precisely within the *nucleus of the family unit* that children can learn how to recognise the value and the beauty of the differences between the two sexes, along with their equal dignity, and their reciprocity at a biological, functional, psychological and social level' (2019, 21). Seeing biological difference as expressing the 'reciprocity' between the sexes recalls our earlier emphasis on biological, heterogenital complementarity. In the case of both sexual and gender diversities, the Church urges educators to teach through a 'Christian pedagogy' based 'upon an *integral anthropology,* capable of harmonising the human person's physical, psychic and spiritual identity' (2019, 30), in other words, in tune with the anthropology detailed previously.

In spite of the emphasis on listening, dialogue, and respect characterising the Congregation's response to the realities of gender diversities, so much of what the Church teaches around sexualities, genders, and education remains unequivocally at odds with the understanding of queer thriving offered in the introduction and second chapter to this volume. In this context, how are we to proceed? Is cultivating the conditions for queer thriving possible in Catholic education, or is it an invariably lost cause? In what follows, I lay the groundwork for what is to come by addressing these questions directly. I argue that what this theological context offers for queer thriving is: (1) an emphasis on the importance of historicity in approaching Church tradition and scripture; (2) a focus on the inescapable realities of pluralism and difference in the Church; and (3) a necessary attention to the body. These points will be expanded upon in different ways in the second chapter of this volume.

Queer Thriving in Catholic Education—Laying the Groundwork

In beginning to think through the question of queer thriving in Catholic education, the Church's earlier emphasis on taking account of the historicity of Church tradition and scripture is significant. For me, what this emphasis offers in laying the groundwork for queer thriving in Catholic education is a necessary focus on the historically contingent nature of Church teaching and theology, and with it, theological possibilities for renewal and change. In this sense, the Church's historical approach to engagements with tradition and scripture offers inroads into more spacious, less absolutist, relations with the Church's theological heritage, which is important in opening up other (more queer) ways of conceiving, reimagining, and responding to that same heritage. This emphasis on historicity and context is also important in ensuring that any account of queer thriving offered for Catholic education is sensitive to the historical and contemporary violences inflicted by the Church to LGBTQ+ people. In this sense, a historical approach to tradition and scripture does not seek to downplay, minimise, undermine, or sugar- coat Church violence, but rather faces it squarely, but in ways that refuse to grant such violence the final word on matters pertaining to sexualities and genders.

What the above survey also offers in laying the groundwork for queer thriving in Catholic education is a focus on pluralism and difference within the Church. Recall the Church's appeal to the *sensus fidei*, and the possibilities this offers in the context of increasing numbers of Catholics who disagree with the institutional Church's approach to the realities of sexual and gender diversities. For me, this focus is significant for queer thriving in bringing to the fore possibilities for attending to the agency of diverse theological voices both within and beyond the institutional Church, voices who understand gender and sexual diversities in different ways to conventional Church perspectives. In this sense, I am thinking of the Congregations for Catholic Education's call for educators to '*respect every person* in their particularity and difference' and am reminded in this vein of the work of Martin (2018), who has offered theological and pastoral arguments in favour of 'building bridges' with LGBTQ+ Catholics in the Church. I am also thinking of LGBTQ+ Catholic organisations like Dignity USA, as well as recent efforts by the Sisters of Saint Joseph Federation. The Sisters (2023) signed an open letter on Trans Day of Visibility with the assertion that trans and non- binary people are 'beloved and cherished by God', alongside a commitment to 'cultivate a faith community where all, especially our transgender, nonbinary, and gender-expansive siblings, experience a deep belonging.'

Finally, what the above context offers in laying the groundwork for queer thriving in Catholic education is a necessary attention to the body. Whereas traditional Church teaching frames the sexed body in terms that have been used to justify and legitimate cisnormativity and transphobia, a focus on the body and on the realities of bodily difference is nonetheless valuable in framing queer thriving in Catholic education in ways that are sensitive to the 'fleshy' materiality of our embodied lives. As Halberstam observes: '[T]here are many gendered bodies in the world and 'male' and 'female' do not even begin the hard work of classifying them' (2018, 154). In his book *Queer Embodiment: Monstrosity, Medical Violence, and Intersex Experience*, Malatino (2019) makes a similar point. He emphasises how trans theories do not erase the body (making it an 'abstraction', to use the phrasing of the Congregation for Catholic Education). Rather he sees trans theory as foregrounding the ontological role the diversities of bodies play in the discursive construction and re-construction of reality. He argues that 'body talk' is a 'transformative social and political force, not merely imprinted or moulded and not ever able to be neatly relegated to a place beyond, outside, or squarely in the margins of the social' (2019, 210). In laying the groundwork for queer thriving in Catholic education, then, what the theological context surveyed in this chapter offers is this focus on the dynamism of the body itself, and the constitutive role an attention to it plays in understanding and transforming the world.

In Chap. 3 of this volume, I take up these foundations, working with and expanding upon them to offer some contours for queer thriving in Catholic education. In fleshing out these contours, I turn to queer theologies specifically, thus taking a different tact to the engagements with traditional Church teaching that have characterised this chapter's survey.

References

Congregation for Catholic Education. (1983). *Educational guidance in human love: Outlines for sex education* [Online]. Available at http://www.vatican.va/roman_curia/congregations/ccatheduc/documents/rc_con_ccatheduc_doc_19831101_sexual-education_en.html. Accessed April 6, 2023.

Congregation for Catholic Education. (2019). *'Male and female he created them': Towards a path of dialogue on the question of gender theory in education* [Online]. Available at https://www.vatican.va/roman_curia/congregations/ccatheduc/documents/rc_con_ccatheduc_do c_20190202_maschio-e-femmina_en.pdf. Accessed April 6, 2023.

Congregation for the Doctrine of the Faith. (1975). *Persona humana: Declaration on certain questions concerning sexual ethics* [Online]. Available at http://www.vatican.va/roman_curia/congregations/cfaith/documents/rc_con_cfaith_doc_197512 29_persona-humana_en.html. Accessed April 6, 2023.

Congregation for the Doctrine of the Faith. (1986). *Letter to the Bishops of the Catholic Church on the pastoral care of homosexual persons* [Online]. Available at http://www.vatican.va/roman_curia/congregations/cfaith/documents/rc_con_cfaith_doc_198610 01_homosexual-persons_en.html. Accessed April 6, 2023.

Congregation for the Doctrine of the Faith. (2003). *Considerations regarding proposals to give legal recognition to unions between homosexual persons* [Online]. Available at http://www.vatican.va/roman_curia/congregations/cfaith/documents/rc_con_cfaith_doc_200307 31_homosexual-unions_en.html. Accessed April 6, 2023.

Flanagan, B. (2015). Gender, sexual orientation, and the sense of the faithful. *Proceedings of the Catholic Theological Society of America, 70*, 86–87.

Fulton, J. (2000). *Young Catholics at the new millennium: The religion and morality of young adults in Western Countries.* University College Press.

Halberstam, J. (2018). *Trans*: A quick and quirky account of gender variability.* University of California Press.

Hoge, D. R., Johnson, M., & Dinges, W. (2001). *Young adult Catholics: Religion in the culture of choice.* University of Notre Dame Press.

Hornsby-Smith, M. (1991). *Roman Catholicism in England: Customary Catholicism and transformation of religious authority.* Cambridge University Press.

Irish Catholic Bishops' Conference. (2014). *Guidelines on relationships and sexuality education* [Online]. Available at http://www.catholicbishops.ie/wp-content/uploads/2014/04/RSE-Guidelines-RofI-for-web.pdf. Accessed April 6, 2023.

Jordan, M. D. (2000). *The silence of Sodom: Homosexuality in modern Catholicism.* University of Chicago Press.

Malatino, H. (2019). *Queer embodiment: Monstrosity, medical violence, and intersex experience.* University of Nebraska Press.

Martin, J. (2018). *Building a bridge: How the Catholic Church and the LGBT community can enter into a relationship of respect, compassion, and sensitivity.* Harper Collins.

Moore, G. (2001). *The body in context: Sex and Catholicism.* Contemporary Christian Insights. Continuum.

Pontifical Biblical Commission. (1994). *The interpretation of the Bible in the Church* [Online]. Available at https://catholic-resources.org/ChurchDocs/PBC_Interp-FullText.htm. Accessed April 6, 2023.

Pope John Paul II. (1981). *Familiaris consortio* [Online]. Available at http://w2.vatican.va/content/john-paul-ii/en/apost_exhortations/documents/hf_jp-ii_exh_19811122_familiaris-consortio.html. Accessed April 6, 2023.

Pope John Paul II. (1992). *Catechism of the Catholic Church* [Online]. Available at http://www.vatican.va/archive/ENG0015/_INDEX.HTM. Accessed April 6, 2023.

Pope Paul VI. (1965). *Gaudium et spes* [Online]. Available at http://www.vatican.va/archive/hist_councils/ii_vatican_council/documents/vat-ii_cons_19651207_gaudium-et-spes_en.html. Accessed April 6, 2023.

Pope Paul VI. (1968). *Humana vitae* [Online]. Available at http://w2.vatican.va/content/paul-vi/en/encyclicals/documents/hf_p-vi_enc_25071968_humanae-vitae.html. Accessed April 6, 2023.

Salzman, T. A., & Lawler, M. G. (2012). *Sexual ethics: A theological introduction.* Georgetown University Press.

Sisters of Saint Joseph Federation. (2023). Vowed Catholic Religious Honor Trans Day of Visibility. [Online]. Available at https://cssjfed.org/2023/03/31/vowed-catholic-religious-honor-trans-day-of-visibility/. Accessed April 6, 2023.

Dr. Seán Henry is a Lecturer in Education at Edge Hill University. Prior to this, Seán worked as a Postdoctoral Researcher at the Research Centre on Inclusive and Equitable Cultures, Technological University Dublin (2021–2022), and as an Assistant Lecturer in Philosophy of Education at Maynooth University (2019–2021). He currently has a monograph in development entitled *Queer Thriving in Religious Schools*, which offers a queer theory of Jewish, Christian, and Muslim education, and is also in the process of co-editing a special issue on gender and adult education for the journal *Studies in the Education of Adults*. He has published around issues of sexuality, gender, religion, and education in several international, peer-reviewed journals including *Journal of Philosophy of Education, Sex Education, Educational Theory, Ethics and Education*, and *Cambridge Journal of Education*. He currently sits on the advisory board for the International Network of Philosophers of Education, as well as the editorial board for *Ethics and Education*. Throughout his career so far, Seán has contributed to a range of funded research projects. These include projects on: building equitable policy responses to the Covid-19 pandemic; crafting resources for responding educationally to so-called radicalisation and extremism in schools; and designing materials for integrating social justice concerns into higher education teaching. In addition to his research on religion, gender, and sexuality, Seán has started research on the queer pedagogical potential of comedy, and on theories of embodiment and intersectionality more broadly. Before starting his academic career, Seán qualified as a teacher of Religious Education and English.

Part I
Catholic Schools as Places of Queer Thriving

Chapter 3
Queer Thriving in Catholic Education: The Role of Queer Theologies

Seán Henry

Introduction

To think affirmatively about the relationship between Catholic education and LGBTQ+ lives can appear to many as a contradiction in terms. Indeed, research on Catholic schooling has suggested that inclusive educational approaches to sexual and gender diversities are often hamstrung by acquiescence to heteronormative Catholic doctrines by staff and students. and Wells (2005), for instance, have pointed to the effects of deference to institutional Church teaching has had in justifying the exclusion of gay couples from student proms in the Canadian context, while the work of scholars like Love and Tosolt (2013), Callaghan (2016) and Bailey (2017) have drawn attention to how traditional Catholic teachings on sexualities and genders can contribute to heteronormative school cultures where the structural causes and effects of homophobic and transphobic bullying are ignored at best, and actively reinforced at worst. This is repeated by Neary (2013, 2017) and Fahie (2016), both of whom foreground the 'chilling effects' Catholic school patronage has had on the personal and working lives of LGBTQ+ teachers in the Irish context.

At the same time, however, efforts at carving out alternative possibilities for the relationship between Catholic education and LGBTQ+ lives have begun to emerge. McDonough (2012, 2016), for example, has argued for a model of pedagogical dissent in Catholic schools that can create the space for heteronormative Catholic teachings to be resisted. Similarly, Herriot and Callaghan (2019), drawing from insights from queer and trans theologies, have offered an understanding of policy enactment in Catholic settings with the potential to disrupt the opposition between Catholic education and inclusive responses to trans students. In keeping with this sensibility, the purpose of this chapter is to map avenues for reimagining Catholic education in affirmative, queer terms. The title of this chapter, 'Queer thriving in

---

S. Henry (✉)
Edge Hill University, Ormskirk, UK
e-mail: Sean.Henry@edgehill.ac.uk

Catholic education: The role of queer theologies', points to my approach to this theme, so I begin by giving it some attention here.

Firstly, I appeal to the image of queer thriving to situate this chapter in a register that can hopefully initiate discussions between Catholic education and LGBTQ+ lives from an alternative starting point. Rather than begin from discourses of vulnerability, trauma, or suicidality that typically characterise engagements across LGBTQ+ and religious concerns, I hope instead to begin from the assumption that LGBTQ+ lives are not 'problems' or 'issues' to be accommodated, tolerated, or 'saved' by Catholic education, but are instead sites of infinite potential from which Catholic education can gain insight and inspiration. I would like to offer an affirmative set of reflections for Catholic education that prioritise educational and theological perspectives committed to queer thriving, that is, to perspectives that afford LGBTQ+ people the chance to live lives that are liveable, fulfilling, and worthwhile (Greteman, 2018). In this sense, the chapter is focused less on 'reconciling' LGBTQ+ lives to the precepts of traditional Church teaching, and more on how to refigure Catholic education so that its historical and contemporaneous heteronormativity can be transformed for, with, and by LGBTQ+ people.

Secondly, I position queer theologies as resources for this work given the capacity of this tradition to disrupt the monopoly that heteronormative theologies have had in discussions around sexualities, genders, and Catholic education. Beginning from this position, I suggest that a greater degree of theological spaciousness is needed in navigating the relation between Catholic education and LGBTQ+ people in more productive, and less homophobic and transphobic, terms. I structure my thoughts in this chapter around two potential contributions queer theologies can offer those in Catholic education who affirm the principal of queer thriving:

1. Queer theologies can offer Catholic education a theological resource that remedies overly disembodied approaches to questions of sexuality, gender, and education.
2. Queer theologies can offer Catholic education alternative, more expansive, understandings of LGBTQ+ and religious subjectivities that foreground the agency of LGBTQ+ people.

From here, I move to some reflections on the kinds of commitments that might be needed for enacting a queer approach to Catholic education. As a proviso to this chapter, I think it is firstly necessary for me stipulate how am I using the term queer, as this will be helpful in getting to grips with the project of *queering Catholic education* that I see as worthwhile.

How Can We Understand 'Queer'?

Queer theologian Professor Susannah Cornwall points to the difficulty of defining 'queer', emphasising how 'the very concept of queer has built into it from the start an idea of elusiveness, uncertainty, non-fixity, and a resistance to closed definitions' (2011, p. 9). For Cornwall, 'queer' is a term that is necessarily uncontainable, subverting the neatness of static classifications. Despite this, there still exists for Cornwall the possibility of us attending to some of the enduring features that have become associated with 'queer', and she sets about this task by indicating queer's 'treble function of noun, verb and adjective' (2011, p. 9). I borrow her understanding of queer as both a noun and verb in this way as it offers a useful route for coming to grips with what queer might mean, without losing its complexity.

It is difficult to determine exactly when queer began to be used as a signifier for identity. Indeed, right up to the 1960s queer was more often used as a homophobic insult directed towards gay men and lesbians particularly. By the 1980s and early 1990s onwards, however, queer began to positively enter the vocabulary of lesbian, gay, and bisexual activism, with groups like Queer Nation using slogans like 'We're here! We're queer! Get used to it!' in their political work, for instance (Pickett, 2009, p. 157). The use of the noun queer in this way became allied with a form of sexual and/or gender-based self-identity that refused to comply to the conformities of heterosexual and cisgender society. To think of queer in this nominal sense is to signify a position that inhabits a tension: on the one hand, it identifies a position (naming it and thus 'fixing' it in a way), yet at the same time attempts to displace the very logic of identity that we call upon to signify our experiences to begin with. In this sense, queer as noun has *active* effects, which brings me to its other function as verb.

Given its roots in the sixteenth century German word *quer* meaning strange or oblique (Bevir, 2010, p. 1131), it is perhaps unsurprising that queer has also come to encapsulate a particular style of *doing* something, specifically in a way that is strange or perplexing. This commitment is grounded in a very specific focus: namely, the interruption of heteronormativity, that is the interruption of the social, cultural, historical, and economic privileging of heterosexuality. To queer, then, involves getting under the skin of something and turning it on its head, making it strange, to expose and disrupt the tools of homophobia, biphobia, and/or transphobia that inform the very thing that one is queering. It is in understanding queer in this active, praxis-oriented way that queer projects can be tied to a disidentifying politics, where the neatness and fixity of identity categories are called into question: it is a practice that refuses to grant heterosexual identity, and indeed identity more generally, ultimacy over our lives and relationships.

This turn towards queer as noun and verb has gained much traction across the humanities and social sciences and has more recently entered the theological realm in the form of *queer theologies*. The main purpose of the next section of this chapter is to offer some notes on the value of queer theologies for Catholic education, so allow me at this stage to give you a sense of how these ideas have translated in the theological realm.

What Are Queer Theologies?

Building on the traditions of liberation, feminist, and wider contextual theologies that gained traction across the latter half of the twentieth century, queer theologies emerged initially as gay and lesbian theologies in the 1970s and 1980s. Gay and lesbian theologies developed as affirmative responses to theological and religious homophobia, particularly in the context of HIV and AIDS and the Church's implication therein. Among other emphases, gay and lesbian theologies foregrounded the importance of a contextual approach to theological and biblical hermeneutics, arguing for an understanding of God that could be gauged through an attention towards, and solidarity with, the lives of gay men and lesbians (Stuart, 2003). Queer theologies emerged slightly later, towards the end of the 1990s and into the early 2000s, and was influenced heavily by wider developments in queer theory taking place across the humanities and social sciences at the time.

At the risk of being too simplistic, one of the ways in which queer theologies developed in distinction from gay and lesbian theologies was in queer theologies' emphasis on the non- ultimacy of identity as a basis for theology. Whereas gay and lesbian theologies were necessarily framed in an attention to the specificity of gay and lesbian identities, queer theologies were characterised more by a focus on the contingency of such identity categories altogether (Greenough, 2019). This contingency is of importance to many queer theologians in building theologies that can enable liberation from sexual and gendered oppression for everyone, irrespective of identity. This is not to suggest that queer theologies have abandoned those who identify as gay or lesbian: rather, many queer theologies begin from the view that normative accounts of identities like 'gay', 'lesbian', or 'straight' are part of the problem, and that the mystery of God is perhaps more helpfully revealed in modes of relationship that actively resist what many queer theologians perceive to be the idolatry of homophobia, transphobia, and other manifestations of heteronormativity. In this sense, what distinguishes queer theologies from gay or lesbian theologies is less a distance from the lives of gay men and lesbians and more a recognition of the fact that our embodied sexual and gendered lives are too complex, too unwieldy, to be contained within neat and essentialised identity labels. In this way, queer theologies have come to attend, not only to gay men and lesbians, but also to the lives and liberation of bisexual, trans, non-binary, and queer people, among others.

Furthermore, queer theologies have developed complex relationships with institutionalised churches, like Catholicism. Some have seen queer liberation as possible within a reframing of traditional theology (so called 'apologetic' approaches, that look on tradition with a 'queer-view mirror', to borrow Chris Greenough's (2019) phrasing, while others have positioned such liberation as a project that is impossible to achieve within the context of an irredeemably homophobic and transphobic tradition. Such perspectives can be likened to the works of queer theologians such as Althaus-Reid (2000) and Linn Tonstad (2016a, 2018), who argue for the need for an 'indecent' approach to theology that refuses apology to heteronormative theological and religious traditions.

Having set the scene for what queer theologies are and how they emerged, I now turn to the first of my substantive claims in this chapter, namely that queer theologies can offer Catholic education a theological resource that remedies overly disembodied approaches to questions of sexuality, gender, and education.

Embodiment and Queer Theologies

The claim that education, and Catholic education in particular, can take an overly disembodied approach to questions of sexuality is not one I would perceive to be particularly controversial. Indeed, it is a largely established trope within sex education research, with many pointing to students' critiques of sex education on the grounds of its erasure of the body, pleasure, and the sensual in how sexuality is understood (Allen et al., 2014). Allen (2020) situates this trend within discourses of human reproduction, risk-reduction, and pregnancy and disease prevention that often saturate sex education curricula. She argues that such discourses have the effect of distancing 'students from the sexual and sensual possibilities of human corporeality, while simultaneously dampening their desire and any curiosity around it' (2020, 6). In response to this landscape, I see queer theologies as valuable resources for Catholic education, for they extend and subvert the limits of religious heteronormativity through an attention to the body, sensuality, pleasure, and their possibilities.

On sketching out what it means to speak of 'queer theology', Marcella Althaus-Reid and Lisa Isherwood write of how queer theologians 'plunge into flesh in its unrefined fullness in order to embrace and be embraced by the divine. Bodies tell very complex and challenging stories and these now become the stuff of the salvific tale' (2007, 310). In these terms, queer theologies are interested less in pinning down an absolutist account of God or of sexual ethics, and more in exposing theologies to the messiness of our embodied and sexual lives, a messiness through which alternative possibilities beyond the (hetero)norm can be necessitated by, and cultivated for, queer people. Althaus-Reid and Isherwood write of how the divine relates to the flesh by drawing from the incarnation in the birth of Jesus Christ:

> That the divine immersed itself in flesh and that flesh is now divine is Queer Theology at its peak. There can be no sanitisation here or something of the divine essence will be lost – it is not the genetically modified, metaphysical son of god that declares the divine-human conjunction, but the screaming baby born amidst the cow shit and fleas, covered in his birthing blood. (2007, p. 310)

Thus, it is through an attention to the complexities of our embodied and sexual lives that heteronormativity collapses. In light of this, an alternative imaginary for

God becomes both necessary and possible, an imaginary Goss (2002) takes seriously, for example, when he frames homosexual sexual acts as expressions of theological and Eucharistic communion with God. In these terms, queer Christian theologies can be seen as operating within a register committed to the building up of an alternative, *fleshy* Kingdom of God, one where the hypocrisies and idols of heteronormativity are overcome in and through the pleasures and pains of the body and of desire (Althaus-Reid, 2001, 2003). To my mind, it is queer theology's focus on the body as something to be embraced and celebrated, rather than denounced and repressed, that renders it so valuable for those of us working within and or alongside Catholic education, particularly for those interested in foregrounding the body, sensuality and desire in ways that are healthy and fulfilling.

Thinking about questions of desire and identity in more expansive and enabling terms brings me to the second claim of this chapter, namely that queer theologies can offer Catholic education alternative, more expansive, understandings of LGBTQ+ and religious subjectivities that foregrounds the agency of LGBTQ+ people.

Queer Agency and Queer Theologies

The claim that education can rely too heavily on narratives of vulnerability in relation to queerness, has emerged as a critique held by several scholars interested in cultivating thriving school spaces for LGBTQ+ youth (Bryan, 2017; Greteman, 2018). The basis of their critique lies in their sensitivity to the ambiguous and potentially pathologising effects of framing queer youth as inevitably 'at-risk', rather than as complex and multi-faceted human beings. Indeed, Tom Waidzunas (2012) has discussed the looping effects of conflating LGBTQ+ lives solely with narratives of victimhood, vulnerability and suicidality, in which the creation of 'at-risk' LGBTQ+ youth is sustained precisely through the discursive construction of queerness in these terms. It is in this sense too that I voice a certain degree of frustration with approaches to LGBTQ+ youth in Catholic education that are framed only in terms of pastoral support or through an anti-bullying lens: while pastoral support and preventative approaches to bullying are important and necessary, I think these approaches also risk reinscribing deficit tropes of the 'poor suffering queer' if they are not also complemented by efforts to expose and sustain the productive aspects of LGBTQ+ life and the agency of LGBTQ+ staff and students in educational settings. In these terms, Jen Gilbert and colleagues (2018), while recognising the ongoing challenges and inequities experienced by LGBTQ+ youth in educational contexts, has pointed to the need to reframe how we think about and engage with the stories of LGBTQ+ people. In particular, she emphasises the importance of attending to the 'intimate possibilities' of LGBTQ+ lives, possibilities that create spaces for school communities to move beyond the constraints of 'damage-centred' narratives to stories of agency and empowerment that expand who LGBTQ+ youth are, who they want to be, and what kinds of social worlds they want to build.

In responding to this need in the context of Catholic education, I see LGBTQ+ theologies as a valuable resource in how they foreground the agency and life-worlds of LGBTQ+ people in navigating questions of theological authority. Indeed, within queer Christian theologies there has been an ongoing appreciation for the need to engage with theology in ways that affirm LGBTQ+ lives without kow-towing these to the limits of homophobic or transphobic traditions. This is showcased in the work of theologian Grace Jantzen, who writes:

> For many who have had the straight rule of Christendom applied in hurtful and destructive ways, the answer is to slam the book shut altogether and have nothing more to do with this story. For some people that is surely a healthy response, not just 'understandable' in a condescending way, but a very good conclusion to the particular script they have been required to read. But for me that will not do. Part of the reason is that Christendom has not only been the worst of my personal past but also the best of it; and the need to deal with the former requires a reappropriation and transformation of the latter. I will not become a more flourishing person by cutting off my roots. (2001, pp. 276–277)

Queer theologies, at least in terms of how they are framed here, are informed by an honest attempt to face, rather than deny, the injustices created and enacted through theology. Queer theologies arise from a need to imagine theology and theological authority differently, and because of this refuse to give homophobia the last word or to allow homophobia to determine what is or is not Christian, or indeed, Catholic. LGBTQ+ people, in this context, are not passive victims to institutional and theological heteronormativity, but are instead active arbiters of theological praxis and renewal.

Erickson's (2018) understanding of queer theology's 'irreverence' goes further in pointing to the capacity of queer theologies to foreground the agency of queer lives. Erickson characterises queer (Christian) theology as a 'poetry and practice of irreverent criticism' (2018, p. 60), luring forth 'responsibilities of wonder and ethical care where we thought they might not bloom' (2018, p. 74). On this meaning, theological endeavour takes on a 'carnivalesque' quality, 'constantly changing shape and drag' as it exposes and sustains the 'manifold instabilities' that inhere within even 'the most stable or ordinary theological constructions' (2018, p. 74). Theological irreverence 'glances back and subtly rolls its eyes' at God, challenging absolutism and religious fundamentalism by embracing an 'indecent' approach to theological inquiry (2018, p. 62). He concedes that an irreverent queer theology necessarily challenges much of what some people of faith might hold dear or sacred about God and religious teachings: 'Disrespect is hardly my intention, though I most certainly flirt with such danger' (2018, p. 61). In spite of this (or, indeed, because of it) Erickson proceeds anyway, for it is through such irreverence that the 'devastation' caused by static, omnipotent, and anthropocentric conceptions of God can be overcome (2018, pp. 61–62).

Irreverence is also at the heart of the queer theology of Althaus-Reid. On sketching out what it means to speak of 'queer theology', Althaus-Reid writes the following: 'Queer theology is basically an example of high theological doubting or queering, irreverent in the sense that it tends to desacralise what has been made sacred for the sake of ideological interests' (2001, p. 58). For Althaus-Reid queer theology enacts its 'theological' qualities when it disrupts, rather than reproduces or solidifies, heteronormative ideologies and constructions that have been supplanted onto God. Indeed, she writes of how 'one of the most important characteristics of Queer theology' is its 'passion and ability to de-familiarise us with the accepted, with the God- norm' (2001, p. 62). In this way, there 'is nothing quite like Queer theology for making fun of idols' (2001, p. 58): it participates in 'Outing' theology by exposing traditional theology's homophobic hypocrisies and idolatries, and through this enabling queer people to construct an alternative understanding of God and of tradition that is life-affirming and life-enhancing (2001, p. 60). Tonstad (2018) takes this up as well in arguing for a non-apologetic approach to Christian theology, one which does not seek to 'correct' the heteronormativity of Christian traditions and institutions, but rather aims at cultivating alternative theologies characterised by 'a revolution in cultural, economic, and social terms' (2016b, p. 127).

So, in summary then, I have proposed that queer theologies can offer Catholic education:

- A theological resource that remedies overly disembodied approaches to questions of sexuality, gender, and education;
- A theological resource that foregrounds the agency of LGBTQ+ people in their relationship to religion and theology.

But of course, engaging with queer theologies is a praxis that, for some, might be quite removed from the day-to-day grittiness of life in Catholic educational institutions. Indeed, the question of accessibility comes into play: how can we translate these theological contributions into a set of concrete commitments that can be lived out in exploring questions of sexuality, gender, and religion in the day-to-day life of Catholic schools, colleges, and universities? It is in response to this that I forward notes on three commitments that are worth reflecting on in how we think about the enactment of a queer praxis in Catholic educational spaces.

Commitments for Enacting a Queer Praxis in Catholic Education

The first commitment I seek to suggest is a commitment to taking seriously the relationality at the heart of education, i.e. the fact that education always necessarily enacts a living with, and being taught by, others. Attending to this relationality is important in exploring questions of sexuality, gender, and religion in Catholic education because it entails a receptivity on the part of teachers and students to the flesh-and-blood experiences of others. In this sense, living with, and being taught by, others can invite a pedagogy of interruption, where the other with whom we relate exposes us to experiences that displace our attachments to ourselves, our identities and our institutions (Biesta, 2013). By interrupting the bounds of our own egos, a commitment to living with, and being taught by, others can grant us access to new ways of relating (of being, acting, feeling) in this world that have the potential to transcend the limits of already existing social structures and discourses. In this sense, a commitment to living with and being taught by others involves transforming what we desire into what is desirable for others: it creates the conditions for us to set our own priorities aside, to engage out of responsiveness to those typically marginalised or ignored, and to work in ways that are receptive to difference, rather than resistant to it. In this sense, taking seriously the relationality at the heart of education calls into question accounts that narrow the purposes of Catholic education to the preservation of an institutionalised and heteronormative faith identity: transforming what is desired into what is desirable for others requires an alternative imagining of Catholic education that is no longer vested in necessarily sustaining Catholic institutions (and the heteronormativity therein) or a supposedly 'shared' Catholic identity. At the interface between sexuality, gender, and Catholic education, this kind of commitment seems especially appropriate if we are to move beyond the kind of identarian defensiveness that often characterises heteronormative resistances to queer thriving.

The second commitment I seek to suggest is a commitment to being sensitive to people's embeddedness within religious traditions. No education is context-free, and is instead always necessarily informed by, and situated within, particular cultural, political, social and religious settings. For me, attending to this contextual embeddedness is important in exploring questions of sexuality, gender, and religion because it exposes Catholic education to the material messiness of religious traditions, with their living and breathing histories. In this sense, religious traditions are not reducible to a disconnected and propositional set of codes about the world and about God, but instead also involve embodied and affective forms of experiences (including ritual and so on) within which we are entangled and from which the potential for transformation depends. Recognising our embeddedness within traditions allows us to be honest about the fact that no tradition is static, and that the absolutism with which heteronormative doctrine are often treated invariably falls short in the face of life's complexity. This is crucial for all those who are seriously committed to challenging heteronormativity, homophobia, and transphobia within Catholicism.

The third and final commitment I seek to forward is a commitment to challenging monolithic understandings of religious traditions. Religious traditions are not uniform entities, but are rather ever-evolving and living traditions constituted by a plurality of perspectives and experiences. While I cannot claim authority on the day-to-day workings of Catholic school life, on the level of school policy and classroom practice this point is significant as it exposes both the limits of articulating school policies in deference to a narrowly defined religious/institutional code, as well as the theological inaccuracy of classroom resources that represent Catholicism in purely heteronormative terms. In this way, queering Catholic education could require Catholic school administrators expanding how religion is framed in the likes of admissions criteria and school enrolment protocols, and could also require educators diversifying how religion is represented in classroom resources and discussions. Relatedly, exploring the pluralities of religion in the classroom space could require providing students and educators with opportunities for discussing, expressing, and embodying their religious, sexual, and gendered identities and experiences in ways that are open, sensitive to others, and affirmative of difference. In this sense, cultivating thriving spaces for LGBTQ+ people in Catholic education would be dependent on classroom and school communities collectively promoting the conditions necessary for honest and enabling conversations and experiences.

Conclusion

To conclude, polarisations at the interface between religious and queer concerns have been a longstanding feature in discourses around religion and sexuality/gender, not least in connection to Catholic education. Over the course of this chapter, I have made efforts to respond productively to this context by reflecting on two potential contributions that queer theologies can make to Catholic education:

1. Queer theologies can offer Catholic education a theological resource that remedies overly disembodied approaches to questions of sexuality, gender, and education;
2. Queer theologies can offer Catholic education alternative, more expansive, understandings of LGBTQ+ and religious subjectivities that foreground the agency of queer people.

Central to this task, I have proposed, is a commitment to taking seriously the relationality at the heart of education, a relationality that entails an openness to others in ways that are attuned to the contextually situated and pluralistic nature of religious traditions. As a note of caution, however, I think it is important to resist framing the work I have proposed through the lens of 'quick-fix' solutions. The Catholic tradition has always been a work in progress, and always will be: as such, no 'pure' or 'perfect' solution to how students and educators can best resist religious heteronormativity is possible. Instead, I think it would be more worthwhile and more productive for all of us interested in Catholic education to begin discussions around religion and LGBTQ+ identity from the vantage point of where we currently find ourselves, and working supportively with each other from this to explore other ways of collectively being, relating, and thriving in this world.

As a parting word, I draw attention to the author Jeanette Winterson, who writes the following about story-telling in her 1985 novel *Oranges are not the only fruit*.

> Of course that is not the whole story, but that is the way with stories; we make them what we will. It's a way of explaining the universe while leaving the universe unexplained, it's a way of keeping it all alive, not boxing it into time. Everyone who tells a story tells it differently, just to remind us that everybody sees it differently. Some people say there are true things to be found, some people say all kinds of things can be proved … The only thing for certain is how complicated it all is, like string full of knots. It's all there but hard to find the beginning and impossible to fathom the end. (2001, p. 119)

Winterson's remarks are interesting in how they point to significant questions to consider further in progressing research on queer thriving in Catholic education. For instance, how can Catholic education challenge theological heteronormativity in a manner that sets about 'explaining the universe' a little, while also 'leaving the universe unexplained'? How can Catholic education do this in a way that can keep Catholic education alive, not boxing it in time? Indeed, are there ways of imagining Catholic education that acknowledge and build upon the fact that the traditions we encounter and live by are determined neither entirely by their 'beginning' nor 'end', but by the messiness of what is 'there' in the complexities of the present?

I wage the claim that we are all (LGBTQ+ or straight, Catholic or not) more than how we identify, and, indeed, are identified, and that it is in the mysteriousness of living that such a view is borne out for humanity. Queer theologies provide much scope in this respect, for they offer us discourses that, in their attentiveness to the body and to the agency of LGBTQ+ people, open up spaces for us to rethink ourselves, the world, and its religions without granting primacy to dogmatic narratives of alienation or shame. While my mapping of what queer thriving might look like for Catholic education is by no means exhaustive, I nonetheless hope it goes some way in opening a conversation between Catholic education and LGBTQ+ lives that delights in the 'knottiness' of it all. Indeed, the only thing for certain is how complicated it all is.

References

Allen, L. (2020). Breathing life into sexuality education: Becoming sexual subjects. *Philosophical Inquiry in Education, 27*(1), 1–13.
Allen, L., Rasmussen, M. L., & Quinlivan, K. (Eds.). (2014). *The politics of pleasure in sexuality education: Pleasure bound*. Routledge.
Althaus-Reid, M. (2000). *Indecent theology: Theological perversions in sex, gender, and politics*. Routledge.
Althaus-Reid, M. (2001). Outing theology: Thinking Christianity out of the church closet. *Feminist Theology, 27*, 57–67.
Althaus-Reid, M. (2003). *The Queer God*. Routledge.
Althaus-Reid, M., & Isherwood, L. (2007). Thinking theology and queer theory. *Feminist Theology, 15*(3), 302–314.
Bailey, S. (2017). From invisibility to visibility: A policy archaeology of the introduction of anti-transphobic and anti-homophobic bullying guidelines into the Irish primary education system. *Irish Educational Studies, 36*(1), 25–42.
Bevir, M. (2010). *Encyclopaedia of political theory*. SAGE Publications, Inc.
Biesta, G. (2013). *The beautiful risk of education*. Routledge.
Bryan, A. (2017). Queer youth and mental health: What do educators need to know? *Irish Educational Studies, 36*(1), 73–89.
Callaghan, T. (2016). Young, queer, and Catholic: Youth resistance to homophobia in Catholic schools. *Journal of LGBT Youth, 13*(3), 270–287.
Cornwall, S. (2011). *Controversies in queer theology*. SCM Press.
Erickson, J. J. (2018). Irreverent theology: On the queer ecology of creation. In W. Bauman (Ed.), *Meaningful flesh: Reflections on religion and nature for a queer planet* (pp. 55–79). Earth, Milky Way: punctum books.
Fahie, D. (2016). 'Spectacularly exposed and vulnerable'—How Irish equality legislation subverted the personal and professional security of lesbian, gay and bisexual teachers. *Sexualities, 19*(4), 393–411.

Gilbert, J., Fields, J., Mamo, L., & Lesko, N. (2018). Intimate possibilities: The beyond Bullying Project and stories of LGBTQ sexuality and gender in US Schools. *Harvard Educational Review, 88*(2), 163–183.

Goss, R. (2002). *Queering Christ: Beyond Jesus Acted Up*. Resource Publication.

Grace, A. P., & Wells, K. (2005). The Marc Hall Prom predicament: Queer individual rights v. Institutional Church Rights in Canadian Public Education. *Canadian Journal of Education/Revue canadienne de l'éducation, 28*(3), 237–270.

Greenough, C. (2019). *Queer theologies: The basics*. Routledge.

Greteman, A. (2018). *Sexualities and genders in education: Towards queer thriving*. Palgrave Macmillan.

Herriot, J., & Callaghan, T. (2019). Possibilities for trans-affirming policy potential: A case study of a Canadian Catholic school. *Journal of Catholic Education, 22*(3), 57–83.

Jantzen, G. (2001). Contours of a queer theology. *Literature and Theology, 15*(3), 276–285.

Love, B. L., & Tosolt, B. (2013). Go underground or in your face: Queer students' negotiation of all-girls Catholic schools. *Journal of LGBT Youth, 10*(3), 186–207.

McDonough, G. (2012). *Beyond obedience and abandonment: Toward a theory of dissent in Catholic education*. McGill-Queen's University Press.

McDonough, G. (2016). Cultivating identities: The Catholic school as diverse ecclesial space. *Philosophical Inquiry in Education, 23*(2), 160–177.

Neary, A. (2013). Lesbian and gay teachers' experiences of 'coming out' in Irish schools. *British Journal of Sociology of Education, 34*(4), 583–602.

Neary, A. (2017). *LGBT-Q teachers, civil partnership and same-sex marriage: The ambivalences of legitimacy*. Routledge.

Pickett, B. L. (2009). *Historical dictionary of homosexuality*. The Scarecrow Press, Inc.

Stuart, E. (2003). *Gay and lesbian theologies: Repetitions with critical difference*. Routledge.

Tonstad, L. M. (2016a). *God and difference: The trinity, sexuality, and the transformation of finitude*. Routledge.

Tonstad, L. M. (2016b). Everything queer, nothing radical? *Svensk Teologisk Kvartalskrift, 92*, 120–129.

Tonstad, L. M. (2018). *Queer theology: Beyond apologetics*. Cascade Books.

Waidzunas, T. (2012). Young, gay, and suicidal: Dynamic nominalism and the process of defining a social problem with statistics. *Science, Technology and Human Values, 37*(2), 199–225.

Winterson, J. (2001). *Oranges are not the only fruit*. Vintage Books.

Dr. Seán Henry is a Lecturer in Education at Edge Hill University. Prior to this, Seán worked as a Postdoctoral Researcher at the Research Centre on Inclusive and Equitable Cultures, Technological University Dublin (2021-2022), and as an Assistant Lecturer in Philosophy of Education at Maynooth University (2019-2021). He currently has a monograph in development entitled *Queer Thriving in Religious Schools*, which offers a queer theory of Jewish, Christian, and Muslim education, and is also in the process of co-editing a special issue on gender and adult education for the journal *Studies in the Education of Adults*. He has published around issues of sexuality, gender, religion, and education in several international, peer-reviewed journals including *Journal of Philosophy of Education, Sex Education, Educational Theory, Ethics and Education*, and *Cambridge Journal of Education*. He currently sits on the advisory board for the International Network of Philosophers of Education, as well as the editorial board for *Ethics and Education*. Throughout his career so far, Seán has contributed to a range of funded research projects. These include projects on: building equitable policy responses to the Covid-19 pandemic; crafting resources for responding educationally to so-called radicalisation and extremism in schools; and designing materials for integrating social justice concerns into higher education teaching. In addition to his research on religion, gender, and sexuality, Seán has started research on the queer pedagogical potential of comedy, and on theories of embodiment and intersectionality more broadly.

Before starting his academic career, Seán qualified as a teacher of Religious Education and English.

Chapter 4
A Call to Reimagine Catholic Education and Schooling—A Response to Dr. Seán Henry

Cora O'Farrell

Introduction

Dr. Henry's writings contained in this volume address the intersection between religion, queerness and Catholic schooling. They are informative and helpful for anyone interested in matters relating to LGBTQ+ and Catholic education. They contain an exposition of the nature of queer theologies and the potential contributions, which they offer to Catholic education. Henry suggests some commitments for enacting a queer praxis in Catholic education and he proposes a radical restructuring in order to disrupt the divide between Catholicism and queerness in schooling. His intention in writing, is to positively engage with Catholic schooling rather than to discard or discredit it. Henry's insights are challenging at times and his invitation to change, is provocative and worthy of attention. Furthermore, Henry presents the subversive idea of Catholic education itself, thriving through a process of queering, which demands a change of mindset, an opening of the imagination and controversially a decoupling of Catholic schooling from Catholic identity.

Henry speaks of how the thriving of LGBTQ+ students in Catholic schools demands more of schools than the provision of pastoral initiatives aimed at supporting such students, who are often viewed primarily in terms of their vulnerability. The clichéd image of an at risk, suicidal, traumatised segment of the school population should not be the starting point for discussion, or the impetus for inclusion according to Henry. Interestingly, the tendency to emphasise this stereotype is not particular to Catholic schooling, and the most recent Irish School Climate Survey (2022) commissioned by *Belong To, LGBTQ+ Youth in Ireland*, provides an example of how reports are often framed in terms of the negative experiences of students. Whilst the statistics contained in the School Climate Survey behove schools not to downplay the risks to LGBTQ+ students and to continue the fine work on the ground in supporting

---

C. O'Farrell (✉)
Dublin City University (Mater Dei Centre for Catholic Education), Dublin, Ireland
e-mail: cora.ofarrell@dcu.ie

students; Henry's point is that the agency of such students needs to be more to the fore. Instead they should be viewed as 'sites of infinite potential from which Catholic education can gain insight and inspiration'. In essence there is a reciprocity there which is not fully realised. This sentiment is reflected in the underlying message of Fr James Martin SJ (2018), advocate for the inclusion of members of the LGBTQ+ community in the Church, when he declares that LGBTQ+ people are a gift to the Church.

The celebration of LGBTQ+ students is happening more frequently in Catholic schools in recent years through Pride week activities and flying the Pride flag.[1] Such celebrations happen within the context of the hetero- and cisnormative dogmas and theologies of the institutional Church. For some in the Church, these celebrations of queer identities are antithetical to what it means to be Catholic and for others, they embrace the very definition of what it means to be Catholic. Pope Francis is an ally for LGBTQ+ people and in 2013, early in his papacy, he spoke critically of the Church for putting dogma before love. In 2016, during an unscripted interview on board a plane, he said that Christians owe apologies to gays and others who have been offended or exploited by the Church: 'I repeat what the Catechism of the Catholic Church says: that they must not be discriminated against, that they must be respected and accompanied pastorally'. More recently, defending the rights of LGBTQ+ people, Pope Francis has called for the global decriminalisation of LGBTQ+.

Pope Francis words are in effect a call for change, but it is one which appears to be reflective of the voice of the People of God who have spoken through the Synodal process. Addressing the inclusion of LGBTQ+ people in the life of the Church, the Irish *Synodal Synthesis* document (Irish Bishops Conference, 2021) states that there is a 'clear, overwhelming call for the full inclusion of LGBTQ+ people in the Church, expressed by all ages and particularly by the young and by members of the LGBTQ+ community themselves' (p. 11). Further afield, a working document entitled *Enlarge the Space of your Tent* (General Secretariat of the Synod, 2022), which was prepared as a stimulus for discussion at the European Continental phase of the synodal process in Prague in February, provided a synthesis of collated national submissions. Paragraph 39 within that document names LGBTQ+ people as 'among those feeling a tension between belonging to the Church and their own loving relationships' (p. 22).

Whilst Pope Francis advocates for the rights of LGBTQ+ people, he has not called for change in official Church teaching. Similarly Fr James Martin who has been an outspoken ally of LGBTQ+ inclusion in the Church for a number of years has also stopped short of calling for a change in Church teaching. An editorial in *The Tablet* (in 2023), expresses the frustration for many with such a stance: 'this is precisely where one of the chief difficulties with the traditional Catholic position arises. It is problematic—if not contradictory—to stand up for the dignity of a gay person of either sex while deploring what it is about them that defines them as gay, namely their desire for intimate personal relationships with others of the same sex'. With regards

---

[1] For a fuller discussion of this see the chapter by Sean Whittle in this volume, discussing RSE provision in Catholic schools in Northern Ireland.

to the possibility of changes to Church teaching, the Synodal Working Document referred to above, which was prepared for the European Continental phase, states that Church teaching on a range of themes including LGBTQ+ was a common issue raised across the continent. Paragraph 51 highlights this point, as well as emphasising differing views and the 'challenges of giving a definitive community stance on any of these issues' (p. 27). Locally, the Irish Synthesis Document for this synod also speaks of divergence in relation to a call for a change in Church teaching. According to the document, those in favour of change asked if the Church is 'sufficiently mindful of developments with regard to human sexuality and the lived reality of LGBTQI+ couples'. Those expressing concern with regards to change were anxious that a change in the Church's teaching would be simply 'conforming to secular standards and contemporary culture'.

An influential voice in the Church has emerged as not only an ally for LGBTQ+ people, an advocate for their inclusion in the Church and the protection of their human rights, but also, more radically, he is calling for change in Church teaching. He is Cardinal Jean-Claude Hollerich of Luxembourg, *Relator General* for the Synod on Synodality and President of the Commission of the Bishops' Conferences of the European Union. Speaking in an interview with the German Catholic news agency (KNA) in 2022, he declared that the 'sociological-scientific foundation of Church teaching on homosexuality is no longer correct'. In Ireland, Mark Patrick Hedderman addressing the debate on gender identity is also seeking change

> The plan of salvation, so ingeniously orchestrated by the triune God before the world ever began........... must be accomplished on a universal scale; and it must include every tribe, tongue, people and nation, but even more importantly, every variety, and every possibility of human identity that presents itself in the multifaceted panoply of our variegated species. As Catholics, of the future, we must face a few biological and theological facts: we are each one of us, God's work of art, and the Holy Spirit is the artist. Our business is to become the unique and original work of art that we were intended to be. (2021)

Dr Henry's chapter coheres with this positionality and he states that 'our embodied sexual and gendered lives are 'too complex, too unwieldy, to be contained within neat and essentialised identity labels'.

Identity is at the heart of Henry's analysis, with disidentification in particular being at the core of his argument. He seeks to move beyond granting legitimacy to 'ossifying and divisive dichotomies' and he calls on Catholic education to begin imagining alternative ways of relating to questions of sexuality and gender. He aligns himself with queer theologies and their emphasis on the non-ultimacy of identity as a basis for theology. Drawing from the literature on queer theologies, he exposes a threefold understanding of the term 'queer' from the perspectives of its use as a noun, a verb and an adjective. Henry suggests that queer theologies provide a resource for a disruption to the taken for granted assumption that Catholic education should exist as a 'site of preserving a narrowly construed understanding of Catholic identity'. Moving into the domain of education more generally, he outlines Biesta's argument for the dissociation of education from identity and he highlights the work of Ruitenberg (2010) who also problematises the limits imposed by identity. Influenced by these theorists, Henry himself calls for a shift in the *identitarian* terms of reference typically used when addressing the divide between Catholicism and queerness in Catholic schooling. The work of the Catholic school, he says, would then become less about confirming or assuming alliance to religious identity on the part of its students, and more about 'exposing the traditions of Catholicism to the formative possibilities created by their own potential self-effacement'. This, according to Henry would entail desacralising what has traditionally been made sacred, in order to understand the very idea of sacredness more fully.

It is clear that Henry's proposal for *disidentificatory* praxes in Catholic education is parabolic in nature. It turns everything upside down and inside out. It is disquieting and feels uncomfortable. It disrupts and queers current modes of practice in Catholic schools. It invites a playful reimagining of the work in Catholic schools, which is energising to those disenfranchised by aspects of current practice which are stuck and unfit for our current cultural context. At its very heart, is the relational; first and foremost, the person. Catholic education is Christocentric and Henry's invitation to an openness beyond rigid forms of identity is not at variance with Jesus' message. Consider the Parable of the Good Samaritan where identities are 'ossifying and divisive' to such an extent that a dying man on the side of the road is bypassed and ignored by all except one person who was willing to discard the mantle of identity and see the person before all else.

Do those who are involved in the project of Catholic education have the courage to take the risk? Can it divert its gaze from the destination of Jericho in favour of accompanying people in the space where they are? It appears that the answer to these questions can be in the affirmative as a different more outward facing approach emerges in the landscape of Catholic education, in the guise of the *Global Compact for Education* (Congregation for Catholic Education, 2019). Recognising that we are living in a context of epochal change, Pope Francis proposes such a global compact on education capable of responding to the current 'transformation that is not only cultural but also anthropological, creating a new semantics while indiscriminately discarding traditional paradigms' (p. 5). He asks for a renewal of our passion for a more open and inclusive education, 'including patient listening, constructive dialogue and better mutual understanding'. It seems that the aspirations of the *Global Compact on Education* and the invitation issued by Dr Henry, have much in common.

Conclusion

On February 25th, 2022, a one day conference organised by the *Network for Researchers in Catholic Education* took place at the *Mater Dei Centre for Catholic Education* (MDCCE), at Dublin City University. Those in attendance experienced a range of paper presentations and discussions on the theme for the day: *What is the research agenda for Catholic Education in relationship to LGBTQ+ matters?* The proceedings from that conference form much of the content in this present volume and their quality is undoubted. However as with many academic conferences, the real value of the day was in its relational dimension and the space it provided for people to tell their stories. Those stories included testimonies from people who are struggling with Catholic education environments in relation to LGBTQ+ and those who are satisfied with the current status quo. The discussions were respectful on the whole and there was an openness to learning. The dialogue which began on that day has continued during four episodes of *Conversations from the Classroom*, a podcast series hosted by Dr. David Kennedy of MDCCE, where the academic, educational and pastoral dimensions of Catholic education's relationship with LGBTQ+ matters are further unpacked. Such spaces for dialogue are imperative, for that which is foreign, strange or queer can appear dangerous and risky. It breeds fear. Breaking down barriers and building bridges happens best in the relational space of deep listening where neither side comes with a set agenda, and where each is open to change and to be changed. Henry captures this idea eloquently in stating that 'it is in our relationships with others that the limits of the existing order of things collapse and alternative possibilities (beyond that which is currently perceptible or intelligible) emerge'.

Henry's contribution to reimagining Catholic education is a very valuable one. His call to transcend the limits of identification is a call to let go of tightly held, perhaps even controlling, modes of education. As has been outlined, this is not anathema to a Christocentric, parabolic way of teaching, which seeks to subvert our righteousness and our comforts. The disruptive quality of Henry's argument is a welcome bedfellow for ongoing changes in approaches to Catholic education.

References

Congregation for Catholic Education. (2019). *Global Compact on Education Vademecum*. Retrieved from https://www.educationglobalcompact.org/resources/Risorse/vademecum-english.pdf

Editor. (2nd February, 2023). *A Church teaching with shaky foundations*. The Tablet. https://www.thetablet.co.uk/editors-desk/1/22771/a-church-teaching-with-shaky-foundations

General Secretariat of the Synod. (2022). *Enlarge the Space of your Tent (Is 54:2) Working Document for the Continental Stage*. https://www.synod.va/content/dam/synod/common/phases/continental-stage/dcs/Documento-Tappa-Continentale-EN.pdf

Hedderman, M. P. OSB (2021). *Saving private Ryan Irish Institute for catholic studies*. Accessed online https://www.youtube.com/watch?v=D7ZA58P09_A

Irish Bishops Conference. (2021). *Synthesis of the Consultation in Ireland for the Diocesan Stage of the Universal Synod 2021–2023*. https://synod.ie/wp-content/uploads/2022/08/National-Synthesis-17-50-Fri-12th-August-.pdf?swcfpc=1

Martin, J. S. J. (2018). *Building a bridge: How the Catholic church and the LGBT community can enter into a relationship of respect, compassion and sensitivity*. Harperone.

Ruitenberg, C. (2010). Queer politics in schools: A Rancièrean reading. *Educational Philosophy and Theory, 42*(5–6), 618–634.

Dr. Cora O'Farrell is an Assistant Professor of Religious Education in the School of Human Development, DCU. She is the Director of the *Mater Dei Centre for Catholic Education*. Cora's research interests include Religious Education, Practical Theology and Children's Spirituality. She has a passion for Montessori inspired forms of Religious Education and has undertaken training in both Catechesis of the Good Shepherd (levels 1 and 2) and Godly Play. Her doctoral research which was completed in 2016, utilised Godly Play to give voice to children with regard to their experience and desire for spiritual education. Cora is a Godly Play Trainer and a founding member of Godly Play Ireland. She is also a Deep Talk practitioner. Cora's background in education is as a primary teacher initially.

Chapter 5
Encounters with LGBTQ+ Lives in Catholic Schools: A Fragile Hermeneutical Space?—A Response to Dr. Seán Henry

David Kennedy

In the opening chapter, Dr. Henry has made a significant effort to open up an informed space for constructive and respectful dialogue to take place about the role and position of Catholic school communities, their tradition, the educational visions it embodies, and people who identify as LGBTQ+ and their lives. It covers a significant amount of ground, much of which requires a more detailed treatment than is possible in this brief response. To assist readers in discerning the positionality of this response to Dr. Henry's chapter, I offer the following non-exhaustive depiction: *I am a 32 year old, white, cisgender, male, he/him, heterosexual, rural/agricultural upbringing, amateur rugby player and musician, married, and father of two children who works as a theologian, philosopher, and educationalist in a secular university in the Republic of Ireland.*

In attempting to offer a response that moves towards some manner of meaningful and constructive engagement with at least a selection of Henry's insights, I have opted to speak to the question that interrupted and confronted the particularity of my thinking as I read the chapter:

> Is it possible for Catholic school communities to arrive at a more nuanced hermeneutical disposition in relation to LGBTQ+ lives while, at one and the same time, sustaining an authentic response to the call of the Gospel, the Catholic tradition and the educational vision it embodies?

In response to this question, I will be orientated by selected points raised in the opening chapter and tentatively tease them out further. I hope to discern a possible way forward for Catholic school communities in terms of their capacity to enter into an authentic and constructive dialogical relationship with people who identify as LGBTQ+ and their lives.

D. Kennedy (✉)
DCU, Institute of Education, Dublin, Ireland
e-mail: David.Kennedy@dcu.ie

Relationality and Interruption: A Hermeneutical Orientation at the Heart of Education

In his chapter in this volume, Dr. Henry emphasises the importance of attending to the relationality at the heart of education—'the fact that education always necessarily enacts a living with, and being taught by, others' (p.). Attending to this relationality, he suggests, 'nurtures a receptivity on the part of teachers and students to the embodied experiences of others' (p.). This invites *a pedagogy of interruption,* where the other with whom we relate exposes us to experiences that displace our attachment to ourselves, our identities, and our institutions. In developing this approach (which ultimately underpins what Henry wants to propose as 'queer thriving') there is a strong reliance on the insights of Biesta (2013). In responding to Dr. Henry's stance I want to begin by challenging the position of Biesta.

Contrary to the work of Biesta (2013), which Henry cites in this instance, I would argue that a pedagogy of interruption speaks positively to a hermeneutical perspective (Kennedy, 2023). Biesta (2013, 2016, 2021) typically maintains that *interruption* is a radically existential reality that one cannot account for in hermeneutical terms. To dismiss hermeneutics, as Biesta does by understanding it as non-existential, is to misunderstand what hermeneutics involves. This point is evidenced most clearly when one considers the philosophical hermeneutical tradition that has developed along the Heideggerian-Gadamerian line which is radically existential in terms of its hermeneutical orientation (Aldridge, 2017; Kennedy, 2021, 2023). It moves, for example, beyond the enclosed hermeneutical circle encountered in romantic hermeneutical theory (Aldridge, 2017; Kennedy, 2023)—a hermeneutical perspective that Biesta (2016) is appropriately unsatisfied with in terms of its capacity to encounter the other and otherness. Philosophical hermeneutics recognises that truth is always encountered in an embodied state (Gadamer, 2013). This hermeneutical way of 'being-in-the-world' is receptive to the embodied nature of truth. Interpretation, therefore, is not simply about the decodification of texts. It is a process, as Kearney (2015a, 2015b) in *Carnal Hermeneutics* suggests, by which novel meanings are generated from one's embodied encounters with the world in which they dwell. Truth, in this context, is embodied 'in-the-world' and encountered 'in-the-world' in a relational and participatory manner—it interrupts (Kennedy, 2021, 2023).

When considered in an educational context such encounters with the other who 'interrupts' are best described as 'truth-events'—moments of truth whereby the 'happening' character of education as well as its transformative nature are appreciated through meaningful encounters with the particularity and difference of the other (Kennedy, 2021, 2023). In other words, the particularity of the otherness of the other *interrupts* and, in this way, challenges persons and communities in their own particularity. Marion (1991, 2013, 2018) speaks of such events as experiences or encounters with truth as '*gift*', as that which is *given* but, in its reception, is always overloaded by the fullness or the excess of that which is *given.* Marion's account of such encounters carries a necessary hermeneutical attentiveness at its centre, particularly in his conception of *givenness* (Kennedy, 2023; Marion, 2013). In this sense, the category of interruption advocated for by Henry in his chapter carries an implicit understanding of truth as disclosure—as the 'other' that interrupts and transforms (Kennedy, 2023). These 'hermeneutical events of understanding' necessitates a respect for the interpretative autonomy of persons and communities in the exercise of critical thinking. This is particularly important when considering communities and their members' relationship with, and interpretation of, tradition in the light of their encounters with the otherness of the other in-the-world.

A Fragile Hermeneutical Space, Open Narratives, and Interpretative Communities

In his chapter, Dr. Henry calls for a reconfiguration of Catholic education by nurturing an openness to LGBTQ+ lives as opposed to attempting to reconcile them to the precepts of traditional Church teaching. Such a reconfiguration is not such a radical proposition when one recognises that 'tradition' is a living, transformative, embodied, relational reality that is characterised in de-traditionalised and pluralised contexts by the hermeneutical fragility of persons in their mode of being-in-the-world. The diversity and plurality among people, for example, illustrates that there are opportunities offered by an open or inclusive society for situating oneself sharply towards established and assumed social, cultural, religious, and ethical traditions (Kennedy & Cullen, 2021). In this sense, people find themselves situated in a 'fragile hermeneutical space' where reality, even one's inner reality, is 'radically marked by a form of polyphony, by a multiplicity of voices, by plurality' (Pollefeyt, 2020, p. 117). In recognising the fragile hermeneutical space that is peculiar to persons, one can come to appreciate the way in which people relate to tradition(s) in de-traditionalised contexts. This hermeneutical space necessitates greater attunement to the plurality and diversity among people as well as the rupture with tradition that is the dynamism of de-traditionalisation (Boeve, 2003). In the light of this attunement, one grounds their understanding of tradition in a well-defined conceptual horizon. A person's way of looking at *tradition* is contextually contingent in that one does not possess the capacity to take up a detached, disengaged, autonomous observer perspective. It is precisely within this context that one encounters a '*recontextualised*' understanding of tradition (Boeve, 2003).

Traditional perspectives on tradition suggest only partial *cumulative* development occurs in terms of the transmission and living out of tradition (Boeve, 2003). A recontextualised understanding of tradition is novel in terms (1) it is grounding in a different theological paradigm to traditional perspectives on tradition, and (2) its stakes the claim that tradition is in a continuous process of development in spite of or thanks to the discontinuity and rupture constituted by interruptive encounters with otherness (Boeve, 2003; Kennedy, 2021). This recontextualised understanding of tradition brings the *sui generis* relationship that exists between identities and rupture into greater focus, particularly when one recognises that people participate, or at the very least, are a part of tradition therefore rendering detachment from tradition an impossibility—even in the exercise of reason in thinking critically. Although some members of the community, for example, may perpetuate the older form of the tradition. Through recontextualisation, it is difficult for communities to live out their faith within the parameters of the older form of the tradition as many of its components—i.e., images, symbols, rites, narratives, terminology, ideas, and concepts, have embraced a novel expression of the tradition (Boeve, 2003). It is important, however, to recognise that many of the components of the older tradition communities sustain their adherence to the original or authentic inspiration of the tradition, and it is precisely through this adherence that communities advance this same narrative and tradition by giving expression to it in an altered context.

'Tradition', therefore, can be understood a as living, transformative, embodied, relational reality that is engaged in a continuous process of development in spite of or thanks to the discontinuity that arises in the wake of the interruption of the other (Boeve, 2003; 2007; Kennedy, 2021). From this standpoint, one can understand the Christian tradition as well as the educational vision espoused and embodied in Catholic school communities as an 'open-narrative' (Boeve, 2003). A narrative that fosters an open sensitivity towards otherness through its receptivity to the particularity of traditions in attempting to attend to plurality and otherness in a non-totalising way. As an open-narrative tradition not only has the capacity to be the other who interrupts, but to be interrupted and transformed by other who interrupts.

In this recontextualised hermeneutical horizon, Catholic school communities can nurture an openness in their encounters with LGBTQ+ lives. This could lead to a transformative efficacy, where encounters with the 'other' can positively impact on individuals, communities, institutions, and traditions. This positive horizon is possible to cultivate while still maintaining an authentic response to the call of the Gospel, the Catholic tradition, and the educational vision that is embodied by the Catholic school community. When Catholic school communities are understood as interpretative communities that are living out their tradition as an open-narrative their capacity and agency to exercise interpretative autonomy becomes most evident (Dillion, 2018; Go, 2019). This interpretative autonomy accommodates reasoned and faithful assent as well as the possibility for legitimate dissent (Dillion, 2018; Go, 2019) by embracing a mode of 'being-in-the-world' that is orientated towards a hermeneutical openness to the transformative encounter with otherness. It is in this context that I welcome, situate, and interpret Dr. Henry's efforts to move towards a reconfiguration of Catholic education by way of an openness to LGBTQ+ lives as opposed to attempting to reconcile them to the precepts of 'traditional' Church teaching.

My response to Dr. Henry's contribution weaves a Heideggerian-Gadamerian thread throughout its argumentation. In this thread human beings are accounted for as *Dasein* [being-there] conditioned by temporality and Being itself. This relationship between Being and human beings points to an orientation of 'all known activity with what is known (Gadamer, 2013, p. 232) such that 'the knower is not standing over against a situation that he merely observes but […] is directly affected by what he sees (Gadamer, 2013, p. 280). What one perceives or turns their interpretative attention towards is inextricably linked to the same world in which they are situated. The temporal-regionality from which understanding arises is the same therefore as that which has coloured the persons' own situatedness in the world. In this sense, all understanding is self-understanding—at least to a certain extent—and *Dasein* as such is intrinsically orientated towards a basic 'openness' to reality'. This point brings the positionality statement offered at the beginning of this response back into focus.

In cultivating an openness to reality my interpretation, and ultimately my understanding, of LGBTQ+ lives is coloured by my temporal regionality as accounted for in my positionality statement. I will never be able, for example, to speak authentically as a person who identifies as a member of the LGBTQ+ community whose understanding and voice is coloured by their lived experience as a person living in a particular time and place who identifies as LGBTQ+. I can, however, be receptive to my own temporal-regionality and cultivate the innate openness of my being to reality and the truth of the other. In this sense, the aspects outlined in my positionality statement have irrefutably affected my response to Henry's contribution. In fact, this temporal-regionality is impossible to avoid in the process of interpretation and understanding. The influence of my temporal-regionality are manifold and might, at first glance, be identifiable to the reader through my choice of thinkers, or the importance that I afford to tradition, or my explicit commitment to a Catholic vision of the human person and the educational vision and mission of the Catholic tradition. What might evade these initial discernments, however, is the way in which this temporal-regionality points beyond the epistemological to a deeper ontological level (Kennedy, 2023).

In encountering the truth offered in Henry's contribution, and by himself as a *being-in-the-world*, my response attempts to contributed to a wider process of interpretation where by our temporal-regional acts of 'seeing' are brought into conversation with our fore-understandings that each of us 'projects' on that which we see which ultimately culminates in a 'fusion of horizons'. It is difficult, therefore, to over-emphasis the role and influence of a persons' particularity and situatedness as a *being-in-the-world* in the process of interpretation and understanding.

This insight is particularly important for Catholic school communities in their efforts to cultivate and sustain educational environments that are conducive to the flourishing of all persons, including members of their community who identify as LGBTQ+. Such flourishing is described by Dr. Henry as 'queer thriving'. It is imperative that readers do not confuse 'queer thriving' with some aspirational initiative or abstract concept that is being imposed or enforced on stakeholders in Catholic schools by an over-reaching neo-liberalist secular agenda, or by some ideological paradigm masquerading as a pseudo-religion. Rather, a Catholic schools efforts to enable persons who identify as LGBTQ+ to flourish must be understood as a justified and meaningful response to a felt need amidst the members of their community. To respond to this need is not a movement away from Catholic tradition, but to educate in a manner befitting to the model of the educator offered by Jesus of Nazareth throughout his earthly ministry. Jesus always saw the person first in their unique dignity as creatures made in the image and likeness of God. The authenticity or validity, therefore, of a schools claim that their ethos is *of* the Catholic tradition need not be negatively affected by their attempts to meet this need in their community, especially in their approach to human development and flourishing.

Conclusion

In response to Dr. Henry's contribution I have entered into dialogue with a selection of his points and tentatively suggested that a possible way for Catholic school communities to enter into a more authentic and constructive dialogical relationship with people who identify as LGBTQ+ and their lives may present itself by way of the following steps:

1. embracing a way of 'being-in-the-world' that operates from a position of hermeneutical openness to the 'given' of existence,
2. in fostering this hermeneutical attunement, Catholic school communities, through their tradition and the educational vision they embody are able to orientate towards transformative encounters with *truth*, the *other* and *its otherness* by way of their own particularity,
3. through this existential and hermeneutical prism, the Catholic school can be understood as an interpretative community that, on both an individual and communal level, affirms and exercises its capacity and agency to engage in critical thinking with the view to establishing fragile hermeneutical spaces. These are spaces where individuals and communities can exercise their interpretative autonomy in response to that which interrupts thereby allowing reasoned and faithful assent as well as legitimate dissent from Church teaching to become an active possibility for individuals and communities in the educational enterprise.

From this standpoint, the commitments called for by Dr. Henry in terms of the exercise of *queer praxis* in Catholic educational spaces—(1) a commitment to the relationality at the heart of education, (2) a commitment to a sensitivity to the embeddedness of persons in religious traditions that are lived out as opposed to a collection of propositions adhered to by believers, and (3) a comment to challenging monolithic understandings of religious traditions—confront Catholic school communities in the particularity of their own educational vision and tradition. It calls on them to be vulnerable in their openness to the other and to embrace its hermeneutical fragility in a detraditionalized and pluralised context.

References

Aldridge, D. (2017). *A hermeneutics of religious education.* Bloomsbury Academic.
Biesta, G. (2013). *The beautiful risk of education.* Routledge.

Biesta, G. (2016). The rediscovery of teaching: On robot vacuum cleaners, non-egological education and the limits of the hermeneutical worldview. *Educational Philosophy and Theory, 48*(4), 374–392.
Biesta, G. (2021). *World-centred education: A view for the present.* Routledge.
Boeve, L. (2003). *Interrupting tradition: An essay on Christian faith in a postmodern context.* Peeters Press.
Boeve, L. (2007). *God interrupts history: Theology in a time of upheaval.* Continuum.
Dillon, M. (2018). *Postsecular Catholicism: Relevance and renewal.* Oxford University Press.
Gadamer, H. G. (2013). *Truth and method* (J. Weinsheimer & D. G. Marshall. Bloomsbury Academic, Trans.). Sheed & Ward Ltd. [Original German Publication 1960].
Go, J.-C. (2019). *Religious education from a critical realist perspective: Sensus Fidei and critical thinking.* Routledge.
Kearney, R. (2015a). In R. Kearny & T. Brian (Eds.), *Carnal hermeneutics.* Fordham University Press.
Kearney, R. (2015). What is carnal hermeneutics? *New Literary History, 46*(1), 99–124.
Kennedy, D. (2021). *Encounters with truth: The hermeneutical task of religious education in the Republic of Ireland.* Ph.D. Thesis. Dublin City University.
Kennedy, D. (2023). The possibility of a truth-beyond-being and givenness: Engaging the work of Jean-Luc Marion in the hermeneutics of religious education. *British Journal of Religious Education, 45*(4), 334–346.
Kennedy, D., & Cullen, S. (2021). So is it true? Time to embrace the hermeneutical turn in Catholic religious education in the Republic of Ireland. *Religions, 12,* 1059.
Marion, J. L. (1991). *God without being: Hors-Texte.* University of Chicago Press.
Marion, J. L. (2013). *Givenness and hermeneutics.* Marquette University Press.
Marion, J. L. (2018). *Givenness and revelation.* Oxford University Press.
Pollefeyt, D. (2020). Religious education as opening the hermeneutical space. *Journal of Religious Education, 68,* 115–24.

Dr. David Kennedy (B.A.; M.A.; Ph.D.; SFHEA) is Assistant Professor in Religious Education at DCU, Institute of Education. He is Associate Researcher at Mater Dei Centre for Catholic Education, DCU. He is a Senior Fellow with the Higher Education Academy. David's research interests include topics from the disciplines of theology, philosophy and education. He is also the creator, host, and producer of the Podcast Series Conversations from the Classroom developed in association with the Mater Dei Centre for Catholic Education, DCU.

Chapter 6
Towards a Theory of Queer Thriving in Catholic Education—A Response to Dr. Seán Henry

Sean Whittle

Introduction

The idea of 'queer thriving in Catholic education' raises a range of intriguing possibilities and challenges for Catholic education, both at the practical and the theological levels. This response to Dr. Henry's arguments (in Chap. 1) will offer a positive assessment of what he is arguing for at both of these levels.

To begin with, it is important to appreciate the intuitive appeal of linking or grounding the idea of thriving or flourishing as someone who is queer with a Catholic education (both formal and life-long). It is a deeply refreshing way to frame the situation. To briefly draw this out, it is helpful to recognise what is being proposed through aligning *queer thriving* with a *Catholic education*. To thrive or flourish raises central themes in Aristotle's anthropology and moral theory (virtue ethics), drawing on his concept of *eudaimonia*. This is to live well in all aspects of life as a human being. By extension, to thrive as a queer person is to live well in all aspects life precisely as a queer person. This is to embrace your identity and humanity as queer. To link queer thriving or *eudaimonia* with a Catholic education is to depict a positive relationship and role between both. This means that it is through a Catholic education that a queer person is enabled to thrive. Thus a Catholic education supports and enhances the ways in which a queer person thrives—both during their school years and in the years beyond school. In past times it might well have been the case that a queer student at a Catholic school learnt to thrive in life despite their Catholic schooling rather than because of it.

To advocate for queer thriving as Dr. Henry does, is of course a very different from the stereo- typical way of framing the relationship between being queer and a Catholic education. Henry likens this to an assumption that the starting point for

---

S. Whittle (✉)
St Mary's University, Twickenham, UK
e-mail: sean.whittle@stmarys.ac.uk

© The Author(s), under exclusive license to Springer Nature Singapore Pte Ltd. 2024
S. Whittle and S. Henry (eds.), *Queer Thriving in Catholic Education*,
https://doi.org/10.1007/978-981-97-0323-4_6

considering LGBTQ+ lives is as "'problems' or 'issues' to be accommodated, tolerated, or 'saved' by Catholic education" (2023, p. 2). This is a discourse that has its starting point in 'vulnerability, trauma or suicidality'. In this context the role which Catholic education plays is to save or protect the beleaguered queer person. This is to give primacy to what might be considered as the 'pastoral paradigm'.

Advocates of Catholic education routinely depict Catholic schools as giving central place to the pastoral care of students (Fincham, 2021). This is to frame Catholic education as a holistic endeavour, and going over and above merely academic concerns to care for the individual needs of each child. Whilst it is a mute-point whether or not Catholic schools do have higher standards of pastoral care compared to other types of school, it is taken as axiomatic that the pastoral needs of the students must come first in genuinely Catholic education. This means that Catholic schools want to offer pastoral care to all students, which of course includes those who are LGBTQ+. This pastoral care paradigm means that a queer child will be seen as someone who stands in need of additional support and even protection. In Catholic schools in countries such as the UK, this pastoral care paradigm is underpinned by Equality legislation and school inclusion policies. Part-and-parcel of these is the policy of recognising 'protected characteristics' associated with certain children, which depicts LGBTQ+ students as standing in need of additional support and protection in a wide range of ways. For advocates of Catholic schools, taking extra special care of any queer students is both a matter of legislation and deeply held principle that is grounded on the ethos and mission of the school. The net result is that in Catholic schools the prevailing ethos is for the majority of these schools to be a places of welcome, inclusion and support for LGBTQ+ students. Where ever practically possible, accommodations will be found to support and protect these students. In giving primacy to pastoral care and support instances of homo-phobic bullying or transphobia tend not to be part of Catholic school experience. The largely positive or benign nature of Catholic education vis-à-vis LGBTQ+ students is given a positive endorsement in Chap. 8 of this volume, which draws on empirical research of the situation for RSE in seven Catholic schools in Northern Ireland.

Although Dr. Henry is not denying the significance of this Pastoral Care paradigm in ensuring almost all Catholic schools are safe-spaces for queer children, he is drawing attention to the negative nature of the vulnerability starting point. This stereotypical starting point needs to replaced by the more positive one of 'queer thriving'. Instead of beginning with being queer as a vulnerability, a protected characteristic, the challenge and invitation is to start with depicting being LGBTQ+ as a positive, life affirming way of being a human. Instead of tolerating or accommodating the problematic nature of being LGBTQ+, Catholic education should be reframed around supporting and fostering queer thriving. This reframing of starting points should not be confused with attempts at advocacy or promotion of any particular sexuality or sexual orientation as part-and-parcel of a Catholic education. Rather it is beginning with the lived experience that some students at Catholic school are LGBTQ+, even if they are not aware of this for some or even most of their time at school. The Catholic school will seek to ensure all students know and understand that their sexual identity is not a vulnerability or a problem to be managed. Rather it is something which can or should help them to thrive as they journey through life.

It is interesting to speculate on what this would mean in practical terms for Catholic schools. One practical challenge would be to reframe school policy statements in relation to LGBTQ+ students along the following lines.

Catholic schools are places of educational excellence that are underpinned by a genuine commitment to inclusion and social justice. As Catholic schools strive to educate and help their students mature and grow up, prepared for the challenges and opportunities of adult life, it essential to recognise the importance of a companionship with the students. This sort of walking alongside the student means the school embraces each child's unique needs, identity and characteristics, including in matters of sexuality, sexual orientation and sexual identity. This means Catholic schools are places where LGBTQ+ students are not merely given appropriate pastoral support or recognised in inclusion terms as having 'protected characteristics'. More importantly, because Catholic schools are underpinned by a theology of companionship this should mean each LGBTQ+ student (and member of staff) are supported to be able to thrive and be recognised, welcomed and liked as valued members of the Catholic school community. Catholic schools as good companions to LGBTQ+ students will, as with all students who belong to the school, be vigilant and highly supportive in providing very good pastoral care. This means Catholic schools are committed to nurturing and supporting any student who is recognising their sexuality and helping them to embrace their sexual identity. However, Catholic schools want their LGBTQ+ students to know and appreciate that they stand alongside them (as companions) to support and affirm both their intrinsic rights in society at large and their value or dignity as children of God who are much loved and liked members of our Church. Moreover, Catholic educators seek to make Catholic schools places which are socially just, and thus be locations where LGBTQ+ students know that they can confidently affirm their sexual orientation and identity without any concern for unfair treatment. Catholic schools are committed, as good companions to their students, to create schools which enable LGBTQ+ students to thrive and flourish as they receive their education and journey into adulthood.

In essence a practical implication of starting with queer thriving is that Catholic education needs to operate with the conviction that the LGBTQ+ students enrich Catholic schools. These students have important insights to offer as the Catholic school as a whole continues to live out the 'joy of the Gospel'.

A second aspect of Dr. Henry's analysis of queer thriving and Catholic education that deserves positive response is around the spotlight he casts on the insights of 'queer theology'. These insights are ones that have the potential to enhance the theory of Catholic education. Elsewhere the case has been made for the challenges of pinning down the theory of Catholic education (Whittle, 2021). In many respects these challenges stem from the way this theory straddles both the philosophy and theology of Catholic education. Paradoxically, it is in being attentive to the insights of leading Catholic theologians (such as Karl Rahner) that fresh progress can be made in teasing out the philosophy of Catholic education. Just as drawing on other branches of theology is helpful (see for example see Kirwan's (2018) discussion of political theology and education), there may well be benefit from drawing on 'queer theology' to develop the theory of Catholic education. In describing and drawing from 'queer theology', Dr. Henry has provided an important service. 'Queer theology' has emerged alongside theologies of liberation (in which there has broad affinity between South American Liberation theology, feminist theology and black theology). According to Henry, 'Queer theologies' arise from a need to imagine theology and theological authority differently. Implicit in queer theology is a challenge to received norms that have implicitly shaped theology. Within queer theology this challenge is associated with an irreverence. It is perhaps in the irreverent challenge to theology and theological authority that fresh insights can be opened up in developing the theory of Catholic education.

In responding to Dr. Henry's analysis it is imperative to reiterate the positive potential in aligning Catholic education with the theme of 'queer thriving'. This is because it allows movement beyond the pastoral care paradigm, where LGBTQ+ students are protected and supported because they have this issue or problem to deal with. However in shifting the starting point (from where LGBTQ+ lives are problems or issues to be 'dealt' with) it allows Catholic schools to begin by framing the inclusion of LGBTQ+ students in more positive terms. The exciting possibilities opened up by Henry's analysis is that it allows Catholic education to become the site where young people can flourish or thrive precisely as LGBTQ+ people.

Ultimately, Dr. Henry is offering an invitation to put 'queer theology' at the service of both the practical reality of school life and the theory of Catholic education.

References

Fincham, D. (2021). *Being the Good Shepherd*. Blessed Hope Publishing.
Henry, S. (2023). In Whittle & Henry (Ed.), *Queer thriving in Catholic education: The role of queer theologies*. Springer.
Kirwan, M. (2018). Catholic schools as an expression of political theology. In Whittle (Ed.), *Researching Catholic education*. Springer.
Whittle, S. (2021). Moving beyond Slogan and Piety: The real challenge facing Catholic Education. In Whittle (Ed.), *Irish and British reflections*. Springer.

Dr. Sean Whittle is a Senior Lecturer in Catholic Education at St Mary's University, Twickenham, and a Research Associate with Professor Gerald Grace. Alongside these academic roles he works as a secondary school RE teacher at Gumley House FCJ Catholic School in West London. His book, *A Theory of Catholic Education* (Bloomsbury 2014), presents a robust philosophy of Catholic education that draws fruitfully on the theology of Karl Rahner. He has edited five books on Catholic Education (*Vatican II and New Thinking about Catholic Education 2016; Researching Catholic Education 2018; Religious Education in Catholic schools in the UK and Ireland 2018; Irish and British Reflections on Catholic Education 2021, and (jointly with Dr Gareth Byrne) Catholic Education: A life long journey (2021)*. Further volumes on Leadership in Catholic Schools and another on Guiding Research into Catholic Education Studies are in preparation for release in 2024. Since 2016 Sean Whittle has been collaborating with other academics working in the field of Catholic Education in order to create the *Network for Researchers in Catholic Education* (NfRCE).

He has also been engaged in a range of research projects (including a Post-Doctoral Research Fellow at Brunel University on a Religious Literacy project, Researching RSE in Catholic schools in Northern Ireland, and a research project of a Catholic Multi-Academy Trust in Birmingham). Prior to that he was a visiting Research Fellow at Heythrop College. Sean continues to serves as the secretary for the NfRCE and is also Chair of the academic association AULRE.

Part II
Research in Relation to Catholic Education and LGBT+ Matters

Introduction

Part I of this volume sketched out some provisional contours for understanding queer thriving in Catholic schooling. Grounded in Seán Henry's account, emphasis was placed on the value of turning to queer theologies as resources for theorising queer thriving in Catholic schools. The value of these theologies are twofold in Henry's view. First, queer theologies can offer Catholic education a theological resource that remedies overly disembodied approaches to questions of sexuality, gender, and education. Second, queer theologies can offer Catholic education alternative, more expansive, understandings of LGBTQ+ and religious subjectivities that foreground the agency of LGBTQ+ people.

Henry's argument was then complemented in Part I by responses from Cora O'Farrell, David Kennedy, and Sean Whittle. All three were united in a positive appraisal of Henry's arguments, though for different reasons. For O'Farrell, Henry's notion of queer thriving is helpful in exposing Catholic education to an 'openness beyond rigid forms of identity'. Kennedy likewise sees value in Henry's approach in how it fosters in Catholic school communities a hermeneutical openness to the 'givenness' of existence, including the 'givenness' of those in such schools who identify as LGBTQ+. An openness to queer thriving, Kennedy contends, lends itself to an understanding of Catholic schools as interpretive communities of both assent and dissent to Church tradition. In a similar vein, Whittle explores the positive potential in aligning Catholic education with the theme of 'queer thriving', though for Whittle its value lies precisely in its movement beyond the pastoral care paradigm. Staying with this, Whittle draws out some implications for practice in Catholic schools, one of which involves Catholic education operating from the conviction that 'LGBTQ+ students enrich Catholic schools'. In this sense, Whittle builds on Henry's notion of queer thriving to suggest that LGBTQ+ students have a positive contribution to make to Catholic schools, and that Catholic schools live out the 'joy of the Gospel' precisely by beginning efforts at inclusion from this perspective (Kennedy's emphasis on the 'givenness' of LGBTQ+ students and teachers comes to mind here too).

Building on this positive appraisal, the purpose of Part II is to offer readers the opportunity to engage with current research at the interface between Catholic education, schooling, and LGBTQ+ identities. Much of the research detailed in this part will be empirical in nature, drawing from fieldwork at the 'coalface' of Catholic education and Catholic schools, or at least from resources that have an eye on the realities of policy and lived experience in Catholic schools. Vivek da Silva's chapter appropriately opens Part II with a focus on the Irish relationship and sexuality education policy landscape, arguing for a reworking of Catholic education that is alive to the realities of the world in which such policies operate. Contributions from Gillian Sullivan, Sean Whittle, Claire Jenkins, Bernadette Sweetman, and Ruth Wareham 'live out' this attunement to the world by: foregrounding the lived experience of building LGBTQ+ inclusive environments for students and staff in Catholic schools (Sullivan and Whittle); centring the voices of trans Catholics (Jenkins) and adults more generally in Catholic education (Sweetman); and attending to those perspectives that lie outside Catholic education altogether (Wareham). Part II's turn to these 'empirical' realities is done to offer readers the chance to nuance and critically appraise the viability of queer thriving against the backdrop of students' and teachers' 'flesh-and-blood' encounters in Catholic schools. This is important given Henry's positioning of embodied life as central to his account of queer thriving to begin with.

Chapter 7
Relationships and Sexuality Education (RSE) in Catholic Post Primary Schools in Ireland: LGBT+ *Matters* in a Church that is Learning to Love

Vivek da Silva

Introduction

We live in times where there has been a considerable shift in societal and cultural norms regarding the expression of sexuality and gender (Nolan, 2018). In this context, this chapter explores the evolving landscape of Irish society regarding the expression of sexuality and the delivery of Relationships and Sexuality Education (RSE) that is cognisant of these significant changes. Noting the tension that exists, especially for Catholic schools, in holding the balance between faith and cultural expression, the chapter calls for a robust dialogue between Catholic ethos and secular rationality (Boeve, 2019; *Christus Vivit*, 2019; *Fratelli Tutti*, 2020; The Identity of the Catholic School, 2022). It accepts that a values framework is essential for any RSE programme. A framework that responds to the lived experience of students and equips them with the necessary competencies and skills for a lifelong journey of informed choices with regard sexual wellbeing and healthy relationships (Martin, 2018a). Keeping in line with the basic principles of Catholic education, namely, fostering an atmosphere that allows every student to realise their potential to the full, and reaching out to those marginalised, this chapter argues that catholic schools are places that celebrate diversity, nurture interiority and foster hospitality particularly to students who feel marginalised, excluded or even rejected (Berry, 2003; Coll, 2021; Educational Guidance in Human Love, 1983; *Gravissimum Educationis*, 1965; Tapestry, 2021).

V. da Silva (✉)
Dublin City University, Dublin, Ireland
e-mail: vivek.dasilva@dcu.ie

Encouraging Encounter and Transformation

In the midst of such change and intense public debate about faith and culture, Lane (2015) reminds us that 'Given the importance of reading the signs of the times for the mission of the Church in the world and its credible proclamation of the Gospel, it is imperative to map out the social and cultural context in which Catholic education takes place today' (p. 28).

A Catholic school today is urged to be a place of encounter promoting participation through relational dialogue so that different points of view can be expressed and understood. Francis (2019) has been insistent on this path of wide-ranging dialogue and mutual understanding which invites all towards a radical transformation of concerns and misunderstandings through collaborative partnership. These learning communities would facilitate every person to express themselves and grow towards a fullness of their humanity.

Jesus was clear in stating that his mission on this earth was to bring people to that fulness of life (Jn 10:10). Throughout his ministry he invited those around him to engage critically with their understanding of how belief and dogma was lived out in contemporary culture. When the woman caught in adultery was brought before him, the baying crowd was clear that the letter of the law, handed down to them by Moses, commanded that such a woman be condemned to death by stoning. Jesus, we are told, responded by staying silent, stooping down, and writing in the dust (Jn 8:1–11). Was Jesus, in this moment of silence, inviting the hostile crowd to revisit their understanding of the law in the context of the human story? Jesus constantly invited people, through his encounter with those on the margins and peripheries of society, to engage critically with how their faith and belief engaged with the rhythm of life. We see this in his encounters with the Samaritan woman at the well (Jn 4:7–27), the Canaanite woman (Mt 15:21–28), Zacchaeus (Lk 19:1–10) and healing the man with the withered hand (Mk 3:1–6). Catholic education, similarly, rooted in values that reflect the teachings of Jesus, invites its students to engage in critical dialogue, at those intersections where people of different races, cultures, beliefs and religions meet.

At these intersections of faith and culture, amidst all the change in society, many may feel that their faith does not adequately provide the explanation for the nature, purpose and meaning of life. Faced with this reality, Feehan suggests we have one of three choices:

> You can refuse to accept the evidence and continue as before. You can abandon the faith you grew up with because it has proved to be inadequate. Or you can accept the new knowledge and use it to develop a more mature understanding of what lies at the core of your beliefs. The first response is intellectually dishonest. The second is intellectual laziness. The third is a stance of critical acceptance, leading to a reinterpretation of core concepts (2012, p. 148).

The Changing Landscape in Ireland

Ireland is no stranger to these radical shifts in societal norms that are demanding *a reinterpretation of core concepts* especially when it comes to the expression of sexuality and relationships. In a relatively short period of time Ireland has seen the proverbial pendulum swing from being an overly conservative and largely religious society to an increasingly liberal and largely secular society. Varadkar (2018) in his address to Pope Francis, observed that while religion might no longer be central to Irish society, it still holds an important place. There is no denying that there has been a gradual erosion of the moral authority of the institutional Catholic Church in Ireland, due to the revelations of clerical sexual abuse, the forced illegal adoptions, and the abuse experienced by women and children in Magdalene laundries and Mother and Baby homes. Many, particularly young people, feel the Church is a 'cold place, legalistic, judgmental and condemning' (McVerry, 2018). Hoban (2019) comments that there has been a tectonic shift for the Irish Catholic Church, and argues that, while the Church might attempt to respond proactively to this shift, it amounts to nothing more than building a scaffolding around a collapsed house. However, Catholic educators committed to the credible proclamation of the Gospel are challenged to hold a mirror up to society, aware that

> If the music of the Gospel ceases to sound in our homes, our public squares, our workplaces, our political and financial life, then we will no longer hear the strains that challenge us to defend the dignity of every man and woman (Fratelli Tutti par. 277).

The lifespan of the 8th Amendment of the *Irish Constitution* is a good timeline as any to signpost the rapid pace of change in Irish society. In 1983, this Amendment acknowledged the right to life of the unborn equal to the right to life of the mother. In 2018, the 36th Amendment of the Constitution repealed the 8th Amendment and permitted the *Oireachtas* (the bicameral Parliament of Ireland) to legislate for abortion with the signing into law the Health [Regulation of the Termination of Pregnancy] Act 2018. Legislation from 1983 to 2018 reflects the change of a nation distancing itself from a conservative attitude to sex and sexuality. In 1985, the Health [Family Planning Amendment] Act liberalised laws regulating contraception. In 1993, the Criminal Law [Sexual Offences] Bill decriminalised consensual same-sex activity. In 1996, the Family Law [Divorce] Act lifted the constitutional ban on divorce. In 2015, the Marriage Act legislated for same-sex marriages, and the Gender Recognition Act, provided for the legal recognition of a person's preferred gender.

In the context of these changes and evolving understanding and expression of sexuality in contemporary Irish society it is important to recognise that sexuality is a product of social and cultural influences of its time and must be viewed within the context of a particular culture (Foucault, 1985). Legislation, cultural practices and social norms and values influence the understanding and expression of one's sexuality just as much as a person's biological constitution.

Moral and Cultural Fault Lines

The change in traditional cultural perceptions, societal norms and religious values has exposed the moral and cultural fault lines in the Irish society (Thunder, 2019). This now ideologically divided society holds radically different opinions on the liberalisation of abortion laws, the legitimacy of same-sex marriage, the rights of transgender people, the place of faith in society, and the authority of the State to determine the nature of the curriculum in schools. In 2018, the then Minister of Education, Richard Bruton, called for a major review of RSE regarding its content and delivery within the school curriculum. The Provision for Objective Sex Education Bill (2018) reflects the call for the RSE curriculum to move from favouring a minimalist, conservative and morally absolutist approach to one which leans more towards a person-centred, liberal and morally relativist approach (Nolan, 2018).

In national debates, one argument has been that Catholic schools are incapable of delivering a non-ethos based, factual, biologically correct and objective RSE curriculum (*Dáil* Éireann, 2018). Archbishop Martin (2018a), counters that negative perceptions to a faith-based approach to RSE in Catholic schools is uninformed and agenda driven. But given the changes in society there is consensus that the current RSE curriculum in schools needs to be updated to give consideration to the significant changes that have taken place in Ireland (DES, 2019).

It is important to recognise that while legislation might point to progress with regard to expression of sexuality, the reality on the ground is quite different as evidenced by continuing hate crimes towards the LGBT+ community. The president of the *Irish National Teachers' Organisation* (INTO), Joe McKeown, highlighted the reality of discrimination against the LGBT+ community in some Catholic schools and called on schools to nurture an environment where LGBT+ teachers and students are safe and celebrated (2022). Coll (2021) recognises that there are features of LGBT+ lifestyle that unsettle Catholic belief and that there is an estrangement that needs to be faced 'to find an ethic that is viable where we do not pretend that there is no issue or difference.' Martin (2018b) acknowledging the fractious relationship between the Church and the LGBT+ community urges the church to exercise compassion and listen to the experiences of the LGBT+ so as to learn, be challenged and inspired. Archbishop Martin (2018a) insisted that RSE in schools must address the challenges facing young people in their lives today in both the virtual and real worlds in which they move and inhabit.

What is Sexuality?

The *Department of Education and Skills* defines sexuality as including all aspects that relate to being a human person and 'is subject to change and development throughout life' (1995, p. 6). Sexuality shapes an individual's personal and interpersonal relationships. It determines their sexual orientation and gender identity and expression.

It concerns sexual activity and procreation, and influences the capacity to give and receive love. Sexuality is an integral part of the human person and is affected by the interplay between biological, psychological, cultural, social, political, ethical, legal and spiritual factors (Crisis Pregnancy Agency, 2019; DES, 1995).

The Catholic understanding of sexuality is deeply rooted in the acceptance that sexuality, just as everything else, is a *gift* from God. It is the intimate nucleus that enriches the whole person and contributes to the person's physical, psychological and spiritual personality. It manifests its inmost meaning in leading the person to the gift of self in love. Sexuality has love, in its giving and receiving, as its intrinsic end and it is realised in its fullness not only by existing with someone but existing for someone (*Educational Guidance in Human Love*, 1983; *Familiaris Consortio*, 1981; *The Religious Dimension of Education in a Catholic school*, 1988; *The Truth and Meaning of Human Sexuality*, 1995). The Catholic concept of sexuality is built on relationality with self, the other and the Divine.

Rolheiser (1998) observing that the word *sex* comes from the Latin word *secare*, which means to be cut off from, says that one's sexuality drives the lifelong desire for communion with something beyond themselves. O'Murchu (1998) speaks of sexuality being at the very heart of the evolving process of each person seeking to come to a fullness of their being as a human. It is, he says, the all-encompassing energy for wholesome relationships that seeks friendship, companionship, family and generativity.

Relationship and Sexuality Education Within the Context of Holistic Education

Consequently, RSE within Catholic education aims to promote an understanding of the human person as created in the *image of God*. It recognises the dignity of the embodied human person. It encourages the need for understanding, respect and love of the other, and it fosters an openness to dialogue that is rooted in faith (*Evangelium Vitae*, 1995; *Familiaris Consortio*, 1981; *Gaudium Et Spes*, 1965; The Truth and Meaning of Human Sexuality, 1995; *Veritatis Splendor*, 1993; Young People, The Faith and Vocational Discernment, 2018). Sexuality education within Catholic education is required to consider the advances in psychological, pedagogical and didactic sciences (*Amoris Laetitia*, 2016), and address the physical, physiological, psychological and biological aspects along with the ethical, moral and emotional aspects (*Educational Guidance in Human Love*, 1983).

RSE as an integral part of a holistic education 'seeks to promote the overall development of the person and which includes the integration of sexuality into personal understanding, growth and development' (Circular 0027/2008). The *Joint Committee on Education and Skills* (JCES, 2019) insist that RSE must reflect the lived experience of students, including the experience of those identifying as LGBT+. It recommends that RSE be taught with 'a mindset of inclusivity which is centred on competence, wellbeing and the development of mutually satisfying relationships' (p. 10). They suggest that the approach to RSE needs to be 'gender-equality based, inclusive, aspiring to be holistic, creative, empowering and protective' (p. 26). Archbishop Martin (2018a), proposes a relevant RSE programme, with active collaboration of parents, that will equip students with the critical sense to debate and discuss issues such as contraception, sexually transmitted infections, same-sex relationships and the full meaning of consent in an age and developmental stage appropriate language and manner. School-based RSE has the potential not only to reduce inequalities in the access to and provision of information, but also to meet that need in the young for reliable and substantive knowledge about sex and sexuality (Tanton et al., 2015).

A Values Framework for RSE

While there is general agreement about the purpose of school based RSE, the point of contention emerges when considering the framework for the implementation of RSE in schools. Most schools have an open-minded approach to RSE, however, some Catholic schools citing ethos choose not to address some topics that appear to be incongruent with Catholic doctrine such as same-sex marriage, abortion, contraception, sex outside the context of marriage and gender identity. The *Department of Education*, in keeping with Article 11.2 of the European Social Charter, indicated that sexuality education must be provided in a manner that is 'objective, based on contemporary scientific evidence and does not involve censoring, withholding or intentionally misrepresenting information, for example as regards contraception or different means on maintaining sexual and reproductive health' (Circular 0037/2010). Schools were reminded of their responsibility and duty to protect students in their care at all times from any potentially harmful, inappropriate or misguided resources, interventions or programmes while promoting the students' wellbeing, and social and emotional learning (Circular 0043/2018).

RSE needs to offer students in Catholic schools the opportunity to address all aspects of human sexuality within a moral, spiritual and social framework respecting the whole spectrum of views be they religious or secular, conservative or liberal. RSE would create the safe space for students to reflect critically, explore honestly and question fearlessly the real issues of their lived experience of sexuality. It is important that RSE, in a plural society such as Ireland, nurtures the capacity of students to engage and dialogue with a variety of views even those that may appear to be incongruent with the ones espoused by them, their faith or their family.

Catholic education within a plural society must show the will and capacity to hold the tension of the multiplicity of religious and secular views that are expressed when it comes to educating the young about the complexities of human relationships and sexuality. Secular rationality and religious belief "need one another and should not be afraid to enter into profound and on-going dialogue for the good of our civilization" (Benedict XVI, 2010). Francis (2019) says that some Catholic schools seem to be structured for the sake of self-preservation. Fear of change makes them entrenched and defensive before the dangers, real or imagined, that any change might bring. A school that becomes a "bunker", he warns, appearing to protect its students from errors "from without" is a caricature of this tendency. Coll (2021) echoes this sentiment cautioning schools that burying their heads in the sand does not help move forward and that there is a potential political threat to the mission of Catholic schools from failing to properly engage with RSE especially where Catholic schools are part of the state sector and expected to conform to all national regulations pertaining to equality and diversity.

With so many new ways of living affectivity and the multiplicity of ethical perspectives (Synod of Bishops, 2019), the Church's stance on many complex and conflictual contemporary realities are seen as intolerably intransigent and incongruent with its core message of compassion and understanding. Many experience the Church as judgemental and condemnatory instead of being more empathetic (McVerry, 2018). The Church is aware that it's teaching regarding matters of human sexuality is not universally accepted. The Church, however, remaining steadfast in "obedience to the truth which is Christ, whose image is reflected in the nature and dignity of the human person … interprets the moral norm and proposes it to all people of good will, without concealing its demands of radicalness and perfection" (*Veritas Splendor*, 1993). This stance on contentious issues creates an awkwardness for those entrusted with the teaching of RSE in Catholic schools as they attempt to balance factual information and the lived reality of their students with the moral code and doctrine of the Church.

Catholic Schools as Leaven and Places of Welcome

Catholic schools, animated by the Gospel and guided by the values of Jesus, seek to be leaven in the community, nurturing the personal development of every student. Pope Francis has been consistent in his call for schools to be communities of encounter and robust dialogue. This would require nurturing the ability to listen deeply and respectfully to the lived experience of all within the school community, including those identifying with the LGBT+ community. A Catholic ethos is characterised by its inclusiveness, quality of welcome and engagement with those marginalised. Catholic institutions have been at the forefront of encouraging inclusiveness. However, in stark contrast to these values, many Catholic schools are experienced as places that are unsupportive towards the LGBT+ community (DCYA, 2018).

James Martin (2021), maintains that Catholic schools, as welcoming places for everybody, particularly for students who might feel in anyway marginalised, excluded or rejected, should be bending over backwards to try to take care of people who are in any way on the margins. And today transgender youth often perceive themselves to be amongst the most marginalised and persecuted of people. The Catholic Bishops Conference of England and Wales (2018) recognising the intense public debate about gender acknowledged the suffering and discomfort of those 'who do not accept their biological sex'. While this raises 'profound questions about human nature, how we understand ourselves, relate to one another and our capacity for self-determination,' they reiterated the need to listen to the experience of transgender people so as to understand them more deeply, and walk with them compassionately. Compassion draws us to act justly and love tenderly. Jones (2019) reiterates the need to tune in to the reality of the experience of trans people. He asks that we engage with each other with the love that casts out fear, and he holds that,

> when irrational fear is cast aside what remains are challenges common to other human situations. Perhaps then we will discover that being trans is one more way to be human and one more way to be Catholic (2019, p. 5).

How, then, do Catholic schools become these places of welcome, inclusion and celebration of all staff and students, including those identifying as LGBT+? How do we celebrate the dignity of each and every individual as being created in the image of God and a unique manifestation of the Divine? How might Catholic schools produce the circumstances that permit all individuals to be fully themselves and allow them to flourish?

The Values of Diversity, Interiority, Community and Hospitality

Berry (2003) in speaking of learning from the evolving story of the Universe notes that 'values are now determined by the sensitivity of the human responding to the creative urgencies of a developing world (p. 84).' The Good Samaritan (Lk 10:25–37) responded with sensitivity to the urgent needs of the man lying half dead after being attacked by bandits. His was a compassionate response towards his neighbour. The priest and Levite, on the other hand, conditioned by the law handed down by Moses, walked by ignoring the pain and suffering of the injured man. They did not risk an act of compassion for fear of becoming unclean. We need values, today, that will enable us to respond sensitively to emerging needs of an ever changing world. Berry (2003) presents us with the values of increasing differentiation (diversity), deepening subjectivity (interiority) and comprehensive communion (community).[1] These values give us the stepping stones on the pathway to ensure a compassionate response towards an authentic inclusion of those identifying as LGBT+ in our schools.

Diversity brings us to recognise the overwhelming complexity and variety within all of creation. It holds the invitation to expand the narrow preconceptions one might hold of the stranger and their strangeness. Jesus invited those who listened to him to experience the spaciousness of God allowing the complexity of the other to expand their image of neighbour. Interiority gives every being their sense of self, their interior dimension. Berry (2003) holds that 'to deprive any being of this sacred quality is to disrupt the total order of the universe…The Universe does not come to us in

---

[1] Thomas Berry in later interviews and articles used the words diversity, interiority and community more widely.

pieces any more than a human individual stands before us with some part of one's being (2003, p. 85). The invitation here is to nurture one's own sense of inner sacred mystery so as to encourage and support the intrinsic creative unfolding of the other (McCormack, 2014). Community speaks of the interconnectedness of all creation, that Pope Francis addresses in *Laudato Si'* (2015). The uniqueness of each being determines a particular manifestation of the Divine. Together, as a communion of subjects, each individual and all of creation gives expression to the vastness of the Divine.

This intricate web of relationship that is required for the flourishing of all humanity is also expressed in the Bantu philosophy of *ubuntu*. Tutu (2011) maintains that the humanity of one is inextricably bound with that of another. It is the delicate network of interdependence that acknowledges that each individual can only come to their fulness if the other is nurtured to their fulness.

Coll (2021) invites us to focus on the Christian understanding of hospitality in the context of the story of the two disciples on the road to Emmaus (Lk 24:13–35) as we respond to the needs of LGBT+ community in Catholic schools. She highlights how genuine dialogue and honest conversation facilitates openness, listening and transformation. Jesus, in the Gospels is both stranger who is welcomed to the table (Lk 24: 13–35), and is host (Lk 15) who welcomes strangers who are on the peripheries of society to the table of fellowship. In being hospitable to the stranger, Jesus risked challenging long held religious and social norms.

Catholic Ethos Animated by the Dream of God

Jesus was proclaiming the dream or vision of God for the world (Casaldáliga, 1994, 82) expressed in the passage that Jesus read in the synagogue (Lk 4:18–19). It is good news for the poor. It is release for those held captive. It is recovery of sight to the blind. It is the promise of freedom for the oppressed. It is the call for a broadening of the vision (*metanoia*); it is the invitation to a new way of encountering God and responding to God's word (*dabar*); and it demands a way of relating among people that is so radically different that it excludes no one from being at the table of fellowship, especially the poor and the marginalised (Mt 8:11; Lk14:16). Jesus challenged the prevalent worldview of the time and this "turned the world, both Jewish and Gentile, upside down" (Nolan, 2007, 50). This dream of God demands a new consciousness. It does not burden people with a blind adherence to the law (Mk 2:18–27; 10:2–9), or systemic traditions (Mk 7:1–23) instead it invites people to do the will of God (Mk 3:35). Jesus recognised the inherent dignity of every individual. He looked upon people with compassion (Mk 6:34). He reminded them of their identity as children of God. Nothing would separate them from the unconditional love of God (Rm 8:38–39).

It is this dream of God that demands of Catholic schools that those identifying with the LGBT+ community in our schools are treasured and genuinely loved (Martin, 2018b). It is this dream of God that should frame the teaching of an inclusive RSE in Catholic schools to facilitate both the inclusion and celebration of the LGBT+ community. Chittister (2019) says, it is this courage of Jesus that is required to speak the truth publicly and to say unequivocally, 'I think differently about that'. It is claiming this right to think differently, she adds, that will turn heads and open hearts.

Catholic Ethos is no Barrier to Compassionate Response

It is a misconception that the Catholic ethos could be a barrier to RSE. Mayock et al (2007) observe that 'ethos was something of a smoke screen, which, in today's world, had little bearing on the reality of what was now accepted and demanded (by parents, by society at large and perhaps by the church) from school-based relationships and sexuality education' (p. 120). Boeve (2005) cautions Catholic schools against the tendency to barricade themselves behind their own 'self-secured identity' to the point of excluding that which is other as *illegitimate.* Francis (2014) urges Catholic schools not to isolate themselves from the world but 'enter bravely into the *areopagus* of current culture and open dialogue, conscious of the gift that they can offer to everyone.'

Ethos based barriers, even when erected with every good intention, create an insurmountable disconnect between what is taught and the experienced reality of students. Cowering behind firewalls of Church doctrine will only risk further widening the chasm between the institutional Church and the lived reality of young people. Catholic education and ethos need to build bridges of compassion, respect and sensitivity through critical dialogue in a manner that engages the unfamiliar and strange as Jesus did.

Catholic Schools Singing a Bold New Song

Greek mythology, in the two stories of Odysseus and Orpheus as they countered the luring song of the Sirens, offers us two approaches to face that which might seem to take us off course. As educators in Catholic schools approach RSE they could, like Ulysses, tie themselves to a cross-piece half way up the mast of the boat and cover the ears of all of their fellow companions with beeswax so that they do not hear the Sirens' enticing song. Alternatively, they can, like Orpheus, sing a bold new song so beautifully that it masks the bewitching song of the Sirens.

Catholic schools, with the capacity to influence transformative change in individuals and society, are well positioned to sing a bold new song in delivering an RSE that is relevant to the lived experience of the students seeking to integrate the knowledge of head, heart and hands. They have the challenge to offer a RSE programme that reflect the basic Christian values of compassionate response, the dignity of the embodied person as created in the image of God, the willingness to encounter the stranger and the openness to dialogue with the human condition. It is an opportunity that would follow the example of Jesus who bent down and wrote in the dust when faced with the baying crowd calling for the stoning of the woman caught in adultery (Jn 8: 1–11).

In a church that is learning to love (Tapestry, 2021), it is time for Catholic educators to engage with RSE listening to the call in *Amoris Laetitia* that invites the Church and all in Catholic education by association to,

> be particularly concerned to offer understanding, comfort and acceptance, rather than imposing straightaway a set of rules that only lead people to feel judged and abandoned by the very Mother called to show them God's mercy. Rather than offering … the light of the Gospel message, some would "indoctrinate" that message, turning it into "dead stones to be hurled at others." (2016)

References

Benedict, X. V. I. (2010). *Address in Westmster Hall*. Meeting with representatives of British Civil Society.
Berry, T. (2003). The new story. In A. Fabel & D. St John (Eds.), *Teilhard in the 21st century: The emerging spirit of Earth* (pp. 77–88). Orbis. (Essay was first published in 1978).
Boeve, L. (2005). Religion after detraditionalization: Christian Faith in a post secular Europe. *Theological Quarterly, 123*(70), 99–122.
Boeve, L. (2019). Faith in dialogue: The Christian voice in the catholic dialogue school. *International Studies in Catholic Education, 11*(1), 37–50.
Casaldáliga, P., & Virgil, J. M. (1994). *Political holiness*. Orbis Books.
Catholic Bishops Conference of England and Wales. (2018). *Guiding principles on issues of transgender*. https://rcdow.org.uk/news/bishops-express-concerns-about-gender-ideology/
Chittister, J. (2019). *The time is now, a call to uncommon courage*. Penguin Random House.
Coll, R. (2021). Hospitality to difference: LGBT, religious education and the Catholic school. *Journal of Religious Education, 69*, 25–36.
Congregation for Catholic Education. (1983). *Educational guidance in human love*. Libreria Editrice Vaticana.
Congregation for Catholic Education. (1988). *The religious dimension of education in a Catholic school: Guidelines for reflection and renewal*. Libreria Editrice Vaticana.
Congregation for Catholic Education. (2022). *The identity of the Catholic School for a culture of dialogue*. Libreria Editrice Vaticana.
Crisis Pregnancy Agency. (2019). *Exploring and understanding sexuality*. https://b4udecide.ie/relationships/sexuality/
Dáil Éireann. (2018). *Debate on provision of objective sex education bill*.
Department of Children and Youth Affairs (DCYA). (2018). LGBTI+ National Youth Strategy 2018–2020—LGBTI+ Young People: visible, valued and included. dcya.gov.ie.
Department of Education and Skills (DES). (1995). *Report of the expert advisory group on relationships and sexuality education*. The Stationery Office.
Department of Education and Skills. (2008). *Circular 0027/2008*. Dublin.
Department of Education and Skills. (2010). *Circular 0037/2010*. Dublin.
Department of Education and Skills. (2018). *Circular 0043/2018*. Dublin.
Department of Education and Skills (DES). (2019). Joint Committee on Education and Skills (JCES). *Report on relationships and sexuality education*. Dublin.
Feehan, J. (2012). *The singing heart of the world*. Orbis.

Foucault, M. (1978, 1985, 1986). *The history of sexuality*. Translated by R. Hurley in 3 Volumes. Pantheon.
Francis. (2014). *Address to participants in the plenary session of the Congregation for Catholic Education*. Clementine Hall.
Francis. (2015). Laudato Si'. On care for our Common Home. Encyclical Letter. Vatican City: Libreria Editrice Vaticana.
Francis. (2016). *Amoris Laetitia, Post Synodal Apostolic Exhortation*. Libreria Editrice Vaticana.
Francis. (2018). *Young people, the faith and vocational discernment, instrumentum laboris*. Libreria Editrice Vaticana.
Francis. (2019). *Christus Vivit, post synodal apostolic exhortation*. Libreria Editrice Vaticana.
Francis. (2020). *Fratelli Tutti*. Libreria Editrice Vaticana.
Hoban, Brendan. (2019). Another Beginning? *Studies: An Irish Quarterly Review, 108*(430), 151–161. https://www.muse.jhu.edu/article/800574
John Paul II. (1981). *Familiaris Consortio, apostolic exhortation*. Libreria Editrice Vaticana.
John Paul II. (1993). *Veritatis Splendor, encyclical letter*. Libreria Editrice Vaticana.
John Paul II. (1995). *Evangelium Vitae, encyclical letter*. Libreria Editrice Vaticana.
Jones, A. (2019). One more way to be human. *The Tablet* (pp. 4–5). April 6.
Lane, D. (2015). *Catholic education in the light of Vatican II and Laudato Si'*. Veritas.
Martin, E. (2018). 'Catholic Schools Supporting Families: Towards a Better Education of Children.' Keynote Address. JMB/AMCSS 31st Annual Conference. Galway.
Martin, J. (2018). *Building a bridge: How the Catholic Church and the LGBT community can enter into a relationship of respect, compassion and sensitivity*. Harper Collins.
Mayock, P, Kitching, K, & Morgan, M. (2007). *Relationships and sexuality education: An Assessment of the challenges to full implementation in post-primary schools*. Crisis Pregnancy Agency.
McCormack, M. T. (2014). *Three principles of the universe. Talk. contemplative assembly*. Ecuador. http://www.sistersofthegoodshepherdcontemplatives.com/sites/default/files/MTM%20-%203%20Principles%20of%20the%20Universe.pdf
McVerry, P. (2018). Dear Pope Francis. *The Irish Times*. August 11.
Nolan, A. (2007). *Jesus today: A spirituality of radical freedom*. Orbis Books.
Nolan, A. (2018). School-based relationships and sexuality education (RSE): Lessons for Policy and Practice. *Spotlight*. Oireachtas Library and Research Service.
O'Murchu, D. (1998). *Reclaiming spirituality*. Crossroad Publishing Co.
Paul VI. (1965). *Gravissimum educationis, declaration on Christian education*. Libreria Editrice Vaticana.
Pontifical Council for the Family. (1995). *The truth and meaning of human sexuality*. Libreria Editrice Vaticana.
Rolheiser, R. (1998). *Seeking spirituality; guidelines for a Christian spirituality for the twenty first century*. Hodder and Stoughton.
Synod of Bishops. (2019). Young people, the faith and vocational discernment. Libreria Editrice Vaticana.
Varadkar, L. (2018). *Speech of an Taoiseach, Leo Varadkar, on the occasion of the Visit of Pope Francis*. Irish Government News Service. MerrionStreet.ie.
Tanton, C., Jones, K. G., Macdowell, W., Clifton, S., Mitchell, K. R., Datta, J., Lewis, R., et al. (2015). *Patterns and trends in sources of information about sex among young people in Britain: Evidence from three national surveys of sexual attitudes and. lifestyles*. BMJ Open 5: http://bmjopen.bmj.com/content/5/3/e007834.full
Tapestry with Mary Hynes. (2021). *59: James Martin*. CBC Listen.
Thunder, D. (2019). Progressive Ireland is a fantasy cultivated by elites. *The Irish Times*. March 29.
Tutu, D. M. (2011) or bbn. *Ubuntu: On the Nature of Human Community, in God is Not A Christian*. E-book: Riderr.

Vivek da Silva is an assistant professor in Religious Education in Dublin City University. From 2016 to 2021 he worked with Veritas as a catechetical writer and a producer of digital audio-visual resources for the Religious Education programs in primary and post- primary schools. He is a member of the Irish Bishops' Council for Catechetics Working Group on Laudato Si'. He spent 25 years working in different parts of India and Africa in the areas of education, religious formation, human development, spirituality and leadership. His current area of research is Relationship and Sexuality Education in Catholic Post Primary Schools.

Chapter 8
On the Journey to Authentic Inclusion: One School's Experience of Empowering Student Voice to Mobilise Positive Change

Gillian Sullivan

Introduction

This chapter describes one Irish Catholic post-primary school's experience of purposefully listening to the marginalised voices of the students it serves. It illustrates steps taken by the school in seeking to meaningfully engage with and respond to its diverse student body on a journey towards authentic inclusion. As a teacher of 12 years in this school community I witnessed the increasing cultural and religious diversity of, predominantly, the student population. I conducted doctoral research investigating student and teacher experience of Religious Education at senior cycle. An important objective of this study was to explore the experience of students with minority religious and non-religious worldviews within this Catholic school. This research identified a significant challenge to an inclusive intercultural education within this school community with students with minority religious and non-religious worldviews being most negatively impacted. 'I think it's very difficult to be different' is the title of the research study, which is a quote from a Muslim student whose words echoed a feeling repeatedly described by participating students.

Listening to these voices describe experiences of exclusion, as captured in the research, offers valuable insight into the marginal and vulnerable position some students can find themselves in. This has helped to inform the school's work in recognising other groups of students who may feel marginalised which is an important step in the journey toward authentic inclusion. While this work is ongoing, it is committed to and inspired by the school's *Presentation* ethos particularly Nano Nagle's mission to respond to and include those repressed and marginalised. This chapter will describe important steps this school has taken to recognise and respond

G. Sullivan (✉)
Dublin City University, Dublin, Ireland
e-mail: gillian.c.sullivan@dcu.ie

to diversity more meaningfully. Integral to this journey towards authentic inclusion has been the school's work in empowering Student Voice to mobilise positive change. With the support of Lundy's Model of Participation (Lundy, 2007) it was possible to create safe spaces where marginalised voices could be purposefully listened to and enabled to influence decision making with the school community (Harmon, 2018).

Previous Research Findings from this Context

The school described in this chapter is a large urban all-girls' *Presentation* school currently under the trusteeship of *Catholic Education, an Irish Schools Trust* (CEIST). There is a broad diversity in terms of the socio-economic status of the attending student population. Its location close to a *Direct Provision* centre for refugees to the country has led to a steep increase in cultural and religious diversity especially in the last 20 years. Indeed, the population of Ireland has experienced an unprecedented rate of growth in terms of diversity of race, culture and religion due to rapid social, economic and cultural change since the mid-1990s (Darmody et al., 2011).

Nagle founded the *Presentation Sisters*, as the religious congregation would come to be called, in 1775, amidst a time of great upheaval and suffering for Irish Catholics under the Penal Laws (Raftery et al., 2018). She had a keen sense of the transformative character of education, and this remains at the heart of this school's mission. Nagle's commitment to those 'made poor' through poverty and oppression can be interpreted today as a commitment to and allegiance with those 'made poor' and marginalised because of their minority status for example a religious or non-religious identity or a sexual orientation (Sullivan, 2019).

My research study purports that students with different religious and non-religious identities are those "made poor" within a denominational context, when it fails to recognise, respect and respond to the religious diversity within it. The Student Voice captured describes how this specific Catholic school failed to recognise, respect and respond adequately to the religious and non-religious diversity within it. Students with minority identities or hailing from minority backgrounds were being 'made poor' and marginalised within this school community. This marginalisation was identified as resulting from written and unwritten policies pertaining to the following:

- The Religious Education Department's plan directing RE teachers only to engage with 'Section C: Foundation of Religion—Major World Religions', the optional section for study, if they had surplus time. This resulted in many students never engaging in a study of their religious or non- religious worldviews within the RE classroom
- The unwritten policy that did not permit Muslim students to wear the hijab
- The expectation for all students to participate in religious practices carried out at school assemblies and whole school gatherings.

This school's culture, as influenced by the leadership of the school, exerted influence on school policies that impacted negatively on some students' sense of identity and belonging. Darmody et al. (2011) identified that some Irish schools' engagement with intercultural education tend to adopt 'an assimilatory approach'. Other research also found a downplaying of difference to be more commonplace than a more explicit engagement with cultural and religious diversity (Bryan, 2010; Rougier & Honohan, 2015). The school community described in this chapter also operated a sameness-over-difference approach that denied the reality of difference and in doing so denied opportunities for authentic intercultural education.

Conceptually Framing an Authentic Inclusion

The philosopher Charles Taylor's work on the ethics of authenticity identifies that the dominant culture in Western societies of *being authentic* or *true to oneself* is ratified as a moral imperative. Critics of the culture of authenticity claim that the narrow focus on the individual promotes a soft relativism that denies anything higher than the allegiance to self-development (1991, p. 31). Taylor, however, works to redeem this problematic understanding of the culture of authenticity as one solely dedicated to self-fulfilment by proposing that through dialogical endeavours people can succeed in transcending the boundaries of the self to encounter the "other", and hence achieve human flourishing through shared projects. An authentic inclusion recognises and engages with the complexities of a pluralism, in which there are often incompatible and contested views on the nature of the ultimate-order-of-things by providing opportunities and space for meaningful dialogue and encounter. In his essay 'The Politics of Recognition' (1994) Taylor alerts us to the danger that nonrecognition or misrecognition of one's identity can have, describing it as a 'form of oppression, imprisoning someone in a false, distorted, and reduced mode of being'.

Contemporary educational research propounds student wellbeing ought to be at the very heart of the educational enterprise (Graham et al., 2022). The OECD recognises how it is essential that students feel they belong within a school community before effective and meaningful learning can take place (OECD, 2018). Students need to feel *I am seen, I am heard, I belong*; these beliefs are tantamount not least to success at school but life in general. Contemporary educational discourse recognises the most effective approach to ensuring academic success is to pay careful attention to Maslow's hierarchy of needs when considering students' potential, indeed Maslow must precede Bloom.

Andy Hargreaves, at an online conference hosted by Education Support Centres Ireland, asked educators from a variety of disciplines working at different levels, how often they considered the self-actualisation of their students? In other words how often are students enabled and empowered to express who they truly are in and through their learning? The influence of such thinking is evidenced in the Junior Cycle

Framework which was introduced in 2015 and constituted the most significant curricular reform at second level in recent Irish history. Wellbeing is an underpinning principle of the Framework along with being incorporated into the key skills students will acquire through their learning at junior cycle and as a distinct area of the curriculum with specific Wellbeing subjects (NCCA, 2015). Effective teaching, learning and assessment at junior cycle is now informed by a philosophy that considers student wellbeing deeply.

Evaluating School Ethos, an Important Step in Effecting Positive Change

As a response to the challenges to inclusive intercultural education it was decided to include Ethos as a distinct area of focus on the school's School Self-Evaluation plan (SSE). This was an important step towards effecting positive change as it allowed for areas of need to be identified, targets to be set and worked towards as part of the school's overall School Improvement Plan. An important element of this evaluation comes in the form of student, parent and teacher surveys, the feedback from which will be referred to later in this chapter. School ethos is a living, evolving entity which can be experienced from the moment you walk through the doors of a school to its influence in high stakes decision making of a school's Board of Management. In short, nothing that is experienced within a school falls outside of its ethos. School ethos is synonymous with a school's culture, the all-encompassing character of which is described by *The glossary of educational reform* (2018) as follows:

> The term school culture generally refers to the beliefs, perceptions, relationships, attitudes, and written and unwritten rules that shape and influence every aspect of how a school functions, but the term also encompasses more concrete issues such as the physical and emotional safety of students, the orderliness of classrooms and public spaces, or the degree to which a school embraces and celebrates racial, ethnic, linguistic, or cultural diversity.

The main objective of including Ethos as an area of focus on the SSE plan was to begin a conversation about issues of diversity and inclusion and how the school's Catholic *Presentation* ethos could support a more robust and compassionate response to them. An example of this came with a review of the policy pertaining to the wearing of the hijab when a consensus was reached that the wearing of the hijab should be open for Muslim students who wish to do so. This review was supported by a framework which included Student Voice, School Ethos and the Joint Managerial Body of Catholic Schools' revised '*Guidelines on the Inclusion of Students of Different Beliefs in Catholic Secondary Schools*' (Mullally, 2019).

The review process involved:

- Consultations with staff for dialogue and the sharing of intercultural material to educate and inform on this issue
- Purposeful listening to Student Voice

- Hearing from a Principal and RE teacher of another *Presentation* school who had previously made a positive change to this policy
- A professional development session for teachers exploring *What it means to be a Catholic school in the 21st C?* facilitated by Dr. Aiveen Mullaly, author of the JMB *Guidelines* referred to above.

These actions sought to build confidence around how a change to policy would strengthen the school's commitment to an inclusive *Presentation* ethos. The inclusion of those on the margins is a central value of the school's *Presentation* ethos and so an authentic inclusion requires a dynamic relationship with those on the margins to ensure they do not remain there but are included and engaged with through opportunities for meaningful encounter and dialogue. Lieven Boeve's work on the project of the Catholic Dialogue School, established by the *Office of Catholic Education in Flanders*, is an example of how schools can rediscover and reaffirm their identity as Catholic schools in and through dialogue with people with different religious and philosophical views in a context marked by 'secularisation and religious pluralism' (Boeve, 2019).

Jacque Derrida's work in the area of poststructuralism, culminating in his theory of "deconstruction", is interesting to consider in terms of plurality and inclusion. In his seminal essay 'Differance', Derrida condemns the use of binary oppositions as an element of essentialism that is not conducive to a post-modern pluralist society. Derrida outlines the concept of "differance" as "it is neither *this* or *that*; but rather this *and* that" (in O'Donnell, 2015, p. 49). Where *this* is the individual and *that* is an authentically inclusive society, the emphasis is on achieving a synthesis of both (2015, p. 49). O'Sullivan considers how Derrida's concept of "differance" is adapted by Homi K. Bhabha to elucidate the need for a middle ground or third space in which negotiation rather than negation can take place (1994, pp. 53–56). Once again, the emphasis of creating a safe place where encounters and dialogue between students of different worldviews and cultures whether that be belonging to a religious tradition or the LGBTQ+ community is central to a moving towards authentic inclusion within this school community.

Nurturing Student Voice and Participation to Mobilise Positive Change

Professor Laura Lundy's Model of Participation (2007) conceptualises Article 12 of the United Nations Convention on the Rights of the Child; a child's right to express their views and to have these views given due weight. The four elements of the model have a rational chronological order: Space, Voice, Audience, Influence. Lundy warns how the obligation to child participation can be diminished if this participation is understood solely in terms of Student Voice (Lundy, 2007). The four components of the model need to be present and activated so meaningful and legitimate child participation can happen. The Irish government's National Strategy on Children and

Young People's Participation in Decision-Making (2015–2020) was informed by the Lundy Model of Participation and a checklist was subsequently developed to support and

> help organisations, working with and for children and young people, to comply with Article 12 of the UNCRC and ensure that children have the space to express their views; their voice is enabled; they have an audience for their views; and their views will have influence. (Department of Children and Youth Affairs, 2016, p. 22)

Lundy's model and checklist are applicable to participation of young people up to the age of 24. It is cited in *Looking at Our School 2022: A Quality Framework for Post-Primary Schools* as a suitable model to support student participation. See Fig. 8.1 illustrating this checklist below.

Space

HOW: Provide a safe and inclusive space for children to express their views

- Have children's views been actively sought?
- Was there a safe space in which children can express themselves freely?
- Have steps been taken to ensure that all children can take part?

Voice

HOW: Provide appropriate information and facilitate the expression of children's views

- Have children been given the information they need to form a view?
- Do children know that they do not have to take part?
- Have children been given a range of options as to how they might choose to express themselves?

Audience

HOW: Ensure that children's views are communicated to someone with the responsibility to listen

- Is there a process for communicating children's views?
- Do children know who their views are being communicated to?
- Does that person/body have the power to make decisions?

Influence

HOW: Ensure that children's views are taken seriously and acted upon, where appropriate

- Were the children's views considered by those with the power to effect change?
- Are there procedures in place that ensure that the children's views have been taken seriously?
- Have the children and young people been provided with feedback explaining the reasons for decisions taken?

Fig. 8.1 Lundy's Model of Participation checklist

This framework is used to support student participation within this school community so that Student Voice can be nurtured, empowered, and mobilised to effect positive change. In an effort to avoid tokenism and to ensure ongoing participation seats were established on the junior and senior Student Council for *Advocates for Diversity and Inclusion* with a pathway process designed for students wishing to be elected to these four seats. The Lundy Model of Participation is used in this election process to ensure that as many students as possible will feel comfortable using their voice and participating in this differentiated election process. The only requirement to apply is to be interested in issues relating to diversity and inclusion, and to date there have been many students who express strong interest. The Lundy Model of Participation is used in the following way to support student participation in the election process:

Space: A suitable time and place is arranged with interested students and this meeting is facilitated by at least two teachers. There are two separate meetings arranged for junior and senior students to ensure students feel safe and more 'at home' in the group.

Voice: Teachers welcome students to the space and provide information on what the role of *Advocate for Diversity and Inclusion* entails. Teachers encourage purposeful listening before the students, who sit in a circle, introduce themselves to one another. They then take turns describing the reasons they are interested in issues of diversity and inclusion, they outline work the Student Council could do to ensure a more authentically inclusive school community along with what they feel they can bring to this work.

Audience: For the teachers and participating students this meeting offers rich insight into the various reasons informing individual student's interest and motivation for applying. Many of these reasons are personal experiences of difference whether it be belonging to a minority religious or non-religious group within the school, accessing Learning Support services in the school, or identifying as gay, transexual or non-binary.

Influence: Following this sharing of experiences and ideas there is a student vote to decide who will sit on the Council. The students who are elected *Advocates for Diversity and Inclusion* view the work of the Student Council through this lens and use their voices to ensure recognition, representation and respect for diversity and inclusion is sustained.

Students who are not elected to these seats are invited to join a Student Intercultural Education Team. This is a forum where the Lundy Model of Participation is used at different times to support the work of the Team, with authentic inclusion as its aim. This work includes:

- Raising awareness of days and months of significance, secular and those important to different religious traditions
- Ensuring that there is an intercultural dimension to school events. For example: Arts Week, Wellbeing Week and Positive Mental Health Week

- Providing Student Voice as part of the school's review of and subsequent change to policy e.g., the policy pertaining to the wearing of the hijab for Muslim students who wished to do so.

These students despite their diverse ethnicities, learning abilities, cultural heritages, ages, sexual orientation, gender identification etc. have a shared interest and common goal in using their voice to mobilise positive change in working towards authentic inclusion within this school community.

Broadening Our Understanding of Diversity

Traditionally diversity and inclusion within the Irish education system is understood in terms religious and cultural pluralism or relating to students with Special Educational Needs. However, increasingly issues of gender and sexual orientation diversity have entered public discourse and become more 'live' issues for many schools. In 2016 the Department of Education along with GLEN, Gay and Lesbian Equality Network, published *'Being LGBT in School': A Resource for Post-Primary Schools to Prevent Homophobic and Transphobic Bullying and Support LGBT Students'* to support schools in becoming safe spaces for all of their students in all of their diversity (DoE, 2016).

The prevalence of this concern is not confined to the educational realm as feedback from the 26 Irish dioceses contributing to Pope Francis' global synodal process, "Synod 2021–2023: For a Synodal Church", indicates the inclusion of LGBTQ+ people within the Catholic Church to be a key priority (RTE, 2022). The Irish Bishops' Conference identify the synodal process as being inspired by the familial vision outlined in the Vatican II document *Gaudium et Spes* (Vatican, 1965),

> we are reminded that the experience of our brothers and sisters that will resonate within our hearts; *"The joys and the hopes, the griefs and the anxieties of the people of this age, especially those who are poor or in any way afflicted, these are the joys and the hopes, the griefs and the anxieties of the followers of Christ. Indeed, nothing genuinely human fails to raise an echo in their hearts"* (GS, 1).

The Church recognises the challenge for people belonging to the LGBTQ+ community to live in a heteronormative world is something that should initiate a compassionate response. For some this can raise the question whether it is acceptable or indeed possible for a Christian to remain unmoved by LGBTQ+ people's efforts to live an authentic life that expresses their true humanity while remaining faithful to the Christian Commandment of Love?

School Response to Gender and Sexual Orientation Diversity

Belong To is a national organisation that provides support services for Lesbian, Gay, Bisexual and Transexual young people in Ireland. It is funded in part by the Irish government along with a host of other sponsors such as Microsoft and the National Lottery. Its 2019 'School Climate' survey conducted was the first of its kind in Ireland with 788 members of the LBGTQ+ young people ranging in age from 13–20 years old reporting on their experience of school. This research garnered startling findings with 73% of LGBTQ+ students reporting they feel unsafe at school and 86% feeling isolated (Belong To, 2019). Moninne Griffith, CEO of Belong To, writes 'for many LGBTQ+ young people in Ireland, school is an unwelcoming environment that excludes their experiences' (Belong To, 2019).

Since including Ethos as an area of focus in the School Self- Evaluation plan the students and parents of this school community have consistently referenced LGBTQ+ matters in response to the survey question:

> In your opinion how can diversity be better recognised and respected in the school community?

A synergy was identified in the suggestions made by some parents and students with regards to introducing trousers as an option to the skirt of the school uniform. Prior to September 2022 the only students granted permission to wear trousers were those with a certificate from a doctor denoting a medical need for them. Students experiencing a gender identity crisis in which wearing the school uniform skirt is particularly difficult were also expected to furnish the school with a medical certificate. The school's senior leadership team recognised that this approach was exacerbating the struggle of students who were already suffering, and trousers became an option as part of the school uniform from September 2022. In this regard, Hargreaves' axiom of *'what is essential for some is good for all'* is fitting as students who feel they cannot wear the school uniform skirt have trousers as an option and everyone else gets a choice. Other suggestions outlined in the SSE surveys related to raising awareness of gender and sexual orientation diversity and making the school a safer place for LBGTQ+ students.

Stand Up Awareness Week: Using Words that Heal Not Hurt

In November 2021, the school participated for the first time in Belong To's initiative Stand Up Awareness Week. This is a week whereby participating schools actively recognise and celebrate their LGBTQ+ community. Belong To describe this week as 'a time when we show solidarity with young people and our colleagues to ensure they feel seen, heard, and safe, and to ensure everyone knows that biphobic, homophobic, and transphobic language and bullying will not be tolerated'(Belong To, 2021). The theme of Stand Up 2021 was 'The Power of Language: using words that heal not hurt'. The school's participation was led by a Guidance Counsellor who is witnessing an increase in students who identify as LGBTQ+ availing of support due to feelings of exclusion and anxiety. A core team of teachers was established and members of this team availed of training from Belong To in order to support the school's engagement with Stand Up Awareness. Following this training, it was decided, given this was to be the school's first time to get involved that the focus would be on school environment and how this could be made more welcoming and affirming for LGBTQ+ students.

It was important to those leading the campaign that all communication around why and how the school had planned to participate would be communicated well in advance of the week. This was to avoid putting teachers and students on the spot or feeling coerced into participating. All participation was presented in the invitational spirit of Catholic education. The main objective was to establish a positive school culture for the holistic development of LGBTQ+ students where they will feel safe, respected and included.

A core team of students was also formed whose members included the senior cycle *Advocates for Diversity and Inclusion* and the president of the Student Council, along with other students who expressed interest in getting involved which included some from the Student Intercultural Education Team. The following activities were planned following purposeful listening to Student Voice on how students felt the school environment could be enhanced:

- Information hubs were set up in the public areas of the school with material on gender and sexual orientation diversity along with support services listed for student who may need help.
- During Form time (time for pastoral care with class tutor) students and teachers were invited to make posters on the week's theme 'The Power of Language: Use Words that Heal not Hurt'. Participation in this activity was very strong and most classrooms throughout the school had walls emblazoned with compassionate words of support and solidarity for LGBTQ+ people.
- Pride badges and stickers were made available to members of staff who wished to decorate their laptops or pencil case with a sticker, a small gesture which can be powerful message of support to a student who is struggling. A positive finding from Belong To's research on School Climate is that LGBTQ+ students who witness 'staff intervene when homophobic remarks were made were 15% more likely to feel like they belong in their school and 8% less likely to miss days due to feeling unsafe' (Belong to, 2019).
- The raising of the rainbow flag on the school campus. This was the action that the core student team felt most passionately about and therefore it was important that they contributed in a meaningful and purposeful way. This school event was structured around and supported by the Lundy Model of Participation.

The Lundy Model of Participation Supporting the Raising the Rainbow Flag

Space: Due to Covid restrictions the whole school community could not attend the flag raising event, however the core student and teacher teams, members of school management, ancillary staff and the school principal gathered and made space for participating students at the front of the school.

Voice: The school principal welcomed everyone gathered and acknowledged the importance of this day not only to members of the LGBTQ+ community but for everyone belonging to our school community. She spoke of the importance of the school's inclusive ethos, how the school must be a safe space for all its students and how homophobia would not be tolerated. The *Advocate for Diversity and Inclusion* from the senior Student Council delivered a speech elucidating the history and rich symbolism of the rainbow flag. She concluded her speech with 'Today we raise the rainbow flag to celebrate everyone in our school community'. Following this the President of the Student Council, spoke about her experience as a young gay woman and how significant it is that the school fly this flag and insist that it becomes a safe space for everyone. Also a talented singer and musician she then sang an acoustic version of the song 'Girls like Girls' by Hayley Kiyoko as the rainbow flag was being raised.

Audience: The uplifted and joyous spirits of young people was palpable and the audience grew as more teachers came from the staff room, students on errands from class delayed longer crossing the main entrance and caretakers and cafeteria staff put their work aside to join in. The statue of the Virgin Mary situated high above the entrance to the school was caught in everyone's gaze as eyes lifted upwards to see the rainbow flag in all its brightness flap against the grey November sky.

Influence: In the preparation for this event the core student team were asked to consider what they hoped to achieve by holding this event. They were asked to meet to reflect on the kind of influence they wanted to wield at such an event. As the ambassadors of this school's first Stand Up Awareness Week it was important that they had opportunity to consider the influence they had and space and time to think about who they wanted to influence and why. As a group they decided they wanted to have positive influence and for this occasion to be marked as significant and special in the school community. They wanted acknowledgment of the challenges encountered by members of the LGBTQ+ community along with recognition that their school ought to be a safe place for all its students in all their diversity. They also felt strongly that the raising of the rainbow flag should be a celebratory occasion, an uplifting and enriching experience that people would be invited to share in.

A reflection on the experience of participating in Stand Up Awareness Week 2021was completed by the core team of students. This comment from a student illuminates theimpact such events can have:

> A flag representing the various groups within the LGBTQ+ was raised in our school and a speech from representatives of the student body and from the Principal were given. This moment felt impactful as it is the first time, within my 5 years at this school, that I have properly seen the LGBTQ+ community properly recognised by our school. It was a very proud moment.

Another student's reflection included her understanding of why participation in such campaigns are particularly important for Catholic schools to engage in.

> Catholic schools should celebrate Stand Up Awareness week. Jesus spent most of his time helping and supporting the marginalised and others that had a difficult time in the society and therefore Catholics would only be more Christ-like if they embraced the diversity in their environment while of course still staying true to their beliefs.

Conclusion

This chapter has described one school's experience of empowering Student Voice to mobilise positive change in response to challenges to inclusion previously identified. The purposeful listening to students along with frameworks of support, such as the Lundy Model of Participation, has assisted this school on its journey towards authentic inclusion. This school recognises that meaningful student participation is central to any robust and significant commitment to diversity and inclusion.

In January 2022 the school celebrated Catholic Schools Week, who's theme was inspired by Christ's words 'I have come that you may have life and have it to the full' (Jn10:10). The journey towards authentic inclusion is understood as ongoing and dynamic and one that necessitates a reciprocal relationship with those on the margins and those being 'made poor'. It is hoped such an inclusive approach will enable all students to live life to the full within this Catholic school community.[1,2]

References

Belong To. (2019). *School climate survey*. Available at: https://belongto.org/wp-content/uploads/2019/11/Key-Findings-School-Climate-Survey-2019-1-1.pdf
Belong To. (2021). *Stand up awareness week 2021*. Available at: https://www.belongto.org/wp-content/uploads/2021/11/A-Guide-to-Stand-Up-Awareness-Week-2021.pdf
Bhabha, H. K. (1994). *The location of culture*. Routledge.
Boeve, L. (2019). Faith in dialogue: The Christian voice in the catholic dialogue school. *International Studies in Catholic Education, 11*(1), 37–50.

---

[1] For a fuller discussion on Nano Nagle and the Presentation Order see Raftery et al. (2018).

[2] A new specification for Junior Cycle Religious Education was implemented in 2019 as part of the major curricular reform at junior cycle. This has helped to ensure the study of RE at junior cycle has become more interreligious in its purpose, nature and scope. Currently the syllabi at senior cycle remains unchanged, however with a redevelopment of curriculum at senior cycle currently underway similar curricular changes are expected.

Bryan, A. (2010). Corporate multiculturalism, diversity management and positive interculturalism in Irish schools and society. *Irish Educational Studies, 29*(3), 253–269.

Darmody, M., Tyrrell, N., & Song, S. (Eds.) (2011). *The changing faces of Ireland: Exploring the lives of immigrant and ethnic minority children*. Sense Publishers.

Department of Children and Youth Affairs. (2016). *Diversity, equality and inclusion charter and guidelines for early childhood care and education*. Dublin: Government Publications.

Department of Education and Skills. (2016). *'Being LGBT in school': a resource for post-primary schools to prevent homophobic and transphobic bullying and support LGBT students*. Government Publications.

Department of Children, Equality, Disability, Integration and Youth. (2019). *National strategy on children and young people's participation in decision-making (2015–2020)*. Government Publications.

Graham, A., et al. (2022). Exploring the associations between student participation, wellbeing and recognition at school. *Cambridge Journal of Education*. https://doi.org/10.1080/0305764X.2022.2031886

Harmon, M. (2018). 'I am a Catholic Buddhist: the voice of children on religion and religious education in an Irish Catholic primary school classroom'. *EdD Thesis*. Dublin City University. Available at DORAS: https://doras.dcu.ie/22639/

Lundy, L. (2007). 'Voice' is not enough: Conceptualising article 12 of the United Nations convention on the rights of the child. *British Educational Research Journal, 33*(6), 927–942.

Mullally, A. (2019). Guidelines on the inclusion of students of other faiths in Catholic secondary schools. JMB/AMCSS.

NCCA. (2015). *Junior cycle framework*. Available at: https://ncca.ie/en/junior-cycle/framework-for-junior-cycle/

New Revised Standard Version Bible. Oxford University Press.

OECD. (2018). 'Chapter 9: A sense of belonging at school'. Available at: https://www.oecd-ilibrary.org/sites/d69dc209-en/index.html?itemId=/content/component/d69dc209-en

O'Sullivan, C. (2015) 'The social, personal and health education curriculum as an agent of inclusion in twenty-first-century Ireland'. In A. O'Donnell (Ed.), *The inclusion delusion?: Reflections on democracy, ethos and education*. Peter Lang.

Raftery, D., Delaney, C., & Bennett, D. (2018). The legacy of a pioneer of female education in Ireland: Tercentennial consideration of Nano Nagle and presentation schooling. *History of Education, 48*(2), 1–15.

RTE. (2022). *Irish Catholics call for more inclusivity*. Available at: https://www.rte.ie/news/ireland/2022/0616/1305337-catholic-church-synod/

Rougier, N., & Honohan, I. (2015). Religion and education in Ireland: Growing diversity-or losing faith in the system? *Comparative Education, 51*(1), 71–86.

Sullivan, G. (2019). 'I think it's very difficult to be different' How does Religious Education contribute to inclusion in an Irish Roman Catholic post-primary school?'. *EdD Thesis*. Dublin City University. Available at DORAS: https://doras.dcu.ie/22896/

Taylor, C. (1994). The politics of recognition. In A. Gutmann (Ed.), *Multiculturalism: Examining the politics of recognition* (pp. 25–73). Princeton.

Taylor, C. (1991). *The ethics of authenticity*. Harvard University Press.

The glossary of educational reform. (2018). Available at: https://www.edglossary.org

Vatican II. (1965). *Gaudium et Spes*. Available from: www.vatican.va

Dr. Gillian Sullivan is a post-primary teacher of Religious Education, English and Philosophy, who is currently seconded to Oide, a national organisation supporting the professional learning of school leaders and teachers. She contributes on a part-time basis to the B.Rel.Ed programme in Dublin City University. Gillian holds a Doctorate in Education from Dublin City University, her thesis investigated how Religious Education contributes to inclusion in a Roman Catholic post-primary school. She holds an MA in Religion and Culture from Mater Dei Institute of Education where she specialised in *Poetry and the Human Condition*. Her research interests include Religious Education, Inclusive Education, Teacher Education, Student and Teacher Voice.

Chapter 9
Relationships and Sexuality Education in Catholic Schools in Northern Ireland

Sean Whittle

Introduction

This chapter presents a summary of research findings about the state of Relationship and Sex Education (RSE) in Catholic secondary schools in Northern Ireland. The research data was gained from fieldwork visits to a sample of Catholic schools in Northern Ireland, conducted in the autumn of 2019. The data and resulting scoping report provides an intriguing and positive assessment of RSE provision in Catholic schools in the north of Ireland. In what follows it will be argued that there are high standards of RSE taking place—certainly in the Catholic schools visited. The evidence indicates that these Catholic schools are good at supporting students well in the RSE provision, and this is true also for students who are LGBTQ+.[1]

The findings summarised in this chapter are drawn from the scoping report commissioned by ACCORD, who are a voluntary organisation operating in Northern Ireland that aims to promote a deeper understanding of Christian marriage, and to offer couples support for their marriage and family relationships, working under the auspices of the Catholic bishops of Northern Ireland. The scoping report sought to identify the main strengths and areas for development in the provision of RSE in Catholic schools in Northern Ireland. To achieve these aims a qualitative study was undertaken, in order to assess the situation across Northern Ireland, through a sample of seven Catholic schools. There are two main reasons driving this methodology.

First, qualitative research allows for a more in-depth exploration of the provision of RSE. Rather than quantifying survey responses or presenting measurable data about student and teacher attitudes to RSE, the attention is on recognising what

---

[1] This report was commissioned by ACCORD in 2019 and was submitted to the Catholic bishops in the North of Ireland in 2020. Requests for a copy of the full report should be directed through Accord Northern Ireland (info@accordni.com). The data in this chapter has been anonymised.

S. Whittle (✉)
St. Mary's University, Twickenham, UK
e-mail: sean.whittle@stmarys.ac.uk

© The Author(s), under exclusive license to Springer Nature Singapore Pte Ltd. 2024
S. Whittle and S. Henry (eds.), *Queer Thriving in Catholic Education*,
https://doi.org/10.1007/978-981-97-0323-4_9

different groupings within the school have to say about this important part of the curriculum. Second, a qualitative approach allowed the research to be framed as a listening exercise—conducted on behalf of Accord (and through them the Northern Bishops). A key goal is to listen carefully to what teachers, governors, young people and their parents have to say about RSE in their Catholic school.

Focusing on a sample of seven schools as part of a qualitative research investigation has generated a rich set of data. It provides a timely and accurate snapshot of RSE in the Catholic secondary schools of Northern Ireland.

A sample of seven Catholic schools, six secondaries and one all-through Special school, were identified as the sample group. Members of the ACCORD team identified the schools in the sample group. This was done in order to ensure a selection that included the following range: single sex girls, single sex boys, mixed schools, schools in more rural areas and schools in urban areas. One Special school was also chosen. Attention was also given to choosing schools across almost all of the northern dioceses in Ireland.

Each of the seven schools was visited for one day by the Principle Investigator and a member of the Accord team. Each day consisted of four sets of focus groups with structured questioning—with the headteacher/senior staff, other staff (Head of RE, SENDCo, Year Heads, Teaching Assistants), students (from the School Council) and parents. When possible, others such as governors and chaplains joined in with the focus group. Each focus group involved a structured discussion of questions raised by the Principle Investigator (PI), and on average each meeting was one hour long. The questions had been sent to the headteacher as part of the original request to visit the school. However, most participants had not seen the questions beforehand. The working assumption is that the responses were not scripted or rehearsed prior to the focus group.

Some of the student groups were split into two, younger and older students. The decision to do this was left with the Safeguarding Lead in each school. Typically the student groups were drawn from the School Council, and as such were used to meeting together. The proceedings of each focus group was recorded on a smart phone in order to be transcribed at a later stage. To comply with ethical research standards and to be Safeguarding compliant, permission to record all meetings was sought from each participant at the start of every meeting. Moreover, anonymity was guaranteed in order to encourage participants to speak more confidently. The participating schools are discussed in an anonymous way. The visits took place during October and November 2019. Each school was visited for a full day. In addition to the focus group interviews, information on RSE policy and other documents were collected. Most schools had a Curriculum map identifying where topics are covered across the entire curriculum. Following the visits the recordings of the focus groups in all seven schools were transcribed and then analysed and scrutinised. The transcripts proved to be a fruitful way of identifying the common themes and issues across all seven schools.

The Main Findings

The visits to all seven schools proved to be a very positive experience. The schools are very committed to delivering high quality RSE and do so in a way which is reflective of their ethos as Catholic schools. The opportunity to meet and engage with so many headteachers, governors, teachers, parents and young people in order to enquire about RSE has generated a rich set of data. In terms of analysing and interpreting this data six central themes are presented here in order to summarise the main findings.

Theme 1: Abundant Evidence of Good Practice in RSE

Each of the schools visited recognise the importance of RSE. They were willing and able to explain the multiple ways in which the curriculum, pastoral care and wider ethos of their school contributed to the effective delivery of RSE. Many of the headteachers and senior staff interviewed were able to describe in eloquent terms the centrality of relationship education within their schools. One described the centrality of 'respect' for self and all others as the guiding basis for every interaction within their school. It was pleasing to see this positive description echoed and reaffirmed not just amongst the other staff interviewed, but also with the parents and the young people interviewed.

All the schools visited had taken seriously their responsibility for RSE and developed a range of appropriate courses. The majority had opted for a cross-curricular approach, in which RSE topics and themes are delivered in a number of different subjects and at various occasions in the year. Typically these are in religious education, science, and through the school's pastoral programme. Most of the schools supplemented what they delivered through the use of external agencies who specialise in presenting themes related to RSE to young people. By far the most popular is *love for life*. Teachers and students found these external providers to be engaging and relevant. Many older students had very vivid and positive recollections of these presentations. The main reservation is around the cost to the school of buying in these services. Typically the *Love for Life* presentation happens through extended assemblies involving half or even a full year group. Follow-up materials are left with the school to use in subsequent Personal Development or Learning to Live Well lessons.

The responses from the teachers, particularly those involved in delivering RSE, consider the cross-curricular approach to be a real strength, signalling to the students that the issues are important and span across multiple aspects of life and the curriculum. In most of the schools these teachers judged that their students would not recognise or appreciate that they were actually covering RSE issues repeatedly in different parts of their work at school. In three of the schools this was regarded as something very positive, in that their young people were soaking a solid RSE without even realising it. No doubt this reflects the assumption that in the future the seeds sown would bear good fruits in the lives of their students.

One of the many positive things revealed by the focus group interviews is that both the studentsand their parents valued what their school did in terms of RSE. The responses indicate that RSE is a relevant and important part of their education. In particular the students like and enjoy the RSE they have received, and any reservations are around wanting to receive more of it. In each of the seven schools the meetings with the students were both full of insights and enjoyable experiences. Repeatedly, the students displayed impressive levels of openness, acceptance and tolerance towards the matters that come up within RSE. Things such as homosexuality or lesbianism that were eschewed within living memory, are regarded as no longer controversial by these young people and certainly not things that would be criticised or be the cause of bullying in their school. Inclusion, acceptance and openness to alternate ways of expressing sexuality and identity were repeatedly demonstrated by the students in each school. In displaying these positive dispositions and attitudes the students demonstrated internalisation of central Gospel values (loving your neighbour). It was evident that they had indeed been well educated in matters of RSE by their respective schools and their parents. The students were a delight to be with because as articulate, polite and socially adept young people they displayed important relationship skills towards each other and to those who were in effect strangers visiting their school. One way of measuring the success of the RSE provision in these schools is to recognise the good fruits that it has already produced in the students they educate. The schools were proud of their students, with many of the teachers and senior staff citing that the best part of the school to be the children and young people who belong to the school.

The open and positive stance found with the students is reflected amongst the parents interviewed. Parents also value the way the school delivered RSE to their children. They were anxious for their daughters and sons to be well prepared for adult life—when they would need to be able form positive relationships with people who had very different attitudes and values, including in areas of sexuality and sexual practice. They were satisfied that their child's school was doing this. A number of the parents who took part were teachers in the school and as such they had an enhanced awareness of how the school delivers RSE. Although all the parents were happy with what the school did, they would appreciate more and regular communication from it about the RSE themes being tackled in any given part of the year. This would allow parents to be informed and ready to discuss with their children what was being covered in school.

Another sign of the good practice identified in all seven of the schools is in relation to navigating some of the complex issues that frequently crop up as part of RSE. The schools were good at dealing with these in a pastorally apt way. An obvious example is in relation to transgender. Six out of the seven schools visited had in recent years had a student who had expressed a desire to transition in terms of their gender. These students self-identified as no longer wanting to identified by their birth gender and requested to be addressed by an alternative name. In each school the needs of the students was accommodated in a way which maintained their dignity and ensured that they did not experience any trans-phobic discrimination or bullying. The issues were handled with pastoral sensitivity, reflecting Gospel values that guide and inform the school's ethos. The students did not raise any reservations over this issue. In a similar way the parents were supportive of the way that the school responded. It was their expectation that a Catholic school would be good at being inclusive and supporting the needs of any child experiencing the desire to transition from one gender to another.

There is much to affirm about the good practice that it clearly evident in the current provision of RSE in the Catholic schools visited. One of the governors taking part spoke poignantly when he observed that the provision for RSE is in safe hands.

Theme 2: Questions Over the Organisation of RSE in Catholic Schools

The schools visited had roughly similar ways of organising RSE, and as already noted a cross-curricular approach is favoured. Inevitably it falls to science lessons to cover the biology of human sexual reproduction, but it is Religious Education that covers many of the wider and more fundamental aspects of RSE. Most schools had 'personal development' lessons and 'Learning to live Well' which also included a range of RSE topics. Most schools had a document that clearly mapped where (in which subjects) and when (at which point of the year) different RSE topics and work are covered. This made clear that the schools are compliant with statutory guidance on RSE. However, despite this evidence and timetable provision the responses from many of the student focus groups showed that some students in the same school had a far greater grasp of many RSE issues than others. There are two main reasons for this. First, some individual teachers were better at delivering RSE issues in a memorable and accessible way. Second is to do with whether or not students followed the *General Certificate of Secondary Education* (GCSE) Religious Studies course (RS). If students were taking GCSE RS they had to study topics such as family life as part of the course. The specification requires students to compare and contrast Catholic Christian beliefs and attitudes to many family life issues, such as same-sex marriage, with the beliefs of others. Class discussions within these religious education lessons were often wide-ranging and give students the opportunity to debate often contentious RSE issues. However, not all students in Catholic schools in Northern Ireland take RS GCSE. This situation has an impact on the RSE provision because those taking the RS GCSE end up with more curriculum time to engage with these issues within the context of Religious Education. As part of the interviews involving senior leaders and teachers there was recognition of the differences between those who took the RS GCSE and those who had just the Personal Development and pastoral lessons. Within the student focus groups it was apparent that some students knew more because they had covered additional work in their RS GCSE.

In many of the schools visited the Religious Education teachers who were part of the focus groups revealed themselves to be skilled at teaching religious education and at being able to open up the social and moral complexity surrounding RSE issues. However, even amongst religious education teachers there can be a difference between those which are adept at delivering RSE in an engaging way and a smaller number who adopted a more a defensive stance towards presenting what they considered to be official Church teaching on many of these matters.

Although the senior leaders and teachers appreciated the benefits of delivering RSE in a cross-curricular way, a common theme in all but one of the schools was the issue of the students not knowing or realising that they are in fact having RSE lessons. Whilst for the teachers this is regarded as a strength, for the students it may well be a weakness. If students do not know that they are learning about RSE it is possible that this will trigger their perception that there are gaps in their understanding. In many of the student focus groups the initial questions had to probe and remind students that they had in fact learnt a lot about RSE, in particular in relation to friendship formation. No doubt the issue is clouded by the student's inability to recollect that they had done RSE work and perhaps this indicates the need for much clearer sign. posting within lessons and topics. During one student focus group some students had observed that in lessons they had looked at St Francis and charity work. When questioned about whether these were part of relationship education the students were emphatic that they were not. Of course in learning about the life of St Francis a range of relationship issues quickly bubble up, particularly around his rejection of his family's wealth. This lesson would be an ideal opportunity to explore family conflict and our changing values as we grow up and face challenges in our life. Naturally any focus on 'charity' (or practical love for others) will bring up a myriad of relationship issues. Crucially the students had not made the link between these topics and RSE. In the focus groups some students commented on the way Personal Development lessons were given over to practical charity work. Whilst they did not mind this, it fuels their perception that they are missing out on other (perhaps more 'real') RSE work. The students might question the way their schools are stretching both the meaning of RSE and best use of this lesson time. However, the real issue is that for the students the links with RSE and say charity work are too subtle or implicit. They are not grasping why this is a genuine part of RSE. It might well be that in the lessons not enough signposting and linking with RSE work is made.

One other issue related to the organisation of RSE is the question of who oversees the RSE programmes. In several of the schools, one member of teaching staff had the post of being 'RSE Co-Ordinator'. In most schools the deputy headteacher/principal or a member of the Senior Leadership Team had this role as part-and-parcel of their overall job description as the Pastoral Lead. In the schools visited the curriculum mapping documents, the RSE policy and the school prospectus demonstrate that this way of co-ordinating and overseeing RSE is working well. However, to tackle the student perceptions over what they cover in these lessons, more thought and attention needs to be given to making the students more explicitly aware of when and where they are doing RSE work. This might be taken as a criteria for quality assurance—can students recognise and identity all (or most) of the occasions and lessons they are having some RSE.

Theme 3: The Range of RSE Topics and Matters of Age-Appropriateness

An important theme that repeatedly came up in almost all focus groups in each of the schools is about the sort of topics which need to be covered in RSE. There is much approval for the current heavy emphasis on 'friendship' issues in the early years of post-primary. Given that children are moving from smaller primary schools in addition to the physical and emotional changes of entering teenage years, it makes intuitive sense to devote time to navigating friendship issues. The teachers considered this focus on friendship issues in the early years to be laying the foundations of later work in older years in RSE. It is here where there is disconnect between the student's perception of what they are doing and what the curriculum intent is seeking to achieve. This is because the students do not realise that the work done on friendship is an integral part of the RSE work. Parents responses indicate that they recognised the importance of focusing on general friendship issues.

Part of the discussion in most focus groups, particularly with students and parents, was on the range of additional topics that ought to be included in RSE lessons. Some of the older students in the focus groups spoke in forthright terms about their rights to be informed about the legal or rights-based aspects of sexuality and sexual activity. Amongst some older students there was a sense of suspicion that because they attended a Catholic school it meant that they were not given the full picture. Topics which ought to be included are the practical use of artificial contraceptives, pornography, sexting, consent, transgender issues and wider questions such as the legitimacy of same-sex marriage. On the whole, parents agreed that these issues should be included, not least because it will equip their children for the future. Other possible issues are about IVF and the difficulties some couples face in conceiving a child. An important part of the student focus groups was going beyond the 'rights-based' ways of framing RSE. The students went on to explain that RSE ought to involve lessons about 'being in love' and the challenges of working out when you are actually in love and knowing when to trust someone. Part of this could include presenting students with positive role models of happy marriages and committed loving relationships. It might also be necessary to devote lesson time to 'on-line' dating and how to navigate the difficulties of maintaining relationships which begin in this way.

Identifying what additional topics should be part of RSE triggers two key questions about both the amount of curriculum time that is needed and secondly, at what age certain topics should be introduced. There is already considerable pressure on the curriculum, which is why many schools have chosen to augment the RSE provision through buying in the services of external agencies. If additional topics need to be blended into RSE, there is inevitably a practical issue of finding the additional time in an already crowded curriculum. Many of the headteachers and senior leaders interviewed drew attention to funding pressures, which are unlikely to disappear.

The second question, about the age-appropriate delivery of certain RSE topics, triggered a range of opinions in the schools visited. Amongst the teachers the consensus in six out of the seven schools is that some issues are more controversial or complex and as such require higher level of maturity from the students. As such they need to be dealt with in the older years. For example, most schools dealt with issues of sexting during the middle years of secondary school. Issues about pornography tend to be dealt with as an aspect of internet safety. However, amongst the parents and students opinions are more divided. Many of the older students and the parent's explained that some issues need to be dealt with at a much younger age. These days the reality is that many primary school children are given smart mobile phones in the last year of primary school, to prepare for the transition to secondary. As such dealing with issues of sexting and pornography are matters that need to be tackled in RSE both in the last year of primary and first years of secondary. However, beyond the issue of on-line safety there are complex issues surrounding the ready availability of pornography that need to be addressed in RSE as the children grow up. In both the distorted presentation of sex and the damage that pornography can do to relationships, these are matters which go far beyond being merely 'safe on-line'. These are aspects of RSE that need to be repeatedly revisited in different years as a student progresses through the school and grow up.

Many of the older students spoke about the need to teach more about issues such as homosexuality, transgender, and contraception in earlier years and perhaps return to these for further work in later years. Amongst parents the opinions were more divided, whilst many agreed with the older students there was a reticence about too much exposure too early. The concerns here pivot on presenting RSE issues in an age-appropriate way. One school however took a notably different stance in making sure students from the youngest years were aware of RSE work. This was at the Special school visited. As a Special school it frequently taught these issues in a clear and age-appropriate way. For example, children from early years were taught the NSPCC guidance known as the 'underwear rule'.

Most of the schools visited augmented their RSE provision through buying in the services from groups such as *Love for Life*. Whilst these are well received by the students and stand out as memorable events there are some issues with how it is done. Typically the presentations are to the whole year groups in the format of an extended assembly. In this sort of context it can be difficult for students to ask questions or to have sufficient time to mull over the issues raised in the presentation. There is an underlying question about whether sufficient time is being given to RSE work. Students and parents would like more time to be given. There is, as yet, no clear consensus over what is right proportion of curriculum time to be formally given over to RSE.

Theme 4: Anxiety Over the Ways Schools Deliver RSE and Official Church Teaching on Sexuality and Sexual Activity

In nearly all schools visited the teachers responsible for RSE expressed a sense of anxiety or a nagging worry that there was a tension between what is being taught in some RSE lessons and what they perceived to be the official Church teaching. Teachers were anxious to properly represent Catholic teaching in a coherent and justifiable way, whilst wanting to be pastorally aware and supportive of students. One example discussed during some visits is teaching about homosexuality. Some teachers identified a tension when teaching openly homosexual students aspects of the official Church teaching on homosexuality. The students, whilst they cited no examples of homophobia in their schools, also had concerns over the way homosexuality is taught. Although they could articulate a difference between homosexual orientation and homosexual sexual practice, they were troubled by what they saw as an unjust description of homosexual sexual intimacy in the Old Testament and in the *Catechism of the Catholic Church*.

Some teachers and parents raised concerns over the relevance for the young people in their school and the official Church teaching about sexual activity. Whether it be the use of artificial contraception, prohibitions about premarital sex or cohabitation before marriage, there were repeated occasions where teachers of RSE were clashing with the sincerely held beliefs of the students and their parents. Notably, for one Head of RE the situation was very much the clash with contemporary society. In this context, the RSE topics are at the front-line and are issues about which students need to be confronted. In the other schools the situation was couched in less confrontational terms, where students are not starkly presented with the innate truth of the traditional Catholic teaching on relationships. Rather, the teachers want to give Church teaching a fair hearing. However, both for their students and for their teachers, there are worries and questions about the coherence of the Natural Law underpinnings of much official Church teaching in relation to sexuality and sexual activity. Whilst teachers could present the guidance on artificial contraception or teachings on homosexual intimate acts using natural law theory, for too many of the students this theory is no longer convincing or coherent. Similarly, the parent responses openly questioned the relevance for their children of what they saw as the traditional church teachings on sex and sexuality.

Throughout the visits an issue repeatedly discussed was around what ought to be the relationship between RSE in Catholic schools and official Church teaching (as summed up in the Catechism of the Catholic Church, 1994). Is it part of the role of RSE in a Catholic school to encourage or invite students to appreciate the wisdom and value of much of this Church teaching? During the student interviews one of the questions was about how 'biased' should RSE be in a Catholic school. The justification for Catholic schools is a philosophy of education built around a theological anthropology. Presumably the whole curriculum has a role to play in teasing this out for the students who freely choose to attend their Catholic school. Although students (and their parents) conceded that there would of course need to be a formal Catholic stance in RSE, they wanted it delivered in a 'neutral' or 'objective' way. However, there was little appreciation of whether this neutrality is either achievable or even actually that desirable.

Moreover, there is a pedagogical dimension to this issue, relating to the style of RSE lessons. One popular approach is that these lessons are primarily discussion based, in which students freely express their opinions on a range of issues that fall under the umbrella of RSE. It might well be described as a 'safe-space' where students are free to dissent and dismiss aspects of official Church teaching. In almost all of the schools visited this is the preferred approach. Amongst teachers there was sense of pride that students could freely give their opinions and that they were not silenced into accepting the official Church teaching. This was reflected by the students who, on the whole, felt able to express their views even if it meant repudiating some of these teachings. Parents also recognised that their children were not forced to believe certain things, with some contrasting this favourably with their own experience about sex education when they were at school.

However, there is an alternative pedagogic stance. This might be summed up as combining the discussion with challenge. Thus, part of the lesson is to challenge young people with the wisdom or insights contained in the official Church teaching. An important part of this is to make students aware of their own assumptions and biases. In the safe-space of RSE students will need to do more than just share their opinions. They will need to think through both what these opinions reveal about themselves and be challenged by the insights that are embodied in Catholic beliefs about relationships and love. Of course self-reflection and being challenged are often difficult activities to engage in within the average lesson and would call for some skilled teaching and careful lesson planning. It is also important to recognise that this alternative stance rejects the claim that there is a neutral (and value-free) way of delivering RSE.

Theme 5: The Connections Between RSE and Mental Health

All seven schools raised questions about mental health whilst discussing their RSE provision.

There is a strong contemporary awareness surrounding the need to promote mental health at school. There is a widely held conviction that young people are now subject to mental health problems and pressures to an unprecedented level. There are a range of ways in which RSE is able to address and engage with it. There are aspects of RSE, such as issues around low self-esteem or body image issues that have a close connection with mental health issues. For the teachers and parents an important priority is to ensure that the RSE dovetails with supporting mental health. Teachers in one of the schools visited were adamant that many issues coming up in RSE, such as transgender, are actually symptomatic of mental health issues. Thus, a student who wants to transition away from their birth gender ought to be regarded as someone in need of additional mental health support. The firm conviction is that relationship issues are a source of pressure or strain on a young person's mental health and as such the pastoral care structures and RSE lessons need to support or mitigate this whenever possible.

It was apparent from both the teacher interviews and the meetings with parents that all seven schools have very well developed pastoral care structures and principles. The pastoral care in each school was evident. In all the focus groups the pastoral care was noted and regarded as a strength of the school. For the students there was a confidence that bullying would be dealt with appropriately. There were teachers whom students could speak with, as well as access to a school counsellor.

For each of the schools an important priority is to support young people in the choices and decisions they make in terms of their sexual identity. The emphasis is on providing pastoral support for each student if and when it is needed. This was seen as an embodiment of beliefs about the dignity and value of each person (as the children of God). It was pleasing to hear that students reported that they feel confident and able to speak with members of staff over any RSE concerns they might have. Parents also expressed satisfaction with the pastoral care their children received.

The overall impression from the student focus groups is that the schools visited are happy places. The students felt looked after and were keen to speak well about their school. Teaching staff, SLT and governors were similarly positive about the school and the relationships between the students and with staff. As part of the student focus groups we met a small number of the students who had come out as homosexual and they felt happy with how their peers and teachers treated them at their Catholic school. This was not simply tolerance but rather a sense of genuine acceptance.

All the schools were aware of the challenges presented by social media and the ways in which this could feed into mental health concerns. Similarly parents are worried about mobile phone use and would appreciate guidance and support on monitoring appropriate use. There may well be generational issues at play in that teachers and the parents of young people are not 'digital natives' in the way the current and up-and-coming generations of schools are. The relationship young people have to social media and their mobile phone are throwing up a range of relationship issues that have yet to be properly distilled. Perhaps the current movement from 'on-line' safety to 'on-line kindness' will help to show more clearly the RSE issues at play with social media and mobile phone usage. However, there remains a need to address the inter-relationships between self-esteem, mental health and social media.

It is also important to draw attention to the challenges faced by some schools to raise student self-esteem. One non-grammar school is acutely aware that all the students join the school in the shadow having not passed the entrance exams for other schools. Raising the confidence of all students throughout their time at the school is a longer term goal and this naturally feeds into different parts of their RSE programme. In another school the high proportion of 'looked after children' has made teachers very aware of the need to create a very caring school community in which students know they are valued and cared for.

Theme 6: The Resources that Schools Need in Order to Enhance RSE

In all seven schools the issue of the resources and support that schools need came up as a point of discussion. There was a clear rejection of the need for a new text book or overarching programme. Schools have now devised the ways in which RSE is delivered (as demonstrated in the curriculum-maps and the various policy documents). A number positively recalled the programme developed by ACCORD in 2002[2] and recognised how it had over the years been weaved into the school's current provision. Although the idea of developing a new programme was rejected by all the schools, there were still a number of ways in which they needed ongoing support. One of the reasons why they could not do this for themselves is because of funding constraints. Although senior teachers were sanguine about neither ACCORD nor the bishops could help with the additional funding needed, they expressed how their desire to improve the RSE provision was hampered through the current financial constraints. They had a strong sense of there being much more they would like to do, but they did not have the funds for this.

Perhaps the most immediate need for support surrounds the request for some more guidance from Church leaders about teaching some aspects of RSE. This is directly related to Theme 4 and the anxiety schools have about fairly representing official Church teaching in RSE lessons. Many of the schools visited would like clearer guidance on what is the 'official line' on a range of RSE issues.

Rather than physical resources headteachers and teachers identified the need for additional training and education (INSET). This request for INSET could usefully take different forms. There are of course and range of complex and tricky issues to teach and INSET on how best to do this is needed. To begin with these topics would include pre-marital sex, cohabitation, homosexuality, contraception, transgender issues and abortion. Navigating between the official Church teachings on many of these issues and the situation facing many young people has become increasingly difficult. For instance, there has been a huge social change over couples choosing to cohabit prior to marriage. What was regarded as 'living in sin' just a generation ago is now regarded as normal practice. Indeed, a 'trial marriage' period is now widely regarded as a necessary first step that family and friends would expect a serious couple to take before getting married. In many respects the challenge here is an age old one—about how to convey official Church teachings in a way that coheres constructively with the contemporary socio-political context.

In addition to guidance on pedagogy (how best to teach about each of the topics) there may well be the need for catechesis over what the actual Church teaching is (and the reasons for this stance) in relation to these topics. There is a need for INSET on what needs to be taught for specific issues such as pre-marital sex, cohabitation, homosexuality, contraception, transgender issues and abortion. In addition there is a need for more general INSET to explore at the bigger theological questions over

---

[2] This programme was published independently by ACCORD Catholic Marriage Care Services (2002) *Love Rejoices in the Truth*, Belfast: ACCORD.

relationships and sexuality. This will give teachers the opportunity to enhance their self-awareness over RSE issues and improve their theological literacy.

Although there was no strong desire for a complete new programme, akin to the one devised in 2002, busy teachers would always welcome new teaching and learning materials. Many schools made use of materials prepared by different groups such as the PSHE Association. These are generic and not specifically prepared for use in Catholic schools.

A recurring request was for some way of generating 'one off' lessons that might be created and shared on a regular basis. These 'occasional' RSE lessons could pick-up on a current issue in society, such as the '*#me too*' movement, or would link with issues sparked off by popular TV programmes (for example ITVs *Love Island*). When it comes to RSE students do not always recognise the mixed messages that they are being presented with through popular media. Regular but more occasional generic lessons could be effective ways of making students more conscious of RSE issues in the wider society. The student focus groups revealed that they wanted more opportunities to discuss what they saw as the controversial issues of RSE.

Whilst parents are happy with what the school is teaching in RSE they did want more information. At the very least there ought to be regular letters home making parents aware of the topics coming up over the half term. The idea of using 'Parent App' to communicate home about the issues coming up in school was well received. Given that some RSE topics are delivered through assemblies and presentations it would be helpful to let parents know via such an App.

In addition the parent focus groups thought that it would be helpful if there were talks or catechesis sessions aimed at parents and guardians. These might be better delivered via the school rather than through the parishes. These talks could be linked with some of the themes coming up in RSE throughout the school year, in particular around social media and the use of mobile phones. It was assumed that people outside of the school would organise these parent sessions.

Concluding Observations

The empirical research findings summarised in this chapter indicate that in the schools sampled the RSE is effectively meeting the needs of students and their parents. The schools are successfully navigating the need to provide high quality RSE with a balanced presentation of official Church teaching on aspects of sexuality and sexual ethics. A firmly pastoral approach is taken in order to ensure that these Catholic schools are safe spaces for all students. In terms of LGBTQ+ students there was only positive evidence of supportive structures and respectful and affirmative relationships. If the seven schools sampled are taken as broadly representative of all the Catholic secondary schools in Northern Ireland, then there is much to affirm about the quality of RSE provision in the Catholic sector. These research findings would also provide grounds for arguing that Catholic schools in Northern Ireland are not places where LGBTQ+ students are adversely affected. The evidence is suggestive of LGBTQ+ students progressing at least as well as non-LGBTQ+ ones. Whilst this is different from claiming that this is evidence of 'queer thriving' (Henry, 2023). The evidence indicates that the Catholic school sampled are good at supporting all students in terms of the RSE provision.

References

Catechism of the Catholic Church. (1994). Veritas.
Henry, S. (2023). *Queer thriving in Catholic education: The role of queer theologies* (Whittle & Henry (Ed)).

Dr. Sean Whittle is a Senior Lecturer in Catholic Education at St. Mary's University, Twickenham, and a Research Associate with Professor Gerald Grace. Alongside these academic roles he works as a secondary school RE teacher at Gumley House FCJ Catholic School in West London. His book, *A Theory of Catholic Education* (Bloomsbury 2014), presents a robust philosophy of Catholic education that draws fruitfully on the theology of Karl Rahner. He has edited five books on Catholic Education (*Vatican II and New Thinking about Catholic Education 2016; Researching Catholic Education 2018; Religious Education in Catholic schools in the UK and Ireland 2018; Irish and British Reflections on Catholic Education 2021*, and (jointly with Dr Gareth Byrne) *Catholic Education: A life long journey (2021)*. Further volumes on Leadership in Catholic Schools and another on Guiding Research into Catholic Education Studies are in preparation for release in 2024. Since 2016 Sean Whittle has been collaborating with other academics working in the field of Catholic Education in order to create the *Network for Researchers in Catholic Education* (NfRCE).

He has also been engaged in a range of research projects (including a Post-Doctoral Research Fellow at Brunel University on a Religious Literacy project, Researching RSE in Catholic schools in Northern Ireland, and a research project of a Catholic Multi-Academy Trust in Birmingham). Prior to that he was a visiting Research Fellow at Heythrop College. Sean continues to serves as the secretary for the NfRCE and is also Chair of the academic association AULRE.

Chapter 10
A Transgender Perspective on Concerns About TGNB Young People in Catholic Schools

Claire Jenkins

Introduction

This chapter is rooted in the author's context as a trans academic—a sociologist within the Catholic tradition. This context is the setting for a series of reflections and observations on what are the potential challenges facing Transgender and gender non-binary (TGNB) young people as they journey through their Catholic schooling in England and Wales. This chapter intentionally draws on personal experience and observations to present how one trans academic reads the current situation for TGNB students in Catholic schools. The final part of this chapter incorporates a reflection on the account of 'Queer Thriving' advocated by Seán Henry in the opening chapter of this volume. In particular, it focuses on the practicalities that need to be addressed in building up inclusive cultures in Catholic education for TGNB young people.

Reservations Over the Speed of Changing Attitudes

It is helpful to begin with some recollections of a conversation with Sam, a trans man who experienced secondary school during the 2010s:

Me: Did you have **personal, sex** or health education?

Sam: I can't recall anything … there **definitely, wasn't anything LGBT** based.

Me: That's amazing, I went to school in the **1960**s it was the same thing then as in the **1980**s [see Steven's story interviewed in 2008].

C. Jenkins (✉)
The Margaret Beaufort Institute of Theology, Cambridge University, Cambridge, UK
e-mail: cj46@mbit.ca.ac.uk

Sam: Really!

Me: We are talking 40 to 50 years ago.

Sam: Well, **I imagine now it is a lot different**, I left secondary school in **2015** and there was nothing … it was pretty **awful**.

What is striking is that Sam imagines that LGBT based education in Catholic schools will be different now from what he experienced. This chapter will ponder this assumption, drawing attention to some ongoing concerns. The ongoing worry is about whether or not TGNB children are negatively impacted by what could be called systemic neglect in schools. This is because it could be argued that the contemporary sociocultural structure of institutional heterosexuality (Ingraham, 2005) and continued appeals to Natural Law help to perpetuate an unhelpful emphasis on binaries.

The reflections offered in this chapter are framed by the findings of the 2017 Stonewall School Report. The report is based on the experiences of lesbian, gay, bi and trans young people in Britain's schools in 2017 where 3713 LGBT young people aged 11–19 completed an online questionnaire. 16% [N = 594] of respondents said they are trans and a further 8% [N = 297] said they are unsure of whether they are trans or are questioning their gender identity. The statistics relevant to TGNB young people include:

1. 64% of trans pupils are bullied;
2. 46% hear transphobic language 'frequently' or 'often';
3. 9% of trans pupils are subjected to death threats at school;
4. 40% are never taught anything about LGBT issues;
5. 77% of LGBT pupils have never learnt about gender identity and what 'trans' means at school;
6. 44% trans pupils say that staff at their school are not familiar with the term 'trans' and what it means;
7. 33% trans pupils are not able to be known by their preferred name at school;
8. 58% of trans pupils are not allowed to use the toilets they feel comfortable in;
9. 84% trans young people have self-harmed;
10. 45% trans young people have attempted to take their own life;
11. 96% of all LGBT young people say the internet has helped them understand more about their sexual orientation and/or gender identity;
12. 97% of LGBT young people see homophobic, bi-phobic and transphobic content online. These statistics demonstrate that there are many issues needing attention in schools particularly the safeguarding concerns raised by the level of self-harm and suicide.

The Challenge of Shifting Terminology

Transgender or 'trans' is a broad term, with terminology constantly changing and new terms emerging in public discourse. 'Cis' is the term for someone who is not trans. A transgender person typically crosses the conventional boundaries of gender in terms of clothing and social presentation themselves. Gender Non-binary (GNB) is used to refer to someone who does not identify with the exclusive binaries of sex/gender. Trans-people often have complex gender identities and may move from one 'trans' category into another over time. The term trans is used in this chapter in a generic sense, rather than teasing out the different variations.

To help illustrate the complexity here it is helpful to recall another conversation, from over a decade ago, which explored the biographical narrative of a trans man. In a conversation in 2008 (see Jenkins, 2019) with Steven a 34-year-old trans man, he told me of the intense feelings he experienced as a child. He had a close twin sister and described how he first became aware of his feelings that his body was developing in a way that is undesirable, compared to his twin. Steven had been assigned the gender of female at birth, and he wanted his body to develop following the trajectory of a cis boy, not of a girl moving into being an adult female. Stephen felt that he was misunderstood as a child and teenager:

> My sister and I have been very close and as we kind of grew up together. [...] I saw her body changing and it never occurred to me that mine was doing the same and somehow, I managed to deny my own body right the way through my teens. I had problems because I was cutting myself. I started self-harming when I was 8 and I couldn't tell you why at the time. [...] At that time I was always able to do my own thing, play football with the boys, hang out with the lads, whereas when I moved from the village to the town we had an all girl's school and the school uniform arrived and we had all that kind of very specific [...] Suddenly the boys in the school were able to play football with each other and the girls were not and I was very aware at that point that there was something wrong [...] I was tremendously lonely, I really was. I tried a very feeble attempt to kill myself when I was 16. I ended up in a psychiatrist's room for an afternoon and then being dragged along each week for a month or so [...] I mean I wasn't in any position to talk about it and I am sure that they weren't, they probably would have thought that it was more to do with being gay more than trans [um...] because it was quite clear that I was masculine. (Jenkins, 2019, p.)

Steven did not understand his feelings at 8 years of age and it was probably the case that neither did anyone else around him. Nevertheless, he was able to recall that he liked doing the sort of things typically regarded as boys' preoccupations. At first, his experience of children's play was non-gendered but after moving to a new school in an urban setting, it became gender segregated. Gendered play separation and the usual body development caused Steven to become distressed. He began a long period, of more than eight years of self-harm culminating with an attempt to end his life at puberty—he did not want a cis young woman's embodiment since it violated his inner sense of self.

Steven's body was, in the typical terms of Western culture, socially understood to be female, however he felt that he was actually male and he expressed this through engaging in what is regarded as masculine play and behaviour. He challenged the received norms of what can be described as institutional heterosexuality, and part-and-parcel of this assumption that a female body should correspond to typical feminine behaviour (Ingraham, 2005). In this way, Steven stepped outside the dominant ideological hegemony of heterosexuality. He refused the everyday understanding that 'gender is a direct product of biology and carries with it natural and eternal differences between men and women' (Shapiro, 2010: 16). Steven's perceived strange behaviour resulted in him being deemed to have a psychiatric problem because he did not conform to the ideological structure of heterosexuality. His conflicting desires caused him to suppress his anxieties and he was silenced and this induced a sense of shame. Steven explained, elsewhere in his interview, how he released his emotions whilst in the school sixth form through, 'free flowing musical compositions'.

For Steven his school enforced a rigid conformity to adult gender patterns, and this triggered devastating consequences for him, because he felt completely silenced. Steven's experience might fuel the concern that schools are places where conventional gender experiences are constructed and other 'gendered experiences are silenced' (De Palma & Atkinson, 2008: xii). Although Steven did not appear to have been bullied but he internalised his distress which led to self-harm and a suicide attempt.

Steven's narrative raises several issues: self-harm (including suicidal ideation), concerns over institutional heterosexuality, silencing, dichotomous gender boundaries and potential academic underachievement. The nagging concern is that despite wide social changes over the past four decades, schools are not always positive places for TNGB children.

How Best to Frame TGNB Children's Experiences in Schools

It might be helpful to use a wider framework to map out the issues in relation to TGNB children's experience of Catholic schools. In what follows Bronfenbrenner's 'ecological framework' is used (Bronfenbrenner, 1979, 1993) is used to map out TGNB young people's experience of discrimination in our schools. The framework helps thinking about the larger system of TGNB experience within all schools—whether faith based or secular.

How Bronfenbrenners framework could be applied to the situation of TGNB young people at school (Fig. 10.1).

This means Institutional Heterosexuality and the reliance on Natural Law ethical theories can be depicted as a having a framing role to play. The essence of both these systems is a series of binaries: sex as either male or female, gender identity as either masculine or feminine, sexual orientation as either heterosexual or homosexual. Typically, in these binaries the first term is dominant over the second. These systems are reinforced through a wide range of socio-cultural conventions (marriage, family, politics, religion, work, education, medicine and through the media).

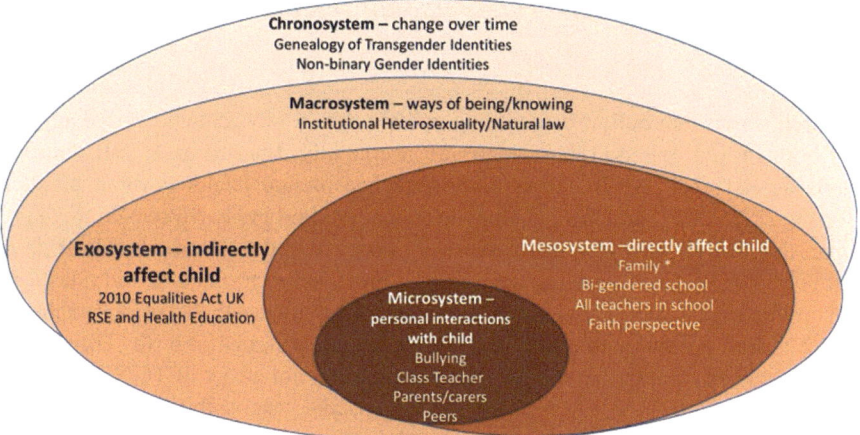

Fig. 10.1 Bronfenbrenner's ecological framework (Bronfenbrenner, 1979, 1993)

An Example of Catholic Teaching for Schools and TGNB Young People

The Congregation for Education at the Vatican issued a document called Male and female He created them: towards a path of dialogue on the question of gender theory in education. Unsurprisingly this document operated with a classic Natural Law depiction of the family, which consists of a married mother and father with children. Humans are described in binary terms as gendered as either a male or female. Fundamentally each human being regardless of their gender have a relationship with God (and this is rooted in scripture, specifically Genesis 1:27). In contemporary Church teaching to be fully human relies on this male-female binary—an expression of the doctrine of complementarity. A problematic part of the text from this Congregation for Catholic education is that it refers to 'TGNB issues' in the semi-pejorative term of 'gender ideology'.

Potential Research Questions

The next part of this chapter is a proposal of three research questions that could frame further investigation of Catholic education in relation to TGNB young people. The first research question is: what are the experiences of TGNB children in schools? This research question needs to be tackled in several ways and it is here that Bronfenbrenners' framework is helpful.

At a Microsystem Level—Interpersonal Interactions with the Child

Research shows that bullying, including cyberbullying, physical and verbal aggression both in and outside school hours are frequently directed at TGNB children (Layla & Krysthel, 2017: 2). As a consequence mental health is often affected (Horton, 2020, 2022) and this can impede educational progress. Moreover, there is a danger that TGNB young people's issues are silenced in the classroom (McBride & Schubotz, 2017). This is perhaps caused by some teaches trying to avoid questions concerning these topics. There is plenty of anecdotal evidence that in primary schools some children articulate that they are not of the sex assigned at birth. There is an ongoing concern that perhaps some schools are often not aware of TGNB children. When this happens it is often up to parents to take responsibility for educating teachers and schools about the issues at stake (Davy & Cordoba, 2019; Neary & Cross, 2018). It is important to realise that some parents might react violently and negatively towards their children who identify as TGNB. As a result schools should proceed carefully, treating it as a safeguarding issue (Callaghan, 2018). Furthermore, because the Catholic school is potentially an environment of institutional heterosexuality and one which assumes natural law to be a coherent ethical theory, there is a danger that peer-pressure might police gender conformity (Layla & Krysthel, 2017; Carrera-Fernández & De Palma, 2020).

At a Mesosystem Level—Whole School Issues that Affect the TGNB Young Person

It is possible that some TGNB teachers and young people could become anxious and feel powerless because of potential silencing in the face of a dichotomy between institutional heterosexuality versus the experienced reality of the presence of TGNB children in schools. There are anecdotal recollections that in the past when schools had not previously encountered TGNB children, they then become reactive after these children's emergence. Such children were seen as a "sacrificial lamb" which sends a school into a panic (Horton, 2020). This resulted in pressure on these 'pioneer children and families'. Headteachers began to engage with the complex problem satisfying the needs of TGNB students in the light of their mission and ethos (as Catholic schools). This is of course part-and-parcel of headteachers engaging with the issues of life in 21st century to provide high quality education for all pupils.

The recent *Department for Education* (England) Relationship and Sex Education (2022) offers no specific guidance concerning TGNB young people. This means school leaders (given their concern for TGNB children) will need to think both structurally and about the whole school ethos, as well as offer practical guidance to teachers in their classroom interactions and around the school with these children. Schools need to recognise that they do not want to be places which have systems which are rigidly bi-gendered. In single sex schools, physical education/sport lessons, use of inappropriate names and pronouns, school dances, overnight trips can all be problematic for TGNB young people (Neary & Cross, 2018; McBride & Schubotz, 2017; Davy & Cordoba, 2019; Layla & Krysthel, 2017). Many of these school activities may cause TGNB young people to hide their identity expression—and potentially drop out of school or face sanctions or be the victim of bullying.

Exosystem Level—Larger Policy Issues Which Indirectly Affect TGNB Children

Although the UK 2010 Equalities Act offers guidance for schools concerning gender reassignment[1]. However, there remains uncertainty, at the time of writing, concerning the legal status of the range of TGNB young people which is contested in the courts. At the same time the Statutory guidance issued by the Department for Education in 2019—*Relationships Education, RSE and Health Education* (Education, 2019), which came into effect 2020–21 (delayed by COVID-19) is silent on TGNB children. Schools have faced potential problems with local faith groups over RSE work. This is a site where religion, sexuality and gender reassignment intersect. It is important to note that despite these difficulties many schools have responded well with good pastoral care. School leaders have often had to engage in the highly politicised nature surrounding the teaching of TGNB issues. Sheila Jeffreys' opinion is described by Carrera-Fernández and DePalma in this way:

> As for trans* children, … practices such as hormonal blocking therapy to delay the onset of puberty to be a social engineering project designed to force children to conform to rigid gender categories. She [a prominent feminist] compares such therapies to early 20th century eugenics campaigns – the forced sterilization of delinquents as well as the poor, homosexuals, and the Roma. (Carrera-Fernández and De Palma, 2020, p. 753)

At a Macrosystem Level—Ways Of Knowing/Being in Wider Western Society

Up until relatively recently in the Western milieux TGNB identities were viciously or at least sarcastically satirised or attacked by some in the media. One illustrative example can be found in the work of Atkinson and De Palmer, who write:

> Have you had The Conversation with your children yet? Not the one about the birds and the bees, but the one about how some bees feel they are actually a bird trapped in a bee's body, or a bee trapped in a bird's body, or neither bee nor bird but somewhere in the middle of the bee–bird spectrum? (Atkinson and De Palma, 2009, 26).

---

[1] Available at https://assets.publishing.service.gov.uk/government/uploads/system/uploads/attachment_data/file/315587/Equality_Act_Advice_Final.pdf.

This attempt at humour runs the risk of trivialising the lives of TGNB students and it might contribute to mental health issues.

Chronosystem Level—Genealogy of Transgender Issues and Emergence of GNB Young people

In the 2010s, more gender affirming approaches to TGNB children developed with a greater recognition of the damage, abuse, rejection by families that these children have experienced. Furthermore, evidence of the inappropriate use of conversion therapies experienced in the past started to emerge (Horton, 2020). Typically TGNB young people explore their identity using socialmedia and the internet (Jones et al., 2015; McBride & Schubotz, 2017). Horton also argues that there is strong evidence that socially transitioned children, who are supported, have good levels of well-being and mental health.

However, there is a paucity of literature concerning GNB people and what exists is often weakened by its reliance on sub-optimal methodology and has little recognition of intersectionality (Chew et al., 2020; Horton, 2020).

Research Question 2—How Well are TGNB 'Toolkits', Policies and Legislation Operationalised to Ensure That There is No Systemic Neglect of TGNB Young People in Schools?

School guidance documents seem not to address the effect of the institutional heterosexuality pervading schools and allow TGNB children a voice (Martino et al., 2020). These issues are exacerbated because relationship and sex education guidance emphasise devolved responsibility of TGNB issues to schools/headteachers which can be a twin edged sword because issues such as sensitivity and age appropriateness are complex, socio-politically difficult and contentious. Furthermore, schools may increasingly have a complex mix of children of different religious affiliation, ethnicity, and range of gender identities to deal with.

Research Question 3—What are the Experiences of TGNB Young People in Catholic Schools and How Best are They Revealed?

The Vatican *Congregation for Education* document, *Male and female He created them* (2019) has the potential to raise a number of dissonances. This document suggests that to be fully human relies on the male-female binary which is posited as an essential basis of Christian theology. If this is how it is read, this might create a difficult situation for TGNB children. There seems to be on the one hand a rigid exclusionary Catholic teaching advocated whereas on the other hand Christian social teaching regarding anthropological pluralism, and the Gospel teaching to 'love thy neighbour as thyself' (Mark 12:31) are contrary in the situation of TGNB children. Pope Francis' (2013) *Evangelii Gaudium* impels Catholics to go forth from our own comfort zone in order to reach all the "peripheries" in need of the light of the Gospel', to a place where Christ is to be found amongst TGNB people who might be found at the margins of society. The perceived rejection of TGNB young people by this 2019 education document encourages them to be less involved in the church compared to their cis counterparts.

In England and Wales, the *Catholic Education Service* model curricula on RSE (Education, 2019) omits explicit reference to TGNB children, with exception of transphobic bullying. This might be interpreted as closing discussion and avoiding repercussions directed at Church leaders. Catholic guidance was issued in 2014 concerning schools and the 2010 Equalities Act, and it refers to the characteristic of gender reassignment which is listed as a protected characteristic, but it is not mentioned anywhere else in the guidance despite the appearance of TGNB children in Catholic schools. One might speculate that this a reaction to anticipated conservative opposition (Callaghan, 2018).

Obviously, some teachers in Catholic schools will act professionally and not discriminate against TGNB children, but they might feel that they are in some ways constrained by fear of contravening church teaching and the lack of support from peers and school leaders—there is a dissonance between their personal and professional beliefs. There is further anecdotal evidence that Early years teachers defer teaching about TGNB issues until the children are older, assuming that they are too young, but some children will nevertheless be struggling with these issues. A generic position adopted as adequate because of both these conflicts can be summed up as 'everyone is equal, we're all the same in God's eyes, etc.'. This reluctance to engage with the issue in a deeper way risks the danger of leaving Natural Law as the default position.

However, some Catholic teachers do explain about TGNB issues because of their experience of the reality of family diversity amongst their pupils. They choose to follow *Catholic Social Teaching* and can be compassionate, showing respect to the human dignity of these children. Furthermore, Catholics who are LGBTQ and also teachers might feel that they are presented with a binary choice of protecting their private lives against being open concerning teaching about LGBTQI experiences. In this situation they may be forced to live inauthentically contrary to Vatican II's *Gaudium et Spes*, which affirms that individuals should be free to follow their conscience in the pursuit of social justice. Wright-Maley et al. (Wright-Maley et al., 2016) list further teaching resources in a Canadian Catholic context and Bayly's (2012) book has a range of both didactic and experiential strategies for use in classrooms; role-play and practice scenarios, formal presentations, videos, and question and comments sessions. However, I found that Bayly's material needs to be creatively adapted for TGNB students because it primarily focuses on LGB issues. Both Stonewall and Gender Intelligence[2] offer secular guidance, and which could be modified to better cohere with Catholic understandings.

Turning now to consider *Relationships and Sex Education* Guidance (Education, 2019) in England. There is no reference in this document concerning TGNB issues and consequently this makes it very difficult to monitor school practice either internally or via Ofsted. Concerning Catholic education, I have argued elsewhere (2019) that the exclusionary heteronormative privileging of natural law is sociologically inadequate in explaining the lived reality of TGNB children's identities and the messy realities of contemporary family life—should this teaching be more flexible? Sex and gender are complexly related and so is determining the understanding of bio-social sex differences. It is important that TGNB children who are affected by these religio-theoretical arguments are respected and receive appropriate pastoral care by the church and in schools—there needs to be a careful process of discernment. Presumably, Church leaders will grasp the opportunity to follow Jesus in its pastoral care; to radically develop its practice in a way that is merciful and releases tenderness and love towards all TGNB people and children. In this way it will compassionately privilege the personal situation of the individual in need over religious ideals and structures that oppress people.

Further Research Agenda

The reflections and observations in this chapter are intended to suggest that research in the field of TGNB children's experiences in education (both inside and outside of Catholic schooling) is limited. Perhaps the real challenge is to develop a methodology for change, Meadows (2008) offers some crucial conceptual points of reference within the school system. Questions for researchers in this field might be to consider where are the boundaries, are they situated outside of Bronfenbrenner's vantage points developed in this analysis? Or are there other ways of considering the issues, perhaps, for example, from the vantage point of race/ethnicity? However, Meadows suggests that a strategy might be to:

---

[2] https://genderedintelligence.co.uk/.

keep pointing at the anomalies and failures in the old. You keep speaking and acting, loudly and with assurance, from the new one. You insert people with the new paradigm in places of public visibility and power. You don't waste time with reactionaries; rather, you work with active change agents and with the vast middle ground of people who are open minded. (Meadows & Wright, 2008, 164).

Plummer (1995) offers a qualitative narrative approach which will allow conceptualisation of the interface between the personal and the social experiences of TGNB children and their associates (parents, teachers, peers) illuminating their personal and psychic investment in the conventional sex/gender identifications of our heterosexual paradigm. Martino et al. (2020) further suggests a case study methodology which focuses on the educators of TGNB children.

Queer Thriving of TGNB Children in Catholic Education

Having offered my series of reflections above, and having thought more about Henry's perspectives on queer thriving earlier in this volume, I have a few final points to make in bringing this work to the concrete contexts of Catholic school and other educational institutions.

To begin, I think it would be worthwhile for the Catholic Education Service and school leaders in my own context of the UK to firstly recognise that TGNB children will be subjected to some form of bullying both interpersonal and online through social media where gender norms are policed. Schools will need to be proactive in addressing this and may appoint a member of staff to be a TGNB champion. This champion might facilitate the setting up of a safe space in schools. This space might be like an after-school club to allow young people's concerns and experiences (including but not limited to bullying) to be discussed with the champion and supportive peers. Unless this happens TGNB young people's mental health and educational progress will deteriorate. However, there is emerging evidence that socially transitioned children, who are well supported, have good levels of well-being and mental health.

Conscious of Henry's framing of queer thriving as calling Catholic education to move beyond discourses of vulnerability and suicidality in how it includes TGNB young people, I suggest that more needs to be done apart from these anti-bullying interventions. In this vein, I think it would be important for the Catholic Education Service and school leaders to also recognise that gender identity issues are different from sexuality issues (this is not something Henry's conceptualisation makes explicit). As such, gender identity issues may for some transgender children arise in their primary schools years, requiring a response from early years teachers that speaks to the specificities of children's experiences, rather than simply deferring to generic statements like 'everyone is equal, we're all the same in God's eyes', etc.

Building on this idea of *how* teachers can respond to these questions in their work, it would be important for Catholic education providers and leaders to acknowledge that teachers' reluctance to engage with TGNB children's issues often comes from a fear of contravening Church doctrine, as well as a fear that they will have a lack of support in their work from peers and school leaders. Bearing this in mind, cultivating the conditions for queer thriving in Catholic schools will require school leaders being explicit in their support for this work. Connections with Church teaching can also be made in justifying this support. For example, school leader could argue that Catholic educators need to reflect Pope Francis' (2013) exhortation in *Evangelii Gaudium* 'to go forth from our own comfort zone in order to reach all the "peripheries" in need of the light of the Gospel', peripheries where Christ can be found amongst TGNB people. Reference could also be made to *Gaudium et Spes*, which states that individuals should be free to follow their conscience in the pursuit of social justice.

This being said, it is important that this support is not romanticised, and that Catholic education leadership is sensitive to the realities of their communities and to wider social and political trends. Indeed, schools will need to tread carefully with parents as some will support their TGNB child and others will not. Discussion with the child and safeguarding professionals may help with this dilemma. Furthermore, supportive parents should not need to be put in the position of educating schools about TGNB issues as this is an unreasonable burden. In this context, School leaders cannot ignore the highly politicised nature of opposition to the teaching of TGNB issues. Backlash should be expected and it needs to be dealt with positively, in ways that recognise and respond to the structural, as well as purely individual, nature of transphobia.

Building on this last point, it perhaps goes without saying that cultivating and sustaining queer thriving for TGNB young people in Catholic schools will require fundamental structural reforms in the context of the Catholic Church. The Congregation for Catholic Education's (2019) *Male and Female He Created Them*, for example, needs to be revisited on the part of the Catholic hierarchy to recognise the reality of TGNB young people in Catholic schools and acknowledge their lived experience. With this in mind, Church teaching needs to respond to contemporary scientific biological and social understandings of alternatives to the male-female binary and heterosexual marriage and come to embrace the messiness of family life. In the UK Catholic education sphere specifically, this structural approach will require revisions to Catholic guidance on the 2010 Equalities Act to include explicit treatment of TGNB issues, as well as more sustained treatment of TGNB experience in the curriculum beyond merely prohibiting bullying or discrimination. And while Wright-Maley et al. (2016) and Bayly (2012) offer insights on Catholic teaching that go some way in cultivating queer thriving in schools, these will need to be adapted for the UK context to explicitly address the gender identity issues of TGNB children.

In summary, the Church should hold together its teaching (which might be applied to TGNB young people) in tension with its pastoral and education approach to the individual situation of such a TGNB child and their close family members. This tension will create an opportunity to explore flexibly and dynamically what is going on concerning their lived experience in the messy realities of family life. This is exactly where the Holy Spirit may become manifest releasing a new vigour, life and interpretation to help us discern what God is calling us to do in this concrete and yet complex situation of TGNB young people.

I hope this chapter relating to the situation of TGNB children in Catholic Schools will not be ignored but accepted as part of the Congregation for Catholic Education's desire for dialogue. Furthermore, I trust that the Church will grasp the opportunity to follow Jesus in its pastoral care—to radically develop its practice in a way that is merciful and shows tenderness and love towards all TGNB children. In this way it will compassionately privilege the personal situation of the individual child in need over the religious ideals and structures that oppress them.

References

Atkinson, E., & De Palma, R. (2009). Dangerous spaces: Constructing and contesting sexual identities in an online discussion forum. *Gender and Education, 20*, 183–194.

Bayly, M. J. (2012). *Creating safe environments for LGBT students: A Catholic schools perspective*. Routledge.

Bronfenbrenner, U. (1979). Contexts of child rearing: Problems and prospects. *American Psychologist, 34*, 844–850.

Bronfenbrenner, U. (1993). Ecological models of human development. In: M. Gauvain, & M. Cole (Eds.) *Readings on the development of children* (2nd ed.). Freeman.

Callaghan, T. D. (2018). *Homophobia in the Hallways: Heterosexism and transphobia in Canadian Catholic Schools*. University of Toronto Press.

Carrera-Fernández, M. V., & De Palma, R. (2020). Feminism will be trans-inclusive or it will not be: Why do two cis-hetero woman educators support transfeminism? *The Sociological Review, 68*, 745–762.

Chew, D., Tollit, M. A., Poulakis, Z., Zwickl, S., Cheung, A. S., & Pang, K. C. (2020). Youths with a non-binary gender identity: A review of their sociodemographic and clinical profile. *The Lancet Child and Adolescent Health, 4*, 322–330.

Congregation for Catholic Education. (2019). *'Male and female he created them': Towards a path of dialogue on the question of gender theory in education* [Online]. Available at https://www.vatican.va/roman_curia/congregations/ccatheduc/documents/rc_con_ccatheduc_doc_20190202_maschio-e-femmina_en.pdf. Accessed April 6, 2023.

Davy, Z., & Cordoba, S. (2019). School cultures and trans and gender-diverse children: Parents' perspectives. *Journal of GLBT Family Studies, 16*, 349–367.

De Palma, R., & Atkinson, E. (Eds.). (2008). *Invisible boundaries, addressing sexualities equality in children's words*. Trentham Books.

Department for Education. (2019). *Relationships education, relationships and sex education (RSE) and health education: Statutory guidance for governing bodies, proprietors, head teachers, principals, senior leadership teams, teachers* [Online] Available at: https://www.gov.uk/government/publications/relationships-education-relationships-and-sex-education-rse-and-health-education. Accessed April 6, 2023.

Francis. (2013). *Evangelii Gaudium* [Online]. Available at: https://www.vatican.va/content/francesco/en/apost_exhortations/documents/papa-francesco_esortazione-ap_20131124_evangelii-gaudium.html. Accessed April 6, 2023.

Grace, G. (2020). Taking religions seriously in the sociology of education: Going beyond the secular paradigm. *British Journal of Sociology of Education, 41*(6), 859–869.

Horton, C. (2020). Thriving or surviving? raising our ambition for trans children in primary and secondary schools. *Frontiers in Sociology, 5*.

Horton, C. (2022). Gender minority stress in education: Protecting trans children's mental health in UK schools. *International Journal of Transgender Health*.

Ingraham, C. (Ed.). (2005). *Thinking straight: The power, the promise and the paradox of heterosexuality*. Routledge.

Jenkins, C. (2019). *Critique of Vatican document on male and female he created them* [Online]. Available at: https://www.academia.edu/40363549/Critique_of_vatican_document_on_Male_and_female_he_created_them. Accessed 6 April, 2023.

Jones, T., Smith, E., Ward, R., Dixon, J., Hillier, L., & Mitchell, A. (2015). School experiences of transgender and gender diverse students in Australia. *Sex Education, 16*, 156–171.

Layla, J. K., & Krysthel, H. C. (2017). School policy and transgender identity expression: A study of school administrators experiences. *International Journal of Education Policy and Leadership, 12*, 3.

Lydon, J. (2009). Transmission of the charism: A major challenge for Catholic education. *ISCE, 1*(1), 42–58.

Martino, W., Kassen, J., & Omercajic, K. (2020). Supporting transgender students in schools: Beyond an individualist approach to trans inclusion in the education system. *Educational Review, 74*(4), 753–772.

McBride, R.-S., & Schubotz, D. (2017). Living a fairy tale: The educational experiences of transgender and gender non-conforming youth in Northern Ireland. *Child Care in Practice, 23*, 292–304.

McCann, C. M. (2014). Contributions of the Vincentians to Catholic education in Ireland and England. *ISCE, 6*(1), pp. 91–107.

Meadows, D. H., & Wright, D. (2008). *Thinking in systems: A primer Vermont*. Chelsea Green Publishing.

Miller, M. (2006). *The Holy See's teaching on Catholic schools*. Sophia Institute Press.

Neary, A., & Cross, C. (2018). *Exploring gender identity and gender norms in primary schools: The perspectives of educators and parents of transgender and gender variant children*. University of Limerick and the Transgender Equality Network of Ireland.

Paul V. (1962-5). Pastoral constitution on the Church in the modern world—Gaudium et Spes. *Vatican II*. Holy See.

Plummer, K. (1995). *Telling sexual stories: Power, change and social worlds*. Routledge.

Shapiro, E. (2010). *Gender circuits, bodies and identities in a technological age*. Routledge.

Wright-Maley, C., Davis, T., Gonzalez, E. M., & Colwell, R. (2016). Considering perspectives on transgender inclusion in Canadian Catholic elementary schools: Perspectives, challenges, and opportunities. *The Journal of Social Studies Research, 40*, 187–204.

Dr. Claire Jenkins is a trans woman and convert to Catholic Christianity. In 2013 she was awarded a Ph.D. from the University of Sheffield for her research into the effect of transitioning on the family members. Subsequently she has advised university research projects and has spoken at academic conferences. Currently she help the pastoral care to LGBT Catholics, giving ongoing support to LGBT Moslem asylum seekers and refugees, belongs to a small working party who advises the Catholic Bishops of England and Wales about transgender issues, and is researching the experiences of Transgender and Gender Non-Conforming young people in schools.

Chapter 11
What Can the Adult Religious Education and Faith Development Project (AREFD) Tell Us About the Research Agenda in Catholic Education in Relation to LGBTQI+ matters?

Bernadette Sweetman

Introduction

The *Adult Religious Education and Faith Development* project (AREFD) began in October 2018 at the *Mater Dei Centre for Catholic Education* at Dublin City University. Funded by the *Presentation Sisters North East Province*, the AREFD project had two broad aims. Firstly, the research team sought to explore the current landscape of religious education and faith development for adults in Ireland. In doing so, a greater focus could be given to the specific realm of adult religious education and faith development as opposed to the school-based sector or sacramental preparation—two areas that have been to the forefront of religious education and faith development for some time. Consequently, the research team aimed to identify possible areas for development in AREFD including potentially new approaches to or models of AREFD.

This chapter will focus on what can be learned from the AREFD project to inform the research agenda in Catholic education in relation to LGBTQI+ matters. Firstly, it is therefore necessary to provide some background information on the AREFD project and the data on which this chapter draws. Secondly, the rationale for returning to the AREFD datasets with a new research question relating to LGBTQI+ matters will be justified. Thirdly, our expectations as a research team in contrast to the reality of the data identified as relevant to this new research question will be discussed. This provides an insight into the current positionality of LGBTQI+ matters in the Catholic

---

B. Sweetman (✉)
Mater Dei Centre for Catholic Education (MDCCE), Dublin, Ireland
e-mail: bernadette.sweetman@dcu.ie

© The Author(s), under exclusive license to Springer Nature Singapore Pte Ltd. 2024
S. Whittle and S. Henry (eds.), *Queer Thriving in Catholic Education*,
https://doi.org/10.1007/978-981-97-0323-4_11

education research agenda. Finally, the pertinent data is interpreted and a commentary provided followed by some concluding comments and recommendations of how research agenda in Catholic education in relation to LGBTQI+ matters could be fruitfully developed.

Context: Overview of the Adult Religious Education and Faith Development Project

Launched in October 2018, this was initially a three-year project and due to the impact of COVID-19, was extended to December 2022. Broadly speaking, the project was created to facilitate a re-energising of adult religious education and faith development in Ireland. In the first year, an extensive literature review commenced and an online survey was designed. This nationwide online survey was live for six weeks during May/June 2019 and was publicised widely through various networks and social media channels to invite as diverse a sample as possible. The purpose of the survey was to ascertain the different forms of AREFD taking place in Ireland and to identify key individuals and groups involved. It invited adults to explore their understanding and experiences of religious education when they were at school but also bring them beyond that, to what matters to them in the present day. It encouraged adults to reflect on how they express their beliefs and values; the opportunities (or lack thereof) for religious education/faith development at various stages of life; and, ultimately, what would Irish adults like to see happening in the future to engage them in ongoing religious education and faith development. The AREFD online survey was designed for self-completion, using mainly multiple choice and *Likert scaling* on five points (very positive to very negative, very important to not important at all, strongly agree to strongly disagree).

Although the total number of respondents to the survey is 738, indicating the sample could not be seen as representative of the entire Irish adult population, there were, however, respondents from every age group and every county in Ireland. The data were analysed by means of SPSS, employing frequencies and correlations according to age and gender. Analyses on the quantitative data of this survey has been reported elsewhere (Byrne & Sweetman, 2021, Sweetman, 2021b). A smaller amount of qualitative data was gathered from the online survey whereby respondents were given the option to elaborate further on comments in open text format. Any responses to each question that included the option of open text responses were copied into individual word documents according to each question and stored for future analysis.

The second phase of the AREFD project consisted of consultations with a diverse sample of individuals and groups working in the area of AREFD in Ireland. All consultations took place between December 2019 and April 2021 in accordance with DCU Ethics regulations. The research team sought to engage with different forms of AREFD in a variety of contexts. Context in this case referred to the size of the projects in which participants were involved, their geographical location i.e. local/ nationwide, and/or rural/urban, and the overall mode or genre of the AREFD taking place. Some participants had voluntarily contacted the research team in the earlier phase of the AREFD project expressing their interest to contribute in some further way, where possible. Other participants were approached where it was considered by the researchers that their context would complement the existing sample. In total, twenty-two people working in adult religious education and faith development, in both the Republic of Ireland and Northern Ireland and across a variety of settings were consulted during this second phase of the AREFD project. Contexts in which they have worked include retreat centres, pilgrimage sites, Catholic school management, academic research in religious education, training for voluntary pastoral ministry, evangelical ministry, diocesan advisory services at primary and post-primary level, youth ministry, and parish ministry. The purpose of these interviews was to gather together the rich insights from the wealth of experience of the interviewees on the practicalities and possibilities central to adult religious education. Interviews lasted for one hour on average. All interviews were transcribed by the research team and stored for analysis.

Exploring How the AREFD Project Could Inform the Research Agenda of Catholic Education

The AREFD project is purposefully broad and did not from the outset focus on any particular cohort or issue within the adult education spectrum. Nonetheless, the data proved beneficial when interrogated with a specific lens such as what could be learned from it in relation to informing initial teacher education in Religious Education (Sweetman, 2021a) and addressing the phenomenon of *detraditionalisation* (Sweetman, 2021c).

When the Network for Researchers in Catholic Education (NfRCE) announced a one- day conference in February 2022 to explore the research agenda for Catholic education in relation to LGBTQI+ matters, the research team sought to methodically explore whether the data from the AREFD project could contribute to the discussion. With this aim, the team returned to the open-ended text responses from the online survey and the transcribed interviews from the consultations. The researchers recollected conversations on LBGTQI+ matters during the consultations and recalled some inferences in the open-text responses to the online survey. It was expected that the data would provide some solid insights as to the opinions of participants that would in turn inform the general discussion on the research agenda in Catholic education in relation to LGBTQI+ matters.

The twenty-two consultations conducted in Phase 2 of the AREFD project had all been transcribed and stored in Word format. The research team conducted a search of all interview files for any reference to LGBTQI+ and related words or phrases. To their surprise and initial disappointment, no references were found despite the team recalling conversations about such issues. Thereafter, the research team searched the data from the online survey. Of the 78 variables in the survey, 16 were open text responses. Respondents were not directly asked about LGBTQI+ matters. Nonetheless, some referenced these issues. Similar to the data from the consultations, far fewer results were found in the search than was expected. Out of the thousands of responses to the 16 open text questions by over 700 participants, just six statements emerged as explicitly referring to LGBTQI+ and related matters. The scant data was a huge disappointment to the research team however it became a significant learning in and of itself when the researchers reflected upon the question of why was there actually such little data. This was happening when the LGBGTI+ discourse continues to be prevalent in media and general commentary, and the researchers also knew it had been mentioned during their fieldwork.

The remainder of this chapter will explore the research team's deliberations as to the reasons for such a dearth of LGBTQI+ data in the AREFD datasets. In addition, it will be described as to how a rich array of possible avenues for research in Catholic education in relation to LGBTQI+ matters was discovered from just those six statements from the online survey.

What Can the Response to the AREFD Project Tell Us About the Research Agenda in Catholic Education in Relation to LGBTQI + matters?

The initial disappointment of the AREFD research team having gathered surprisingly little data related to LGBTQI+ matters in fact led to worthwhile point of learning. Given that LGBTQI+ matters feature increasingly in general public discourse, media and educational arenas, these issues should naturally have featured in the AREFD datasets, as all aspects are parts of the same broad society and culture. That LGBTQI+ matters were not officially referenced in the substantial amount of data gathered in the consultations of phase 2, comprising of several hours of interview transcripts suggests either of two things. Firstly, it suggests that LGBTQI+ matters do not in fact matter when it comes to Adult Religious Education and Faith Development in Ireland. The research team quickly dismissed this possibility on foot of a related finding while conducting the online survey. During this survey there was a mixture of prompts that encouraged participants to comment on past experience such as their school memories of religious education or influences on their faith. These were retrospective and respondents provided a lot of information in this regard. Other sections of the survey were more innovative where respondents were invited to suggest approaches or topics that they would like to see more of in AREFD. The invitation to comment on possible future endeavours or suggesting innovative approaches yielded fewer contributions than the retrospective items in the survey. For the research team, this led to the second and more likely reason for the lack of formal data on LGBTQI+ matters in the AREFD datasets. There is a reticence to formalise LGBTQI+ matters within the Catholic education research agenda. It was during the pre- and post- interview informal conversations in some of the phase 2 consultations that mention was made of LGBTQI+ matters. In contrast, when recording and documenting the statements, other issues were more to the fore, leaving LGBTQI+ matters essentially 'off the record'. The research team considered it to be a significant finding that in spite of a large scale approach with experienced adults with high levels of religious literacy, the absence of such a culturally prevalent topic in the AREFD data underscores the reticence to formally address LGBTQI+ matters in relation to the Catholic education research agenda. If progress is to be made, this reticence must be overcome and commentary in this regard is provided in the concluding section of this chapter.

Contributions to the Research Agenda in Catholic Education in Relation to LGBTQI + matters Based on the Data from the AREFD Online Survey

During the online AREFD survey conducted in May/June 2019, six statements were offered by participants in open text optional comments. These related to LGBTQI+ matters and are presented hereunder. The sections of the survey from which they arose are noted and the statement provided verbatim. An interpretation of this statement by the research team is subsequently offered followed by prompts for discussion and/or possible items for consideration of inclusion in any future research agenda on Catholic education.

Statement 1

> 'Homosexual, so once established that it's sinful, key reason I lost my faith.'
>
> (P1)

This statement came from a respondent (P1) when given the opportunity to elaborate on what may have been significant influences on their faith development.

It is implied that this participant identified at one stage as being both homosexual and having a faith. An external authority (neither seen as positive or negative) was perceived by this participant as stating that homosexuality is sinful. The participant appears to have held the perspective that one cannot have both identities (homosexual and faithful), and therefore the participant 'lost' the faith identity while seemingly retaining the homosexual identity. The word 'lost' intimates that this was not the desirable outcome for the participant, but an inevitable and unavoidable one.

Prompts for discussion arising from *Statement 1*

- Is identity a choice? If so, why? If not, why not?
- Can a person choose to be faithful? If so, how?
- Can a person choose their sexual orientation? If so, how?
- Can a person have multiple facets of identities?

- Is there a sense of inevitability that one cannot be both LGBTQI+ and faithful? If so, where does this sense have its source? Do you agree or disagree and why?
- Is there an implicit understanding of which of these two identities is culturally 'preferable' or 'more acceptable'? If so, where does this come from and do you agree or disagree and why?

Statement 2

> 'My experiences as a gay man greatly shaped my relationship with my faith'
>
> (P2)

This comment by P2 was provided in the same section of the survey as the previous statement by P1. This is neither a positive or negative comment by P2. It suggests for this man that there was a causational relationship in that his sexual identity impacted upon his faith. The man does not indicate the reverse, that is, he does not imply that his relationship with his faith shaped his experiences as a gay man.

Prompts for discussion arising from *Statement 2*

- How does sexual identity impact upon faith?
- Is this a question that only some people (generally those in the LGBTQI+ community) are forced to reflect upon?
- Should all sexual identities reflect upon this question? If so, how can this be done?
- Is there a further distinction between sexual orientation and gender identity and their impact on faith? If so, what is it?

Statement 3

> 'In all societies, groups of people are demonised and isolated, Irish society has been guilty of demonising homosexuals and travellers. Today, as a Catholic I feel demonised for my beliefs'
>
> (P3)

This statement from P3 comes from the section of the survey where respondents were invited to provide any other comments on beliefs and values. This participant identified with one (or more) of the groups of people considered demonized [and isolated]. This person also identifies as Catholic. P3 feels demonised for beliefs in this statement, and not necessarily demonized for gender or sexual orientation. Homosexuality is listed as one of a selection of groups of people who have been demonized by Irish society.

Prompts for discussion arising from *Statement 3*

- How might we explore the linguistic implications in such statements such as the term 'demonise' which itself has religious connotations?
- What is the role of faith within a society?
- What power does faith hold in society, particularly when it comes to the status structure in a society according to certain identifies such as those mentioned in this statement?

- What is the role of gender identity and/or sexual orientation within a society?
- What power does gender identity and sexual orientation hold in society particularly when it comes to the status structure in a society according to certain identities such as those mentioned in this statement?
- Is there a difference in the power of faith upon a society and the power of gender identity and sexual orientation in a society? Is this contextually or temporally based and if so, how?

Statement 4

> 'I am well-educated in doctrine, but I am uneasy with the Church and the failure of Pope Francis to allow married priests, women priests and to allow gay relationships to take place in a loving physical manner (presently considered sinful) and not just in concept.'

(P4)

This comment by P4 also comes from the same section of the online survey as P3. This respondent distinguishes between doctrine, Church and the Pope. P4 sees loving gay relationships as a positive and implies that either the Church and/or Pope Francis allows the concept or idea that relationships between gay people can be loving. A distinction is made between gay relationships that are physical and those which are not and the participant intimates that the physical gay relationship is not allowed by either the Pope and/or the Church and P4 deems this to be a 'failure' on the part of the Pope and/or the Church with which they are 'uneasy'.

Prompts for discussion arising from *Statement 4*

- Is it three separate things to explore LGBTQI+ matters in relation to doctrine; to Church; and to the Pope? If so how and why?
- Is there a different in the understanding of the nature of relationships and nature of love?
- What is the correlation implied in this statement between 'lovingness' and 'physicality'? What might be the pertinence of this?
- How does introducing the specificity of LGBTQI+ into a conversation about relationships and love alter such a conversation? If so, how and why?

Statement 5

> 'I would like to understand more from the Church teachings on moral / social issues such as family planning, LGBT within the Church and the role of women in the Church.'

(P5)

This statement by P5 comes from the section of the online survey where respondents were asked to provide other suggestions for what adults would like to learn about and/or activities they would like to see offered. This statement indicates that the respondent (P5) wishes to learn more about Church teachings on moral/social issues. One of these issues is named as LGBT within the Church. This participant indicates that Church teaching has some authority on moral and social issues. P5 lists three moral/social issues with no priority given to any. All issues relate to gender, sexual orientation or sexual practice.

Prompts for discussion arising from *Statement 5*

- Is Church teaching on moral/social issues in general unclear? If so, for whom and why? How might this be addressed?
- Is there a particular deficit in the clarity of Church teaching on these elements of moral/social issues?
- Why might these issues be mentioned and not others?

Statement 6

> 'The church reimagined with female priests, expressing the true meaning of Christ's life i.e. expression of unconditional love to all including migrants, gay people etc.'

(P6)

This comment by P6 also comes from the same section of the online survey as P5. This statement suggests a possible reality in which the Church exists, but in a reimagined way, in other words, in some way different from its current state. The suggested characteristics 'female priests, expressing the true meaning of Christ's life i.e. expression of unconditional love to all including migrants, gay people etc.' are implied to be not fully existent in the current state of the Church, but would be in the alternative 'reimagined' Church. Gay people are mentioned as one group in a list (including etc.) of groups to whom unconditional love is currently not seen as being expressed by the current Church.

Prompts for discussion arising from *Statement 6*

- Is there anything specific about LGBTQI+ issues amidst other groups with whom they are often heaped together under the umbrella of marginalised/othered/isolated and so on?
- How might LGBTQI+ Christians specifically reimagine the 'expression of the true meaning of Christ's life'?

Conclusions and Recommendations

LGBTQI+ issues increasingly feature across a myriad of political, media and educational discourses. Catholics in Ireland live in the same society as non-Catholics in Ireland. As a result, Catholics should be as engaged with such issues as LGBTQI+ matters as any other group. The AREFD project gathered a substantive amount of data about adult religious education and faith development but not specific to LGBTQI+ issues. One may argue that the research team did not directly include LGBTQI+-related questions in the data collection process. Instead, participants were invited to discuss that which was relevant and pertinent to them. The paucity of reference offered by participants to LGBTQI+ matters suggests that while such issues exist, they float rather than currently being grounded in any formal agenda in discourse of religious education and faith development. Perhaps, the desire to acknowledge the existence of LGBTQI+ matters in AREFD and to somehow address them is combatted by a lack of understanding and confidence in how exactly to go about that task. Is fear of offending, further excluding or 'rocking the boat' keeping LGBTQI+ matters off the agenda?

The first recommendation concerns the acknowledgement of LGBTQI+ matters being a lacuna in the overall Catholic education research agenda and a strong call to redress this. In the initial phase of conducting a literature review for the AREFD project, LGBTQI+ matters did not arise. On reflection at this later point in the project, the research team notes that much of the academic literature focussing on LGBTQI+ and religious education and faith development is recent in nature (Coll, 2020; Huchting & Fisher, 2019; Merry, 2021). Previous work was more prevalent in broader sociological areas (Dahl & Galliher, 2012; Deguara, 2018; Irby, 2014; Rodrigquez, 2010). It is hoped that as an outcome of this NfRCE conference and subsequent publications, more targeted research will be conducted, shared and valued in areas that intersect between all aspects of culture and society with religious education and faith development, such as that of LGBTQI+ which has been shown as a lacuna in the research agenda.

The second recommendation concerns the perception of the role of LGBTQI+ matters in the Catholic education research agenda. LGBTQI+ matters, RSE programmes and the generation of anti-bullying policies in educational settings has for many been the main arena in which discourse has been prompted. This context, though important, by itself only serves to promulgate the perception of LGBTQI+ matters of one of the problems to be addressed. It promotes the view of LGBTQI+ as one of the marginalised groups on the periphery of a normative core. Hospitality (Coll, 2020) and ongoing dialogue is required so as to honour that actual experiences of all involved in Catholic education. LGBTQI+ people are stakeholders in Catholic education and it is recommended that further research be conducted to accurately document these voices (see for example Neary & Cross, 2018; Fuist, 2016; Rodriguez & Ouellette, 2000).

In conclusion, we return to the final statement of P6 and wonder what might be discovered if the research agenda in Catholic education were to truly 'reimagine [how we may express] the true meaning of Christ's life'.

References

Byrne, G., & Sweetman, B. (2021). Opening up religious education and faith development: The AREFD project. *British Journal of Religious Education* (April (online). 2023), *45*(2), 138–147.

Coll, R. (2020). Hospitality to difference: LGBT, religious education and the Catholic school. *Journal of Religious Education, 69*, 25–36.

Dahl, A., & Galliher, R. (2012). LGBTQ adolescents and young adults raised within a Christian religious context: Positive and negative outcomes. *Journal of Adolescence, 35*, 1611–1618.

Deguara, A. (2018). Destroying false images of God: The experiences of LGBT Catholics. *Journal of Homosexuality, 65*(3), 317–337.
Fuist, T. (2016). "It just always seemed like it wasn't a big deal, yet I know for some people they really struggle with it": LGBT religious identities in context. *Journal for the Scientific Study of Religion, 55*(4), 770–786.
Huchting, K., & Fisher, E. (2019). Introduction to the special issue: The challenges and opportunities of including the LGBTQ community in Catholic education. *Journal of Catholic Education, 22*, 3 [online].
Irby, C. (2014). Moving beyond agency: A review of gender and intimate relationship in conservative religions. *Sociology Compass, 8*(11), 1269–1280.
Merry, J. (2021). LGBTQI+ and inclusiveness. *The Furrow, 72*(10), 593–599.
Neary, A., & Cross, C. (2018). *Exploring gender identity and gender norms in primary schools: The perspective of educators and parents of transgender and gender variant children.* University of Limerick and the Transgender Equality Network of Ireland.
Rodriguez, E., & Ouellette, S. (2000). Gay and lesbian Christians: Homosexual and religious identity integration in the members and participants of a Gay-positive Church. *Journal for the Scientific Study of Religion, 39*(3), 333–347.
Rodriguez, E. (2010). At the intersection of Church and gay: A review of the psychological research on gay and lesbian Christians. *Journal of Homosexuality, 57*(1), 5–38.
Sweetman, B. (2021). Learnings from the AREFD project for the Initial Teacher Education of Religious Educators. *Journal of Religious Education, 69*, 453–466.
Sweetman, B. (2021b). Adult religious education and faith development in Ireland: Pushing the boat out. In G. Byrne, & S. Whittle (Eds.), *Catholic education: A lifelong journey* (pp. 49–62). Veritas.
Sweetman, B. (2021). Reimagining adult religious education and faith development in a detraditionalised Ireland. *Religions, 12*(11), 963–978.

Dr. Bernadette Sweetman is the post-doctoral researcher investigating Adult Religious Education and Faith Development at the Mater Dei Centre for Catholic Education (MDCCE). Ongoing since 2018 when Bernadette joined the MDCCE team, this project is researching the nature, scope and potential of religious education and faith development for adults in Ireland. Formerly a primary school teacher, Dr. Sweetman completed her doctoral studies in religious education in 2016. She has written a number of catechetical resources for use in homes, schools and parishes as well as building an international publications portfolio. She has been a researcher at third level since 2013 and has lectured across a range of undergraduate and postgraduate programmes at DCU.

Chapter 12
Faith-Sensitive RSE and Catholic Schooling: An Educational Goods Approach

Ruth Wareham

Introduction

Following decades of campaigning by educationalists, children's rights activists, and others, September 2020 saw the introduction of mandatory Relationships and Sex Education (RSE) in all secondary schools and relationships education in all primary schools in England. In 2022, the launch of the new *Curriculum for Wales* brought with it an even more expansive RSE policy, with relationships and sexuality education introduced for all pupils aged 3–16 with no parental right to withdraw.[1]

While polling suggests that most UK citizens (81%) believe that RSE is an important curriculum subject, at least at secondary level (YouGov, 2022), its introduction has not been uncontroversial. Across the UK, disputes about the content of RSE are relatively common.[2] Indeed, the world over, sex education is a 'touchy' subject (Bialystock and Andersen, 2022) which throws into relief tensions between the authority of the state, parents, and religious groups in a uniquely fractious manner (see also Zimmerman, 2015).

In different jurisdictions, these tensions are managed differently. In most countries in the UK (England, Scotland, and Northern Ireland), schools with a religious character are legally permitted to teach RSE in accordance with their faith ethos. In the context of state-funded schools the right to withdraw can be seen as acting as a

---

[1] This right still exists for sex education in England, although there is no such right for relationships education (DfE, 2019a, p.8).

[2] Most notably in Birmingham in 2019 (Ferguson, 2019) but also in Nottingham (Busby, 2019), as well as in Wales, where a group of parents recently brought an unsuccessful judicial review against the new RSE Code and Guidance (O'Neil, 2022).

R. Wareham (✉)
University of Birmingham, Birmingham, UK
e-mail: r.j.wareham@bham.ac.uk

safety valve against 'indoctrination'.[3] However, in Wales, since there is no longer such a right, all schools—including schools with a religious character—must teach the subject in an 'objective, critical and pluralistic' manner (Dojan and Others v Germany, 2011; Kjeldsen, Busk Madsen and Pedersen v Denmark, 1976). That is, in a way that 'must not direct pupils towards adopting a particular comprehensive worldview or position on controversial issues' and '[covers] a range of different perspectives on those issues.' (Wareham, 2022, p. 710).

Given that, according to guidance issued by the Catholic Bishops of England and Wales through its Department of Catholic Education, 'the principal purpose of Catholic education is the formation of disciples of Jesus Christ' and RSE forms 'an important part' of the Church's 'holistic approach' to this formation, this makes the position in Wales appear somewhat more at odds with Catholic education than such policies in the rest of the UK. Nevertheless, in this chapter I argue that, if the distinctive package of educational goods (Brighouse et al., 2018) provided by RSE is to be adequately realised, faith-based concessions or exemptions[4] to policy pertaining to the subject (such as those adopted in England) should be scrapped.

I go on to argue that this does not mean Catholic educators need to entirely abandon the idea that RSE pedagogy involves or should be partially shaped by faith, merely that, particularly in the context of state-funded schools, the subject should be 'faith-sensitive' (Sell & Reiss, 2021; Wareham, 2022) rather than 'faith-orientated'. Religiously-minded educators may teach about their faith-based perspective(s) on sex and relationships, but (as is already the case in the context of schools without a religious character) this teaching should explicitly recognise that there are a plurality of views on such matters, not only between different religion and belief traditions but, as Henry notes in this volume (Henry, 2023), within them.

Responding to the potential concern that the adoption of the suggested approach would 'dilute' or otherwise remove the religiously distinctive nature of Catholic and indeed other types of faith schools, and acknowledging that, as an 'outsider' there is a (necessary) limit to the recommendations I am able to make regarding the substantive content of authentically Catholic RSE, I end by linking my position to some recent work by Christian educators involving what I call 'priming pedagogies' (Wareham, 2018). These are religiously distinctive ways of teaching that nevertheless avoid the kind of heavy-handed formation (or indoctrination) that is inimical to the development of educational goods, both in RSE and the rest of the curriculum.

---

[3] Here it is important to note that, while the term 'indoctrination' has acquired pejorative connotations in ordinary language (Callan and Arena, 2009; Gatchel, 1972), in the context of human rights law it refers only to teaching from or that is biased towards a particular religion or belief perspective and for which no (parental) opt-out is granted (see Wareham, 2022, p. 710). The state may not indoctrinate, but the law largely permits parents to do so.

[4] I have argued elsewhere that these ought to be framed as 'faith based carve-outs'. (Wareham, 2018).

RSE Policy in England and Wales

As noted above, the introduction of compulsory RSE in England was largely lauded as a positive step for children's rights. However, as highlighted in recent reports to the UN Committee on the Rights of the Child by the Children's Rights Alliance for England (CRAE, 2022) and the Equality and Human Rights Commission (EHRC, 2020), there are gaps in the law pertaining to the coverage of LGBTQ+ content, particularly at primary level. In England, the Government has said it expects 'all pupils to have been taught LGBT content at a timely point' (DfE, 2019a, p. 15) and primary schools are 'strongly encouraged and enabled to cover LGBT content when teaching about different types of families' (DfE, 2019b). However, the statutory guidance leaves primary headteachers to determine when (or indeed if) this content is 'age appropriate' (DfE, 2019a, p. 15) and thus it appears to be discretionary.

This apparent loophole is further exacerbated by what could be described as faith- based carve-outs (Wareham, 2022) which allow religious schools to teach their 'distinctive faith perspective on relationships' (DfE, 2019a, p. 12). This may include the view that same- sex relationships are morally impermissible or sinful,[5] as long as this 'does not subject individual pupils to discrimination' under the Equality Act (DfE, 2014, p. 14) or misrepresent the law (DfE, 2019a, p. 13), e.g., on the existence of same-sex marriage.

The persistence of the parental right to withdraw children from sex education until three terms from their sixteenth birthday also plays a part in restricting access to inclusive RSE provision. After this point, pupils may attend lessons in sex education irrespective of their parents' wishes (DfE, 2019a, p. 18), although, presupposing that older pupils are even made aware of this right, it seems unlikely that very many will be sufficiently confident to avail themselves of it, especially in the face of strong parental opposition.

Furthermore, the section of the statutory guidance dealing with religion and belief states that all schools (including those without a religious character) must take account of the religious background of pupils when planning their teaching of RSE 'so that the topics that are included in the core content…are appropriately handled' (DfE, 2019a, p. 12). Of course, a requirement that teachers pay due care and attention to the backgrounds of their pupils when planning the curriculum is not problematic in and of itself—as I will emphasise below, displaying adequate sensitivity to the particularities of the children one is teaching (and of the broader community context) is a key feature of best practice in RSE pedagogy. Nevertheless, as the anti-RSE demonstrations in Birmingham in 2019 illustrate (Ferguson, 2019), there is a need to ensure that such sensitivity is not confused with a need to radically

---

[5] Many Catholics, including Catholic educators, are accepting of LGBT individuals—in fact, research suggests that, in Western Europe, the majority of Catholics support gay marriage, with 78% of UK Catholics saying they favour allowing gays and lesbians to marry legally and 86% saying homosexuality should be accepted by society (Pew, 2020). Nevertheless, the Catechism of the Catholic Church denounces same-sex acts as 'grave depravity' and labels same-sex attraction as 'objectively disordered' (Catechism of the Catholic Church, 2357).

alter or omit content on the basis that children from certain religious groups should not be exposed to particular ideas or information simply because these are perceived to conflict with the beliefs of their family or the wider community.[6]

Since the teaching of LGBTQ+ content is a regular flashpoint in discussions about the RSE curriculum, the concern that inclusive lessons about same-sex relationships and the increasing recognition of *trans* people run the risk of being more likely to become a casualty of faith-based concessions or adaptations than other RSE content. The media storm that arose during the Birmingham protests is one that few educators would like to experience—who could blame school leaders (particularly at primary level) for avoiding similar controversies which might bubble up under the current legal framework? Elsewhere, there is an anxiety that the right to withdraw could be used to enable some faith schools (for example, those adhering to the tenets of Charedi Judaism), not to simply omit LGBTQ+ content, but to avoid teaching RSE altogether (Nye, 2019). Further, at the time of writing (2023), the UK Government has announced an urgent review of the statutory guidance which, although not (explicitly) faith orientated, appears to be strongly motivated by concerns relating to the teaching of *trans issues* or what is often called 'gender ideology' (New Social Covenant Unit, 2023a) that looks as if it may potentially lead to a more inhospitable climate for the discussion of such matters (and support for trans identified children and young people) in schools.[7]

In Wales, the new curriculum offers teachers a high degree of autonomy with respect to how precisely RSE is taught. However, required content—including content on LGBTQ+ lives and diversity—is mandatory via the *RSE Code* (Welsh Government, 2022). There is no parental right to withdraw from any aspect of the curriculum, a fact which, as noted above, means the subject must be taught in an objective, critical, and pluralistic manner; that is to say, all schools (including those with a religious character) must teach about a diverse range of perspectives and not use RSE as a vehicle to inculcate a particular view on sex and relationships.

In the Welsh context, LGBTQ+ content, which is evident across all three of the curriculum's broad thematic strands,[8] is built-in to each phase in a developmentally appropriate manner. For example, in the *relationships and identity* strand, learners in phase 1 (age 3 and up) begin by developing an 'awareness of the diversity of families and relationships, including friendships and peer relationships' (Welsh Government, 2022, p. 6). Then, at phase 2 (age 7 and up), they will begin to learn 'how families, relationships and parenting are shaped by social and cultural norms and laws that have changed over time' (ibid.) before, at phase 3 (age 11 and up), relating this knowledge

---

[6] At the height of the protests in Birmingham, the DfE pointed out that 'consultation does not provide a parental veto on curriculum content' (DfE, 2019b). However, little to no guidance was provided on what it might mean to ensure that topics were 'appropriately handled' (DfE, 2019a, p. 12).

[7] The organisation behind the report, the *New Social Covenant Unit*, was founded by two evangelical Christian MP's who have been particularly vocal on this issue (NSCU, 2023b).

[8] These are 'relationships and identity', 'sexual health and wellbeing', and 'empowerment, safety, and respect' (see Welsh Government, 2022, p. 3).

to a 'diversity of relationships including marriage and all types of civil partnership' and considering how norms might impact on such relationships in different contexts.

RSE and Educational Goods

Although the precise aims of RSE are clearly a matter of dispute and often engender further controversies regarding the content of the subject, political disagreement about whether it is necessary to teach the subject should not be overplayed. In England, just 21 MPs voted against the introduction of the new regulations and guidance (Bartlett, 2019) and there was similarly strong support for the introduction of compulsory RSE in Wales.[9]

Public opinion is also largely supportive of RSE. As noted above, most people (81%) in the UK believe that sex education is an important part of the curriculum. In Wales, this figure rises to 83% of the population compared with 81.5% in England (YouGov, 2022). This level of support—which outstrips that for many other long-established curricular subjects, including history, geography, physical education (PE), and modern foreign languages (YouGov, 2018)[10]—is reasonably easy to explain by appeal to the educational goods RSE generates. A framework for theorising the kinds of educational (and other) goods produced by RSE,[11] which are goods in a philosophical rather than a material sense, has been developed by Brighouse et al. (2018). They set out six distinct (but connected) categories for such goods. These are:

1. economic productivity;
2. personal autonomy;
3. democratic competence;
4. healthy personal relationships;
5. treating one another as equals; and
6. personal fulfilment.

While some may dispute whether these categories provide an exhaustive account of the range of educational goods[12] and Brighouse et al. acknowledge that other, non-educational or external goods (e.g., childhood innocence or public health), may be promoted (or indeed stymied) by education, most will agree that they are (a) generally speaking, goods (in the sense that they make the lives of people who

---

[9] Although the Curriculum and Assessment (Wales) Act 2021 enjoyed less than unanimous support due to the absence of compulsory lessons on Welsh history. This led Welsh nationalist party Plaid Cymru to withdraw its support for the Bill despite being supportive of the introduction of RSE (see e.g., Gwenllian, 2021).

[10] In this YouGov poll, the only subjects deemed more important were English, maths, ICT, and science.

[11] For a fuller discussion of this see Wareham (2022).

[12] For example, Michael Hand has criticised the omission of 'rationality or responsiveness to reason' (Hand, 2020, p. 1371).

have them go better) and (b) can and should be promoted via education. Further, focusing more squarely on the matter in hand, it is not difficult to identify the expectation that some of these goods will be produced in a distinctive manner by RSE. This is clearly illustrated by the existing policy documentation for the subject. For example, in a section pertaining to RSE at secondary level, the 2019 guidance for England states:

> The aim of RSE is to give young people the information they need to help them develop healthy, nurturing relationships of all kinds, not just intimate relationships. It should enable them to know what a healthy relationship looks like and what makes a good friend, a good colleague and a successful marriage or other type of committed relationship. It should also cover contraception, developing intimate relationships and resisting pressure to have sex (and not applying pressure). It should teach what is acceptable and unacceptable behaviour in relationships. This will help pupils understand the positive effects that good relationships have on their mental wellbeing, identify when relationships are not right and understand how such situations can be managed. (DfE, 2019a, p. 25)

This passage emphasises the need to cultivate healthy relationships, to develop autonomy and, through also respecting the autonomy of others, treat them as equals. Similarly, the Welsh guidance on RSE curriculum design states that the subject is important because 'understanding how relationships are formed, developed and maintained enables children and young people to develop skills and attitudes to support them in their own relationships throughout their lives' (Welsh Government, 2023). It goes on to highlight the necessity of learners having 'the knowledge and skills needed to make sense of their thoughts and feelings' as well as to 'feel equipped to challenge harmful stereotypes and perceptions and seek help and support.' (ibid.) In a section on inclusivity, which explicitly refers to LGBTQ+ inclusivity, the fact that learners are growing up in a rapidly changing world is given as one reason that RSE 'must start early' and explore 'diversity in relationships, gender and sexual identity'. This part of the guidance goes on to say that the subject 'should help learners to develop understanding of different values, religious beliefs and non-religious convictions that can inform our values and identity around relationships and sexuality.' (ibid.)

If, seemingly in line with the position of the UK and Welsh governments, one accepts that good RSE will characteristically focus on the production of a package of educational goods—particularly autonomy, healthy personal relationships, and treating one another as equals—it should nevertheless be recognised that there may be circumstances when such goods conflict. For instance, if one conceives of autonomy as the capacity to make one's own decisions about how to live life, it is not difficult to think of scenarios in which sustaining a healthy relationship, respecting someone else's freedom to make their own self-regarding decisions, or simply living alongside other people will, at least in part, restrict this capacity.[13] On this basis, good RSE will

---

[13] The extent to which such tensions will arise will, nevertheless, depend on the conception of autonomy one adopts. For instance, in other work I rely on a 'global' conception developed by Colburn (2010) which enables agents to adopt lives that may look rather heteronomous from the outside, as long as they genuinely endorse such lives and came to the decision to do so independently (see Wareham, 2018).

need to equip pupils to make wise decisions regarding trade-offs between different goods and, at the macro level, policymakers will themselves need to consider such trade-offs when selecting which policy to adopt. Likewise, whether by accident or design, educational interventions may well distribute goods in an uneven manner (e.g., so they accrue more readily to members of a certain social or cultural group). While there are instances when this might be justifiable (such as when these differences have been introduced to make up for systemic inequalities or disadvantages), this will not always be the case.

Indeed, the upshot of my argument is that the current faith-based system of exemptions to RSE policy in England amounts to an instance of uneven distribution[14] that is not, in fact, justifiable.

RSE, Parental Rights and Catholic Education

Of course, even if there is a reasonable degree of agreement regarding the idea that RSE benefits children and young people, as well as broader society, in terms of a package of some distinct educational (and other) goods, not everyone will be convinced that these consequentialist considerations (so-called because they focus on the consequences of teaching the subject) are all that should influence how, what, and to whom we should teach these lessons. Some may argue, with the Conservative MP Miriam Cates, that it is sufficient for schools to teach 'the biological facts about sex, how to stay safe and what the law says' (Cates, 2023), but leave any teaching of sexual morality and values solely to parents.

It may be possible for individual entitlements, such as parents' rights, to outweigh the need to maximise a particular benefit/good. To illustrate, Eamonn Callan imagines the case of a musically talented child whose parents face a choice between purchasing a piano or an expensive holiday. While it may be 'unfortunate, even stupid' for the parents to opt for a trip to Disneyland over a long-term investment in the cultivation of their child's musical skills, Callan maintains that 'scarcely anyone would think the parents were not in their moral rights in choosing as they did' (Callan, 1997, p. 145). To put it another way, parents are considered to have a 'zone of personal sovereignty' that, in at least some circumstances, warrants respect regardless of whether the actions carried out within this zone will impact negatively on the production of educational goods.

This kind of reverence for the rights of parents is central to the Catholic stance on education. The view that parents 'must be recognised as the primary and principal educators' of children (Vatican Council II, 1965a, s. 3) is a key plank of the Second Vatican Council's *Declaration on Christian Education* (*Gravissimum Educationis*) and is echoed in the Catholic Education Service (CES) guidance for RSE. For instance, a CES document entitled, 'Who is responsible for the teaching of RSE?',

---

[14] An instance that results in fewer goods going to those from religious backgrounds or who attend faith schools.

opens with a quotation from a Vatican document, *The Truth and Meaning of Human Sexuality*, which states:

> Sex education, which is a basic right and duty of parents, must always be carried out under their attentive guidance, whether at home or in educational centres chosen and controlled by them. In this regard, the Church reaffirms the law of subsidiarity, which the school is bound to observe when it cooperates in sex education, by entering into the same spirit that animates the parents. (Pontifical Council for the Family, 1995, s. 43)

Interestingly, this language is mirrored by the Secretary of State's foreword to the DfE guidance which avers: 'We are clear that parents and carers are the prime educators for children on many of these matters. Schools complement and reinforce this role and have told us that they see building on what pupils learn at home as an important part of delivering a good education' (DfE, 2019a, p. 4).

In both its secular and religious guises, the view that parents have a right to direct and shape their children largely derives from the idea that, in most cases, parents will have the best interests of their children at heart and are, due to a special kind of intimate relationship, uniquely well-placed to act on these interests (The Pontifical Council for the Family, 1995). Indeed, parenthood is considered to engender the duty to protect these interests, including by instilling various virtues and acting as a good role model (Catechism of the Catholic Church 2223, n.d.).

Nevertheless, this deference to the rights of parents cannot be unlimited. Children are not the property of their parents to do with what they will; they are human beings in their own right and have their own needs, interests, and entitlements. While childrearing, including the ability to 'contextualise sex education in accordance with [one's] values' (Bialystok & Andersen, 2022, p. 130), will form an important part of many parents' expressive identity when acting *qua* parent,[15] this is necessarily subordinate to the rights of the child. This is a view that is supported by a host of laws and policies; from those prohibiting child abuse to those requiring school-aged children to have some form of education (in school or otherwise). It also seems implicit in the Catholic idea that parenthood is a 'grave responsibility' that should not be taken lightly (CCC 2223, n.d.).[16]

Not only could a policy of unchecked parental power lead to serious physical or emotional harm, but there is a danger that children subject to it may end up (psychological) 'prisoners to the family they happened to be born into' (Bialystok & Andersen, 2022, p. 130), in the sense of being unable to revise their beliefs or values even when the evidence suggests they are untrue or it would otherwise benefit them to do so.

In the context of RSE a further danger posed by a complete lack of constraint on parental authority stems from the fact that most parents are unlikely to have well-developed knowledge and understanding of the broad range of sexual health

---

[15] Parents have their own interests in forming relationships with, bringing up, and shaping their children. For an illuminating discussion of parents' rights and interests, see Brighouse and Swift (2014).

[16] Although this obviously includes a further related duty to God (which is absent from the secular formulation).

and wellbeing issues covered by the subject, or the pedagogical skills necessary to transmit such understanding to children and young people. As Bialystok and Andersen argue, these gaps in knowledge necessitate a more distributed model of authority which enables parents, educators, policymakers, and (as their capacities evolve) children and young people themselves, to share responsibility for the development and implementation of good RSE (ibid.) According to such an approach, while parents will usually be their children's 'first educator', this need not amount to wrongheaded insistence that the authority of parents is unquestionable or that they will always know best.

A further issue with the 'retreat to basics' (Archard, 2000, p. 28) approach advocated by Cates is that it does very little to address difficult questions about what is to count as basic and what should be ruled out because it belongs in the sphere of morals and values (which is, supposedly, the rightful domain of parents). A possible solution to this problem is to sanction teaching only on those fundamental moral precepts that we (regardless of our broader moral framework) can all agree. However, even this is not without tension. For some, the mere mention of the existence of LGBTQ+ people or same-sex relationships strays over this line,[17] while for others the phrase 'it's OK to be gay' simply reflects the reality of living in a liberal democracy in which, amongst other things, same-sex marriage is legally sanctioned and sexuality (including homosexuality and bisexuality) constitutes a protected characteristic (Equality Act, 2010).[18]

A related response to irreducible disagreements about moral questions in RSE involves being what Archard calls 'neutral and comprehensive' (Archard, 2000, p. 31). According to this approach, children and young people should, gradually (and presumably according to their age and developmental stage) be made aware of 'the full range of possible sexual activities' in a way 'which does not beg any moral questions' (ibid.) For example, if teaching about same-sex relationships, one might explain that some regard sexual activity between members of the same sex (or outside of marriage) to be sinful, whereas others 'regard it as a perfectly legitimate choice of sexual activity on the same moral footing as heterosexual sex.' (ibid., p. 32) RSE taught in this way mirrors the teaching of non- confessional Religious Education (RE); namely, by considering a range of options in an objective manner but not attempting to direct children to accept one as correct. This too raises difficult questions, not least about how broad to draw the boundaries pertaining to the kinds of sexual activity that ought to be discussed. As Archard puts it:

> Could one really countenance an education which merely informed children that "some people believe necrophilia to be an abhorrent and perverse violation of the dead; others, on the other hand, view it as an odd sexual taste which harms no-one living"? (ibid.)

---

[17] For example, in the High Court case pertaining to the Birmingham protests, the defendants argued that the 'teaching of LGBT issues… [represented] unlawful discrimination against British Pakistani Muslim children… and those with parental responsibility for them'(Birmingham CC v Afsar (No 3) [2019], para. 37).

[18] Under the Equality Act 2010, these characteristics include sex, race, religion or belief, sexual orientation and gender reassignment.

This is clearly an extreme example. However, some of the material deemed objectionable in the *New Social Covenant Unit* report (2023a) commissioned by Miriam Cates includes references to masturbation, oral and anal sex. These are practices which the report appears to suggest are (or should be) outside the norm and are thus not suitable for RSE, perhaps not even if taught in the neutral manner suggested above.

Given that, whatever one's moral stance on these acts, the prevalence of oral and anal sex in particular appears to be on the rise amongst younger age groups (Lewis et al., 2017; Hirst et al., 2023) combined with the potential risks to health and wellbeing associated with these practices (Burki, 2011; Gana & Hunt, 2022), it would seem that a decision to leave them out of the curriculum altogether risks leaving young people (LGBTQ+ youth included) potentially in the dark with respect to topics which are increasingly likely to have an impact on their sexual lives. Worse still, it threatens to leave a vacuum that, instead of balanced, fact-based information provided by experts, will be filled by misinformation and half-truths gleaned from peers and online pornography.[19]

It would seem that, even if it is important to retain the aim that aspects of RSE are as objective as possible (e.g., statements of scientific fact), it would be both foolish and undesirable to attempt to deliver a subject that is 'neutral all the way down'(Archard, 2000, p. 33). Many of the questions that will be considered in the context of RSE are necessarily value-laden—they relate to what constitutes a good life and the implications this has for how we ought to treat others. And, while some might wish to suggest this area of influence ought to be the sole dominion of parents, this cannot be assumed. It is a sad fact that the interests of parents and their children do not always align, but also that parents may not have the expertise nor the inclination to pass on accurate information which reflects the plurality of reasonable views that exist on sexual (and indeed other forms of) morality, or the range of issues that may affect the sexual health or wellbeing of their child. Further, while some parents take their role as moral educators seriously, others may neglect it entirely. As Halstead and Reiss put it:

> If children are not given direct guidance and help in school but are left to pick up their values as and when they can, this may leave them open to manipulation at the hands of those less concerned for their wellbeing than the school is'. (Halstead & Reiss, 2003, p. 24)

On this basis, we can begin to see how the educational goods approach offers a framework by which to determine what should go on the RSE curriculum, how this should be taught and to whom. Although there will be a presumption that parents will want what is best for their child and will (usually) be uniquely placed to determine what that is, in line with the distributed model of power suggested by Bialystok and Andersen, the state will have a duty to ensure that each child receives the basic package of educational goods necessary to become a good citizen who is capable of navigating and sustaining positive personal relationships by making informed,

---

[19] For a review of the literature on the impact of pornography on the sexuality and behaviour of young people, see Massey et al. (2020).

self-regarding decisions on these matters. To do this, individuals will need to be provided with not only factual information (from the names of body parts to the types of contraception that are available, from pregnancy options to the different ways in which people understand their gender and/or sexuality), they will also need to develop their critical faculties, their empathy, and their moral consciousness—the dispositions (indeed, virtues) necessary to distinguish fact from fiction and to choose wisely and authentically which life path they wish to follow.

There will undoubtedly be ongoing disputes about the best way to deliver this package of goods. Amongst other things, this seems likely to include debates over when to teach certain topics so as not to impinge on the ability of children to enjoy the (non-educational) good of childhood innocence.[20] Nevertheless, it seems reasonably uncontroversial to suggest that, at the very least, RSE lessons that adhere to the educational goods model will need to discuss the diverse range of families and, at the appropriate juncture, sexualities, evident in society and that this must, therefore, contain some reference to LGBTQ+ people.

Less clear is what the admission that RSE must include some form of moral education means for the view the subject ought to be taught from a particular religious perspective and the extent to which this can alter LGBTQ+ inclusive teaching. Does it, as the UK Government appears to have decided in the context of England, really necessitate faith-based exemptions that allow what can be seen as quite strongly partisan forms of RSE? Or is the best way to realise the distinctive package of goods the subject is designed to promote via the more pluralistic version favoured in Wales?

In the next section, drawing on examples from Catholic education, I will analyse the impact that faith-based exemptions to RSE policy can have and suggest the problems they generate mean that such carve-outs should not be tolerated in the context of state schools in liberal democracies. However, in the final section I go on to explain why this may not be an insurmountable issue for religiously-minded educators who are keen to provide an RSE curriculum that authentically articulates and introduces children and young people to a faith.

The Problem with Faith-Based Exemptions to RSE Regarding RSE

In England and Wales the Catholic Bishops published a guidance document, *Relationship and Sex Education in Catholic Schools*, which is organised around a set of 10 frequently asked questions (FAQs). Tellingly, the first two of these questions relate not to RSE itself, but to the purpose of Catholic education and the reason the Church has its own schools (Bishops' Conference of England and Wales, 2020, p. 1).

---

[20] Although, as the recent IICSA (2021) report into child sexual abuse illustrates, we should be cognisant that there is a line between nurturing innocence and fostering ignorance. Allowing the latter to thrive can be just as (if not more) harmful as stripping away the former too soon (see also Wareham, 2022, p. 720).

The reader is told that the purpose of Catholic education is 'the formation of disciples of Jesus Christ' and Catholic schools exist to 'assist in [the Church's] mission of making Christ known to all people' as well as to 'assist parents… in the education and religious formation of their children' (ibid.). This firmly anchors Catholic education around parental rights.

This guidance makes it quite clear that, while 'a fundamental principle of Catholic education is the formation of the whole person' and RSE is deemed 'an important part of this holistic approach' (ibid.), the subject is very much a vehicle for teaching the faith. There are sections in which the need to produce other educational goods is explicitly recognised.[21] For instance, the response to the question about Catholic schools also notes that RSE plays a 'vital role in keeping children safe' from the 'dangers of the modern world' (ibid.) However, not only is there a sense that these 'dangers' are somehow external to the Catholic community[22] or arise because of a failure to remain faithful to Church teachings, but also that this aim is subordinate to the formation of good Catholic Christians.

At a practical level, this is rendered problematic simply by the demographics of Catholic schools. According to the recent CES census data, only 58.5% of the pupils attending Catholic schools and colleges in England identify as Catholic[23] (CES, 2022, p. 19) and while most of these pupils (46.7%) are from other Christian backgrounds, nearly a third (27.7%) have no religion and 10.9% are Muslim (ibid., p. 21). It seems clear that the purpose of the Catholic school is not to convert these pupils to Catholicism. Indeed, while 'the Church Fathers of Vatican II gave the invitation to non-Catholics, Christian and non-Christian alike, to send their children to Catholic schools' (Donlevy, 2007, p. 295), the view that parents are the primary educators of their children read in tandem with the declarations in Sects. 2 and 10 of Vatican II's *Dignitatis Humanae* that 'the human person has a right to religious freedom' and 'no one is to be forced to embrace the Christian faith against his own will.' (Vatican Council II, 1965b) suggests that evangelisation is not considered a priority in this context.

However, setting aside the growing issue of non-Catholic students attending Catholic schools in England and Wales,[24] the claim that the purpose of RSE in Catholic schools involves 'preferentially [promoting] the Church's teaching on the

---

[21] Here it is worth acknowledging that living one's life according to the tenets of a faith may well be conducive to the good of personal fulfilment. However, as I have argued elsewhere (Clayton et al., 2018; Wareham, 2018), the threat to autonomy posed by conscripting children into a particular worldview means that children should be taught about religion non-directively, especially since autonomy is itself a contributory factor to such fulfilment.

[22] A view that clearly flies in the face of the evidence. See for example the Independent Inquiry into Child Sexual Abuse report on Child protection in religious organisations and settings (IICSA, 2021).

[23] In independent schools, this figure falls to just 30% (compared to 59.8% in state funded schools and colleges).

[24] 2021 marked the first Census of England and Wales in which fewer than half the population (46.2%) said they were 'Christian'. The biggest rise was in those with 'No religion', who now make up 37.2% (ONS, 2023a). In light of this trend, the question of how to appropriately accommodate pupils from non-Catholic backgrounds in Catholic schools is likely to remain a pressing one.

dignity of the human person and the sanctity of life' (Bishops' Conference of England and Wales, 2020, p. 2) suggests that it is religious ideology rather than the need to provide accurate information that is driving the subject.

To illustrate how this can go wrong in practice, consider the case of *A Fertile Heart*, a Catholic RSE resource produced by a group of priests from the dioceses of Birmingham, Cardiff, Clifton, and Shrewsbury. The programme, launched in 2019, was originally mandated by the Archdiocese of Cardiff for use in all its schools (which straddle England and Wales). A textbook aimed at secondary pupils included the claim that men are 'initiators' and women are 'receiver-responders' in sexual relationships. It also stated that the contraceptive pill is morally dangerous and prevents young women from understanding their fertility and femininity, and that gay people cannot legitimately marry and must, therefore, abstain from sex (AFH, 2019). Ultimately, the resource was condemned by the DfE on the basis it contained 'gender stereotypes' that 'could normalise non-consensual behaviour or encourage prejudice' (Gibb, 2021). In a letter to MP Jesse Norman, whose constituency, Hereford and South Herefordshire, is in the Archdiocese, Schools Minister Nick Gibb also stated the resource included information about contraception that was 'inaccurate and appears to be included to alarm pupils' (ibid.)

A secondary school that was teaching using the resource in Hereford was also forced to 'change the language' in order to pass an Ofsted inspection and ensure compliance with equality law (Humanists UK, 2021). Nevertheless, in its defence of the resource the Archdiocese simply stated it was 'shaped by the Catholic understanding of the human person and human relationships and sexuality, and authentically [reflected] Catholic teaching' (Garcia, 2021).

Other religious organisations, such as Lovewise, the Society for the Protection of the Unborn Child (SPUC) and LIFE, that operate in the RSE space have also been found to promulgate what can be considered pseudoscience about abortion and contraception (Humanists UK, 2012). Indeed, recently, The *Faculty of Sexual and Reproductive Healthcare* (FSRH) and the *Royal College of Obstetricians and Gynaecologists* (RCOG) launched a factsheet on abortion and abortion care, the primary motivation for which was to counter the spread of 'junk science' on the subject in many schools (FSRH/RCOG, 2021).

The problem with these distortions to content is not only that they lead children and young people to believe untruths that could have negative implications for their sexual health. There are also ramifications for wellbeing (including mental wellbeing) more generally. This is particularly the case if there are instances of narrow or discriminatory teaching on LGBTQ+ issues, including in the context of discussions about marriage.

The proportion of LGBTQ+ people is on the increase, particularly amongst younger age-groups. According to the 2021 Census, 6.91% of people in England and Wales aged 16–24 now identifies as lesbian, gay or bisexual—making people in this demographic more than twice as likely to be LGB than the overall population. 1% of people in this age group identify as trans (compared to 0.54% of the overall population) (ONS, 2023b, 2023c).[25] Furthermore, despite religious prohibitions on homosexual relationships (at least as far as orthodox interpretations are concerned), many religious people, including Catholics, will grow up to be LGBTQ+.[26]

The evidence suggests that the manner in which LGBTQ+ young people are treated by their peers and teachers has a significant influence on their mental health, wellbeing and educational outcomes. For instance, Bradlow et al. (2017) found that 45% of LGBT pupils aged 11–19 (including 64% *trans* pupils) had been bullied for being LGBT at school. As a result, 40% had skipped school, and 52% felt that the bullying had had 'a negative effect on their plans for future education'. Perhaps more concerningly, of those surveyed 84% of *trans* and 61% of LGB young people had self-harmed, and 45% of trans young people had attempted to take their own life (compared to 22% of LGB young people) (Bradlow et al., 2017). These alarming findings are further supported by a 2019 US study by Kosciw et al., which found LGBTQ+ students were more likely to miss school and to have lower grades than their non-LGBTQ+ peers (Kosciw et al., 2019, p. xxi).

In Bradlow et al.'s survey, 40% of respondents said they were 'never taught anything about LGBT issues at school' and 53% said there was not 'an adult at school they [could] talk to about being LGBT' (Bradlow et al., 2017). Although, in the intervening years, the introduction of compulsory RSE may already have gone some way to ameliorate this situation—a wide-ranging review of the evidence on comprehensive sex education by Goldfarb and Lieberman (2021) examined three decades of research, much of which supports the view that, when taught in an inclusive way, RSE enhances attitudes that promote gender equality and contribute to better mental health.

From this small snapshot of evidence, it seems clear that a curriculum which surrenders too much ground to anti-LGBTQ+ positions, for instance by failing to include LGBTQ+ lives within the subject content or by doing so in a negative way, risks being actively harmful to young LGBTQ+ people. It is also likely to damage the ability of non-LGBTQ+ pupils to treat all others as equals in a diverse society.

In fairness, it should be noted that cases where religion has distorted (or attempted to distort) the RSE curriculum are far from limited to Catholic schools.[27] Nevertheless, the strong emphasis on promoting fidelity to the official teaching of the Church in a system where compliance is decided by the local Diocesan Bishop may make Catholic schools particularly vulnerable to the problem.

Of course, not all (or even the majority) of Catholic schools will use resources like *A Fertile Heart*.[28] Many will use or adapt the model curriculum produced by the CES.

---

[25] Both questions were voluntary. However, 92.5% of those aged 16 and over answered the sexual orientation question and 94% answered the question on gender identity (ONS, 2023b, 2023c).

[26] For some fascinating first person accounts of the experiences of LGBTQ+ religious people see Richardson (2019).

[27] I examine some of these cases, including the Charedi Jewish schools where parents were pressurised to exercise their right to withdraw(mentioned above), in more detail elsewhere (Wareham, 2022).

[28] Although it is difficult to ascertain how widespread use of the resource is, the DfE appear to think only one English secondary school is using it. Most of the schools listed as using AFH on its own

At secondary level, this says pupils should be taught about a comprehensive range of issues and emphasises the need to offer 'a broad and balanced RSE programme which provides [pupils] with factual scientific information when relevant and meets the statutory requirements placed on schools' (CES, 2019a, p. 2). It underscores the need to teach about 'equalities legislation, including the Marriage (Same Sex Couples Act, 2013)' and makes it clear that 'discriminatory language and behaviour' including that which is homophobic and transphobic 'is unacceptable, explicitly referencing the protected characteristics in the Equality Act (CES, 2019a, p. 11). At primary level, which also has provisions on a broad and balanced curriculum, the model curriculum mentions 'similarities and differences between people' that 'arise from several different factors' and highlights the Equality Act. No references are made to homophobia or transphobia, but the section on personal relationships for Early Years and Foundation Stage (EYFS) and Key Stage 1 (KS1) states pupils should be taught that 'there are different family structures and these should be respected' (CES, 2019b, p. 7).

The CES model curriculum is far superior to *A Fertile Heart* and, taught in the right way, could well help to cultivate a wide range of important educational goods. Nonetheless, because of the way Church teachings are foregrounded and expressed as truths (rather than as what the Church takes to be true), this model could still generate quite a restrictive (and potentially indoctrinatory) RSE programme. To illustrate, on the topic of personal relationships at Key Stages 3 and 4, we are told that pupils should be taught 'about diversity in sexual attraction and developing sexuality, including sources of support and reassurance and how to access them' (CES, 2019a, p. 8). Elsewhere, multiple references make it clear that (sacramental) marriage is deemed the (only) proper context for sexual relations (e.g., where we are told that pupils should be taught that 'sexuality is a God-given gift and that sexual intercourse is the most intimate expression of human love and should ideally be delayed until marriage', p. 3). Doubtless these issues could be discussed in a way that makes it clear what the Church teaches while also emphasising this position is not 'the only game in town'.

However, there remains the danger that these matters could also be taught in manner that focuses on the purported sinfulness of homosexual relationships; one that—although it may go as far as to explain such relationships are permitted by law and, by dint of their inherent dignity as human beings (ibid., p. 7), people in such relationships are entitled to equal respect[29]—deems them worthy of strong moral censure. Not only does the one-sided nature of this approach deserve the label 'indoctrination'—because it involves the transmission of a belief about which reasonable people disagree as unquestionably true—it also makes autonomous decision-making about

---

website (AFH, 2023) are based in Wales where, under the new curriculum, RSE provision taught in this way would now be unlawful.

[29] This is what political liberals might refer to as 'recognition respect', that is, 'a reciprocal positive regard owed to all persons in virtue of their status as free and equal citizens, regardless of characteristics such as sex, race, and sexual orientation'. As Christina Easton puts it, 'this respect extends to individuals who you believe have made poor life choices and are mistaken in their beliefs about religious and ethical matters' (Easton, 2023, p. 4).

the good life a more difficult prospect. This is because it fails to furnish pupils with a wide enough range of ideas about what this might mean. One might also conclude that, despite attempts to 'love the sinner and hate the sin', such an approach is likely to result in feelings of guilt and shame about same-sex attraction—feelings which are apt to stymie one's ability to live a flourishing life and alienate LGBTQ+ youth from the Church (Hillier & Harrison, 2004; McDermott, Roen & Scourfield, 2008). Indeed, Christina Easton argues that the harms caused by the feelings of guilt and shame associated with a lack of LGBTQ+ 'approval', as opposed to mere 'respect', give political liberals good *prima facie* reasons to treat the latter as a basic moral precept of the kind that may legitimately be taught directively (Easton, 2023).

Furthermore, as Henry's contribution to this volume (Henry, 2023) highlights, the narrow, monolithic approach enumerated above overlooks the fact that there are a variety of views on matters of sexual ethics *within* the Catholic tradition (and indeed other religious traditions).[30] It conveniently forgets that dissent—conceived of as 'the liminal space and action where one awkwardly retains full membership in a group while also sitting apart from the lead attitudes in that group'(McDonough, 2012, p. 172)—can be a space in which criticism is an act of loyalty rather than subversion (ibid., p. 15). If, instead of promoting one perspective to the exclusion of all others, this diversity of viewpoints can be acknowledged and explored, it seems this will not only provide children and young people attending Catholic schools with a real opportunity to develop an authentic religious faith (rather than having that faith imposed upon them), but also open up a space for a fuller kind of LGBTQ+ acceptance within the school community.

This brief survey of approaches to faith-based RSE demonstrates that religious adaptations to policy may tacitly license (or appear to license) teaching which limits the production of important educational goods, including autonomy, the ability to form and sustain healthy personal relationships, and to treat one another as fully equal. These exemptions could potentially also lead faith educators to distort or cherry-pick facts in order to serve their religious ideology, instead of ensuring that students are provided with more objective, evidence-based information.

On this basis, even if the removal of legal concessions was likely to have a negative impact on the ability of religious schools to provide RSE that complied with the tenets of their faith, it would nevertheless be legitimate to argue for their removal. This is particularly the case in the context of state-funded schools which are public institutions that are directly answerable to the wider community and should, therefore, only symbolise and enact values upon which reasonable people can agree.[31]

---

[30] Henry explores the resources 'queer theologies' might offer Catholic education in terms of 'overly disembodied approaches to questions of sexuality, gender, and education' and suggests they can provide 'alternative, more expansive, understandings of LGBTQ+ and religious subjectivities that foreground the agency of queer people' (Henry, 2023, p. 9).

[31] Given the importance of educational goods, both to individuals and the community as a whole, there is, I think, also good reason to prevent private schools from distorting or omitting information from the RSE curriculum in the way faith-based carve-outs allow. Indeed, the notion that there is a fundamental need to receive RSE is already reflected in policy by the fact that the subject has been

As noted above, the need to cultivate the distinctive package of goods developed by RSE should also prompt us to remove the parental right to withdraw children from such lessons. As illustrated by the changes in Wales, this is a move which, from a purely legal perspective, necessitates that (state) schools avoid the kind of religious indoctrination which is prohibited by Article 2 of the First Protocol (A2P1) of the *European Convention on Human Rights*[32] and thus the *Human Rights Act 1998* (HRA, 1998). However, the absence of individual exemptions on grounds of conscience also strengthens the moral argument for RSE teaching that is objective, critical, and pluralistic as, in a situation where there is no escape from such teaching, it is especially vital that the identities, values, and beliefs of all pupils are fully recognised and respected.[33]

Conclusions: Faith-Sensitive RSE?

If one accepts the view that RSE should nurture educational goods, then policies designed to limit access to pluralistic, fact-based information about sex and relationships on faith grounds cannot be adequately justified.

On this issue, appeals to freedom of religion or belief will not do. Essentially, such appeals ask policymakers to restrict the freedoms of one group of more vulnerable people (children) in order to advance them for another, more powerful, group (adults). This actively undermines the very right it purports to protect. This is not to say that parents should not enjoy the right to pass on their faith in the home.[34] However, it is so important for policymakers to safeguard children's access to the valuable educational goods produced by RSE, that it is incumbent upon them to guarantee access to these lessons for all children regardless of the religious affiliation of parents.

Given the avowed purpose of Catholic schools laid out in the Catholic Church documents discussed above, some may see the removal of faith-based exemptions as a serious threat to authentically Catholic RSE and as such something that will dilute Catholic education in a harmful way. As a non-Catholic, I cannot pretend to have the theological understanding necessary to ascertain the extent to which this is the case. Nevertheless, while the position I advocate opposes the kind of

---

made part of the 'basic curriculum' for all schools, including private schools (for further discussion see Wareham, 2022, p. 717).

[32] For further information on the application of A2P1 (otherwise known as the right to education) see European Court of Human Rights (2021).

[33] Despite the changes to the law in Wales, it is not clear that the Church has taken the demand for objective, critical, pluralistic RSE fully on board. The CES's non statutory guidance on the Curriculum for Wales still advocates for a subject that foregrounds the 'Church's vision of human wholeness' (CES, n.d.) and is vague about how Catholic RSE that accords with the RSE Code and Guidance will differ from more traditional faith- based models of the subject.

[34] Although I do think it is true to say that parents do not have the moral right to unquestioningly inculcate their children into a particular worldview, I concur with Tillson (2019) that attempts to legally enforce such a policy would be thoroughly indefensible.

faith-orientated RSE that would result from using a resource like AFH or a more authoritarian interpretation of the model curriculum, I do not think a prohibition on faith-based exemptions to content need concern all religiously-minded educators.

The thrust of the analysis and argument of this chapter, which is reflected in the provisions of human rights law, is that good RSE will necessarily include religion and belief perspectives. In fact, as I put it elsewhere, 'the relevant package of educational goods will only be generated if the subject is provided in a way that is sufficiently attentive to the plurality of views that exist on matters of sexual ethics' (Wareham, 2022, p. 720). Good RSE must not only be *faith sensitive* (Sell & Reiss, 2021), but will take full and proper account of all of the relevant particularities of learners (including background, belief, values, identity and the broader community context). In other words, it will be *student sensitive* (ibid.) Here it is worth pointing out that the CES guidance for both England and Wales refers to RSE that is 'sensitive to the needs of individual pupils' (e.g. CES, 2019a, p. 1; CES, n.d., p. 7). However, it is important to appreciate that the sensitivity demanded in the context of student sensitive RSE involves more than mere awareness of difference; it requires genuine support and acceptance of students which is not exhibited in the context of a classroom where the underlying aim is to inculcate or promote one perspective.

As the changes taking place in Wales illustrate, faith-based exemptions to RSE are not actually required to enable teachers to focus on the teachings of a religious tradition. Catholic schools may prioritise discussion of Catholic perspectives, as long as the attention given to other viewpoints remains proportional and these alternatives are treated with equal respect.[35] To be sure, owing to the need for objectivity, no religious position (including a Catholic one) may be taught as true, indeed only basic morality which passes the test for public reasonableness may be taught directively. However, it is a matter of debate whether a traditionally confessional approach is necessary to authentic Catholic education. Along with Henry (2023) and McDonough's (2012) views on the importance of diversity and dissent, Whittle's theory of Catholic education—which sees it not as a means to create Catholics, but instead as a way of bringing pupils to the 'threshold of theology' through encounters with 'mystery' (Whittle, 2015, 2016)—demonstrates that there are non-confessional forms of Catholic education which could be accommodated in a faith—and student-sensitive RSE framework. Similar 'priming pedagogies' (Wareham, 2018; Wareham, 2024) can also be identified within the broader Christian tradition (e.g., Cooling et al., 2016).

Although it is an open question whether these religiously distinctive but non-directive forms of pedagogy can bear (authentic) fruit in the context of RSE (be that in Catholic or other religious traditions), the importance of granting all children access to comprehensive lessons on relationships and sexuality, which are fact-based, pluralistic, and properly inclusive of LGBTQ+ people, puts the onus on religiously-minded educators to consider this issue more deeply. Faith-based exemptions to RSE must become a thing of the past because they could lead to distortions and omissions in vital content and leave young people potentially ill equipped for their future lives

---

[35] For a discussion of what this means in the related context of religious education, see Juss (2016).

and relationships. However, this proposal should not necessarily be seen as a threat to the religiously-minded educator. Instead, it represents an exciting opportunity for more creative practice that simultaneously promotes the wellbeing of all children and young people.

References

AFH. (2019). *A fertile heart: Receiving and giving creative love stone*. Panda Press.
AFH. (2023). Schools. *Fertile heart* [online]. Available from: https://fertileheart.org.uk/schools/. Accessed March 24, 2023.
Archard, D. (2000). *Sex education*. Impact, 2000 (7): vii–47 [online]. Available from: https://onlinelibrary.wiley.com/toc/2048416x/2000/2000/7. Accessed March 15, 2023.
Bartlett, N. (2019). 21 MPs who voted against teaching kids about gay families. *The Mirror*, 28 March 2019, [online]. Available from: https://www.mirror.co.uk/news/politics/21-mps-who-voted-against-14198149. Accessed March 20, 2023.
Bialystok, L., & Andersen, L. M. F. (2022). *Touchy subject: The history and philosophy of sex education*. University of Chicago Press.
Birmingham CC v Afsar (No 3) [2019] EWHC 3217 (QB) [online]. Available from: https://www.judiciary.uk/wp-content/uploads/2019/11/Birmingham-CC-v-Afsar-No-3-2019-EWHC-3217-QB-Final.pdf. Accessed March 24, 2023.
Bishops' Conference Department of Education and Formation. (2020). *Relationship and sex education in Catholic Schools* [online]. Available from: https://catholiceducation.org.uk/images/RSE_in_Catholic_Schools.pdf. Accessed March 20, 2023.
Bradlow, J., Bartram, F., Guasp, A., & Jadva, V. (2017). *School Report: The experiences of lesbian, gay, bi and trans young people in Britain's schools in 2017* [online]. Stonewall. Available from: https://www.stonewall.org.uk/system/files/the_school_report_2017.pdf . Accessed April 5, 2022.
Brighouse, H., & Swift, A. (2014). *Family values: The ethics of parent-child relationships*. Princeton University Press.
Brighouse, H., Ladd, H., Loeb, S., & Swift, A. (2018). *Educational goods: Values, evidence, and decision-making*. University of Chicago Press.
Burki, T. (2011). 'Is oral sex safe?' *Lancet Oncology*; London, Vol. 12, Iss. 3 (11 March 2011), p. 223.
Busby, E. (2019). 'LGBT+ protests: Demonstrations spread to primary school in Nottingham', *Independent*, 23 July 2019, [online]. Available from: https://www.independent.co.uk/news/education/education-news/lgbt-protests-nottingham-fernwood-primary-school-birmingham-amir-ahmed-a9016741.html. Accessed March 20, 2023.
Callan, E. (1997). *Creating citizens*. Oxford University Press.
Callan, E., & Arena, D. (2009). Indoctrination. In: H. Siegel (Ed.), *The Oxford handbook of philosophy of education*. Oxford University Press.
Cates, M. (2023). Stop sex-education radicals from infiltrating schools'. *The Telegraph*, March 8, 2023 [online].
Catechism of the Catholic Church 2223. (n.d.) [online]. Available from: http://www.catholic-catechism.com/ccc_2214-2231.htm. Accessed March 20, 2023.
Catechism of the Catholic Church 2357. (n.d.) [online]. Available from: http://www.catholic-catechism.com/ccc_2357.htm. Accessed March 20, 2023.
CES. (2019a). *A model Catholic secondary RSE curriculum* [online]. Available from: https://catholiceducation.org.uk/schools/relationship-sex-education. Accessed March 24, 2023.
CES. (2019b). *A model Catholic primary RSE curriculum* [online]. Available from: https://catholiceducation.org.uk/schools/relationship-sex-education. Accessed March 24, 2023.

CES. (2022). *Catholic education service digest of 2022 census data for schools and colleges in England* [online]. Available from: https://cescensus.org.uk/downloads/CensusDigestEngland2022.pdf. Accessed March 20, 2023.

CES. (n.d.). *Curriculum for Wales: Supporting non-statutory guidance for Catholic schools* [online]. Available from: https://www.catholiceducation.org.uk/guidance-for-schools/item/download/76768_b181001740d2ce8b7e79f7010ed8550d. Accessed March 24, 2023.

Colburn, B. (2010). *Autonomy and liberalism.* Routledge.

Clayton, M., Mason, A., Swift, A., & Wareham, R. (2018). *How to regulate faith schools.* Impact, 2018 (25): 1–49 [online]. Available from: https://onlinelibrary.wiley.com/doi/full/10.1111/2048-416X.2018.12005.x. Accessed April 6, 2022.

Cooling, T., Green, B., Morris, A., & Revell, L. (2016). *Christian faith in English Church schools.* Peter Lang.

CRAE. (2022). *UK implementation of the UN Convention on the Rights of the Child Civil society alternative report 2022 to the UN Committee—England* [online]. Available from: https://crae.org.uk/sites/default/files/fields/download/CRAE_UN-%20CIVIL-SOCIETY-REPORT_22-DIGITAL.pdf

DfE. (2014). *The Equality Act 2010 and schools: Departmental advice for school leaders, school staff, governing bodies and local authorities* [online]. Available from: https://assets.publishing.service.gov.uk/government/uploads/system/uploads/attachment_data/file/315587/Equality_Act_Advice_Final.pdf

DfE. (2019a). *Relationships education, relationships and sex education (RSE) and health education statutory guidance for governing bodies, proprietors, head teachers, principals, senior leadership teams, teachers* [online]. Available from: https://assets.publishing.service.gov.uk/government/uploads/system/uploads/attachment_data/file/1019542/Relationships_EducationRelationships_and_Sex_EducationRSEand_Health_Education.pdf. Accessed February 14, 2023.

DfE. (2019b). Relationships education, relationships and sex education (RSE) and health education: FAQs. *Gov.uk*, April 5, 2019 [online]. Available from: https://www.gov.uk/government/news/relationships-education-relationships-and-sex-education-rse-and-health-education-faqs. Accessed March 20, 2023.

Dojan and Others v. Germany. (2011). [online]. Available from: https://hudoc.echr.coe.int/fre#{%22itemid%22:[%22002-424%22]}. Accessed March 20, 2023.

Donlevy, J. K. (2007). 'Ten dimensions of inclusion: Non-Catholic students in Catholic schools' *Catholic Education: A journal of inquiry and practice.* 10(3). Available at: https://ejournals.bc.edu/index.php/cej/article/view/758. Accessed March 20, 2023.

Easton, C. E. (2023). LGBT-inclusive education in liberal pluralist societies. *Journal of Applied Philosophy.*

EHRC. (2020). *Children's Rights in Great Britain—Submission to the UN committee on the rights of the child* [online]. Available from: https://www.equalityhumanrights.com/sites/default/files/childrens_rights_in_great_britain.pdf. Accessed March 14, 2023.

Equality Act 2010 [online]. Available from: https://www.legislation.gov.uk/ukpga/2010/15/contents. Accessed April 6, 2022.

European Court of Human Rights. (2021). *Guide on Article 2 of Protocol No. 1 to the European convention on human rights: Right to education* [online]. Available from: https://www.echr.coe.int/documents/guide_art_2_protocol_1_eng.pdf. Accessed March 24, 2023.

Ferguson, D. (2019). "We can't give in": the Birmingham schools on the frontline of anti- LGBT protests. *The Guardian*, May 26, 2019 [online]. Available from: https://www.theguardian.com/uk-news/2019/may/26/birmingham-anderton-park-primary-muslim-protests-lgbt-teaching-rights. Accessed March 14, 2023.

FSRH/RCOG. (2021). *Abortion and abortion care fact sheet* [online]. Available from: https://www.fsrh.org/documents/abortion-and-abortion-care-factsheet-2021/?preview=true. Accessed March 17, 2023.

Gana, T, & Hunt, L. M. (2022). Young women and anal sex. *BMJ: British Medical Journal,* 378, 1–2, August, 11 2022.

Garcia, C. (2021). Professor calls on Herefordshire school to axe 'medieval' sex education lessons. *Hereford Times*, 25 March 2021 [online]. Available from: https://www.herefordtimes.com/news/19187716.professor-calls-herefordshire-school-axe-medieval-sex-educationlessons/. Accessed February 24 2024.

Gatchel, R. H. (1972). The evolution of the concept. In: I. Snook (Ed.), *Concepts of indoctrination: Philosophical essays*. Routledge & Kegan Paul.

Gibb, N. (2021). Letter to Jesse Norman MP [online]. Available from: https://humanists.uk/wp-content/uploads/2021-0019914-Jesse-Norman-Fertile-heart-1.pdf. Accessed April 6, 2022.

Goldfarb, E. S., & Lieberman, L. D. (2021). Three decades of research: The case for comprehensive sex education. *Journal of Adolescent Health, 68*(2021), 13–27.

Gwenllian, S. (2021) Statement to Welsh Senedd, March 9, 2021 [online]. Available from: https://record.assembly.wales/Plenary/11183#A65150. Accessed March 14, 2023.

Halstead, J., & Reiss, M. (2003). *Values in sex education: From principles to practice*. Routledge Falmer.

Hand, M. (2020). Two worries about educational goods. *Journal of Philosophy of Education, 54*(5), 1371–1374.

Henry, S. (2023) Queer thriving in Catholic education: The role of queer theologies.

Hillier, L., & Harrison, L. (2004). Homophobia and the production of shame: young people and same sex attraction. *Culture, Health & Sexuality, 6*(1), 79–94.

Hirst, J., Pickles, J., Kenny, M., Beresford, R., & Froggatt, C. (2023). A qualitative exploration of perceptions of anal sex: implications for sex education and sexual health services in England' Culture. *Health and Sexuality, 25*(2), 241–255.

HRA. (1998). Human Rights Act 1998 [online]. Available from: https://www.legislation.gov.uk/ukpga/1998/42/contents. Accessed March 24, 2023.

Humanists UK. (2012). 'Anti-choice group's school presentations spread misinformation about abortion and contraception'. July 20, 2012 [online]. Available from: https://humanists.uk/2012/07/20/news-1083/. Accessed March 21. 2023.

Humanists UK. (2021). 'School forced to amend 'misogynistic' Catholic RSE resource to pass Ofsted inspection', May 28, 2021 [online]. Available from: https://humanists.uk/2021/05/28/school-forced-to-amend-misogynistic-catholic-rse-resource-to-pass-ofsted-inspection/. Accessed March 24, 2023.

Independent Inquiry Child Sexual Abuse (IICSA). (2021). *Child protection in religious organisations and settings* [online]. Available from: https://www.iicsa.org.uk/reports-recommendations/publications/investigation/cp-religious-organisations-settings. Accessed March 16, 2023.

Juss, S. (2016). *High court ruling on religious education: Legal guidance on what it means for local authorities, academies, schools, teachers, agreed syllabus conferences, and SACREs* [online]. Available from: https://humanists.uk/wp-content/uploads/2016-04-28-FINAL-High-Court-ruling-on-Religious-Education-legal-guidance.pdf. Accessed March 24, 2023.

Kjeldsen, B. M., & Pedersen v Denmark (1976). [online]. Available from: https://hudoc.echr.coe.int/fre#{%22itemid%22:[%22001-57509%22]}. Accessed March 6, 2023.

Kosciw, J. G., Clark, C. M., Truong, N. L., & Zongrone, A. D. (2019). *The national school climate survey: The experiences of lesbian, gay, bisexual, transgender, and queer youth in our nation's schools*, GLSEN [online]. Available from: https://files.eric.ed.gov/fulltext/ED608534.pdf. Accessed March 24, 2023.

Lewis, R., Tanton, C., Mercer, C. H., Mitchell, K. R., Palmer, M., Macdowall, W., & Wellings, K. (2017). Heterosexual practices among young people in Britain: Evidence From three national surveys of sexual attitudes and lifestyles. *Journal of Adolescent Health, 61*(2017), 694–702.

Massey, K., Burns, J., & Franz, A. (2020). Young people, sexuality, and the age of pornography. *Sexuality & Culture, 25*, 318–336.

McDermott, E., Roen, K., & Scourfield, J. (2008). Avoiding shame: Young LGBT people, homophobia and self-destructive behaviours. *Culture, Health & Sexuality, 10*(8), 815–829.

McDonough. (2012). *Beyond obedience and abandonment: Towards a theory of dissent in Catholic education*. McGill-Queen's University Press.

New Social Covenant Unit (NSCU). (2023a). *What is being taught in relationships and sex education in our schools?* [online]. Available from: https://www.newsocialcovenant.co.uk/RSE%20BRIEFING%20FINAL%201631%20(IS)_small.pdf. Accessed March 13, 2023.

New Social Covenant Unit (NSCU). (2023b). 'About NSCU'. *NSCU* [online]. https://www.newsocialcovenant.co.uk/about/. Accessed March 23, 2023.

Nye, C. (2019). Jewish schools "pressurise parents to take children out of sex ed lessons". *BBC* [online]. Available from: https://www.bbc.co.uk/news/education-50566453. Accessed March 20, 2023.

O'Neil, R. (2022). Campaigners lose legal challenge against teaching school pupils about gender identity in Wales. *Wales Online*, December 22, 2022 [online]. Available from: https://www.walesonline.co.uk/news/education/campaigners-lose-legal-challenge-against-25817993. Accessed March 20, 2023.

ONS. (2023a). Religion, England and Wales: Census 2021. *Census 2021* [online]. Available from: https://www.ons.gov.uk/peoplepopulationandcommunity/culturalidentity/religion/bulletins/religionenglandandwales/census2021. Accessed March 24, 2023.

ONS. (2023b). Sexual orientation: Age and sex, England and Wales: Census 2021. *Census 2021* [online]. Available from: https://www.ons.gov.uk/peoplepopulationandcommunity/culturalidentity/sexuality/articles/sexualorientationageandsexenglandandwales/census2021. Accessed March 24, 2023].

ONS. (2023c). Gender identity: Age and sex, England and Wales: Census 2021. *Census 2021* [online]. Available from: https://www.ons.gov.uk/peoplepopulationandcommunity/culturalidentity/genderidentity/articles/genderidentityageandsexenglandandwalescensus2021/2023-01-25. Accessed March 24, 2023.

Pew. (2020). How Catholics around the world see same-sex marriage, homosexuality. *Pew research centre* [online]. https://www.pewresearch.org/fact-tank/2020/11/02/how-catholics-around-the-world-see-same-sex-marriage-homosexuality/. Accessed March 15, 2023.

Richardson, S. (2019). *Unorthodox: LGBT+ identity and faith*. Five Leaves Publications.

Sacred Congregation for the Doctrine of the Faith. (1976). *Persona Humana* [online]. Available from: https://www.vatican.va/roman_curia/congregations/cfaith/documents/rc_con_cfaith_doc_19751229_persona-humana_en.html. Accessed March 14, 2023.

Sell, J., & Reiss, M. (2021). Faith-sensitive RSE in areas of low religious observance: Really? *Sex Education, 22*(1), 52–67.

The Pontifical Council for the Family. (1995). *The truth and meaning of human sexuality* [online]. Available from: https://www.vatican.va/roman_curia/pontifical_councils/family/documents/rc_pc_family_doc_08121995_human-sexuality_en.html. Accessed March 20, 2023.

Tillson, J. (2019). *Children, religion and the ethics of influence*. Bloomsbury.

Vatican Council II. (1965a). *Gravissimum Educationis* [online]. Available from: https://www.vatican.va/archive/hist_councils/ii_vatican_council/documents/vat-ii_decl_19651028_gravissimum-educationis_en.html. Accessed March 10, 2023.

Vatican Council II. (1965b). *Dignitatis Humanae* [online]. Available from: https://www.vatican.va/archive/hist_councils/ii_vatican_council/documents/vat-ii_decl_19651207_dignitatis-humanae_en.html. Accessed March 20, 2023.

Wareham, R. J. (2018). *Prohibition, accommodation or transformation? A philosophical investigation into the moral permissibility of faith schools in liberal democratic societies*. Ph.D. Thesis submitted to the University of Birmingham.

Wareham, R. J. (2022). The problem with faith-based carve-outs: RSE policy, religion and educational goods. *Journal of Philosophy of Education., 56*, 707–726.

Wareham, R. J. (2024). 'Non-cognitive religious influence and initiation in Tillson's "children, religion and the ethics of influence". *Journal of Philosophy of Education.*

Welsh Government. (2022). *The curriculum for Wales—Relationships and sexuality education code* [online]. Available from: https://www.gov.wales/sites/default/files/publications/2022-01/curriculum-for-wales-relationships-sexuality-education-code.pdf. Accessed March 13, 2023.

Welsh Government. (2023). Cross-cutting themes for designing your curriculum. *Relationships and sexuality education: Statutory guidance*. [online]. Available from: https://hwb.gov.wales/curriculum-for-wales/designing-your-curriculum/cross-cutting-themes-for-designing-your-curriculum. Accessed March 20, 2023.

Whittle, S. (2015). *A theory of Catholic education*. Bloomsbury Academic.

Whittle, S. (2016). What might a non-confessional theory of Catholic education look like? *Journal of Beliefs & Values, 37*(1), 93–102.

YouGov. (2018). *English, maths, science and computing are the most important school subjects* [online]. Available from: https://yougov.co.uk/topics/politics/articles-reports/2018/02/14/english-maths-science-and-computing-are-most-impor. Accessed March 17, 2023.

YouGov. (2022). *How important is it to teach Sex education at secondary school?* [online]. Available from: https://yougov.co.uk/topics/education/trackers/how-important-is-it-to-teach-sex-education-at-secondary-school. Accessed February 14, 2023.

Zimmerman, J. (2015). *Too hot to handle: A global history of sex education*. Princeton University Press.

Dr. Ruth Wareham is a Lecturer in Philosophy of Education at the University of Birmingham. She was previously Education Campaigns Manager for Humanists UK, where she continues to work as an Education Policy Researcher. Ruth is a qualified primary school teacher and, before entering academia, worked in schools across Birmingham and the West Midlands for six years. Ruth's primary research interests sit at the intersection between religion, belief, and education. She is currently working on a book about the place of faith schools in liberal democracies.

Chapter 13
Conclusion: Queer Thriving in Catholic Education: Progressing the Research Agenda

Seán Henry

Introduction

This volume has collected diverse perspectives on the question of queer thriving in Catholic education. It has sought to explore queer thriving from a variety of educational and theological priorities and vantage points. To my mind, what unites these varying accounts is their core commitment to challenging the opposition often set up between LGBTQ+ and Catholic identities, and with it a commitment to making Catholic educational settings genuinely inclusive for LGBTQ+ staff and students. The volume is replete with examples of this inclusive set of priorities.

In her response to my work, for example, O'Farrell (2023) identifies the potential of queer thriving in Catholic education to turn 'everything upside down and inside out', but in a way that simultaneously 'invites a playful reimagining of the work in Catholic schools, which is energising to those disenfranchised by aspects of current practice.' In this, O'Farrell is realistic around the challenges facing Catholic schools that seek to be inclusive of LGBTQ+ staff and students, but is nonetheless attentive to the value of this in foregrounding other ways of imagining those practices that make up our current contexts.

Kennedy (2023) is similarly attuned to the importance of LGBTQ+ inclusion in Catholic education, calling for the need to cultivate fragile hermeneutical spaces of interruption that curate 'openness to LGBTQ+ lives as opposed to attempting to reconcile them to the precepts of 'traditional' Church teaching.' In this, Kennedy's interpretation of queer thriving is a real pedagogical challenge to institutional structures, calling for a potentially radical departure from the Church's historical approach to LGBTQ+ experiences. Ruth Wareham's response has a similar tenor to Kennedy's

S. Henry (✉)
Edge Hill University, Ormskirk, UK
e-mail: Sean.Henry@edgehill.ac.uk

in that hers is also motivated by the educational good of teaching in an LGBTQ+ inclusive way, even if this inclusion necessitates dissenting from institutionally-endorsed, faith-orientated carve-outs and the primacy of 'parental rights' in these matters.

Whittle's (2023) account begins from a different starting point to Wareham's in his emphasis on the inclusive work he has identified in some Catholic schools in Northern Ireland already. He writes of the primacy of pastoral support structures in many of these settings, and indicates in particular the appetite for more inclusive approaches to subjects like relationships and sexuality education in these contexts. The contributions of De Silva (2023), Sullivan (2023), and Jenkins (2023) are also characterised by a refusal to set into opposition Catholic and LGBTQ+ identities. De Silva and Sullivan both signal the primacy of attending to the specificities of students' lives and perspectives in Catholic school contexts, something Jenkins also points out in her assertion that Catholic schools need to 'privilege the personal situation of the individual child in need over the religious ideals and structures that oppress them.'

This desire to make Catholic education LGBTQ+ inclusive, however, is nonetheless contested across the volume. Indeed, Bernadette Sweetman, in the spirit of the initial impetus that brought Whittle and I to this project, notes the need for Catholic education research to move beyond anti-bullying and pastoral approaches to queer inclusion in Catholic education given their tendency to promulgate the view of LGBTQ+ people 'as one of the marginalised groups on the periphery of a normative core.' In other words, LGBTQ+ inclusion is not quite as straightforward as one would suppose, with important dynamics of power and privilege to be considered in including people of diverse genders and sexualities in Catholic education.

From my perspective there is a potential tension across the chapters in this respect. Many of the authors foreground resources from traditional Catholic theology that can be appealed to in making the case for queer thriving, while others (sometimes in the same instance) bring to the fore aspects of Church tradition that have been historically and to the present day actively deployed by the Church to undermine queer thriving in educational contexts. In this sense, a binary between 'normative' and 'non-normative' approaches to queer thriving risks developing, where some approaches are coded as being 'less apologetic' and 'more radical' than others.

It is this point that brings me to mapping out future directions for research on queer thriving in Catholic education. I emphasise below the importance of pursuing research on queer thriving that challenges, without ignoring, the tensions that exist between normative and non-normative accounts of queer praxis. Building on this, I suggest the need for future research in Catholic education to attend to the complexities of educational encounters that lie in excess of binary logics around sexualities and genders, and turn to queer and trans pedagogical theories as frameworks for engagement in this respect. Finally, I offer some thoughts on the need for future research on queer thriving in Catholic education to reflect more closely on the field's relationship to Catholic theology itself, as well as on the role interfaith dialogue can play in cultivating the conditions for queer thriving in Catholic educational settings.

Future Research Directions

> It is a theology from the margins which wants to remain at the margins ... Terrible is the fate of theologies from the margins when they want to be accepted by the centre! Queer theology strives instead for differentiation and plurality .... (Althaus-Reid & Isherwood, 2004, p. 3)

So write Lisa Isherwood and Marcella Althaus-Reid in reflecting on the relationship between queer theologies and so-called mainstream Christian theologies and traditions. In concluding this volume, Isherwood and Althaus-Reid's note of caution is noteworthy as it signals the need to pursue queer thriving in Catholic education in ways that refuse to kowtow to the heteronormative and cisnormative structures that continue to characterise many Catholic institutions.

In researching queer thriving in Catholic education, keeping Isherwood's and Althaus-Reid's critique in mind is important, lest we fall into an overly sentimental, even amnesiac, approach that glosses over millennia of theological and institutional Church violences against LGBTQ+ people. At the same time, however, in charting future trajectories for Catholic education research, I also suggest that there is a need to move away from parsing approaches to queer inclusion too easily around 'normative'/'non-normative', or 'central'/'marginal' binaries. I make this suggestion, not to discount the realities of heteronormativity and cisnormativity in Church theologies and structures, but rather to caution against appeals to binary thinking altogether, and the spatial imaginaries (of 'inside'/'outside', 'centre'/'margin') that often underpin it.

As queer and trans theorist Hil Malatino argues, appeals to 'the marginality and centricity dyad' characteristic of much recent queer and feminist scholarship risks becoming yoked too closely to 'reductive debates about radicalism and assimilation, in which outsiderhood is too neatly linked to queer radicality' (2019, 210). For Malatino, the too-easy conceptual linking of queer radicality with outsiderhood is inadequate for queer theorising as it does not produce 'as much pragmatic political action and empathic support as it could' (2019, 210). In this vein, Malatino suggests that normative/non-normative binaries presume 'a neat division between normativity and resistance, a division ill-equipped to consider the complex complicities and concessions all subjects are forced to make in late-capitalist, neoliberal milieus' (2019, 210). In other words, such binaries fail to account for the complexities of our lives under systems of power and privilege, and in this way divert our attention away from the actual workings of violent majoritarian practices.

As an alternative to this, Malatino suggests that we focus less on setting up binary distinctions between the normative and non-normative, and more on developing relational ontologies that expose the interconnections between that which has otherwise been coded as 'central', and that which has otherwise been coded as 'marginal'. Thinking with these insights for my purposes, I see Malatino's critique of normative/non-normative binaries as helpful for future research on Catholic education as it calls on researchers to work less within the kinds of categorical and identitarian divides that often shape discourses around Catholicism and LGBTQ+ inclusion, and more on the specificities of religious and LGBTQ+ experiences that expose other ways of relating to, and resisting, heteronormativity and cisnormativity in and beyond the Church.

In tandem with this sensitivity to the flesh-and-blood textures of LGBTQ+ and religious lives, I also think it would be worthwhile for future research on queer thriving to engage more directly with research around queer and trans pedagogical approaches and educational research. Beginning from the assumption that education is situated, embodied and relational, queer and trans pedagogies offer critical accounts of pedagogical practice that are sensitive to the machinations of normative sexualities and genders in schools and beyond, as well as to possibilities for relating to such normativities differently (Britzman, 1995; Keenan, 2017). For research on queer thriving in Catholic education, what makes this kind of approach worthwhile to pursue is that it represents a tradition of pedagogical scholarship that speaks from, with, and to LGBTQ+ communities. This is important for three reasons. Firstly, the voices and experiences of LGBTQ+ students, teachers, and scholars is foregrounded in this scholarship, something that Catholic education research continues to lack (as Sweetman notes in her chapter). Secondly, engaging with queer and trans pedagogical research offers an opportunity for Catholic education research to extend its emerging engagements with Freirean traditions of critical pedagogy (Eick & Ryan, 2014), feminist pedagogy (Cullen, 2011), and anti-racist pedagogy (Brecht, 2019). Finally, engaging with queer and trans pedagogies offers Catholic education research an opportunity to re-orient itself methodologically, moving from a research approach that begins from a position of deference to institutional orthodoxy to a position of openness to LGBTQ+ experiences in classrooms, schools, and beyond.

Relatedly, this methodological point brings me to the bigger question of the relationship between Catholic education research and Catholic theologies. From my reading of Catholic education research, traditional Church theologies are often appealed to as a justification and conceptual cornerstone for arguments for and/or against particular educational interventions, theories, and approaches. We see this across some of the chapters in this volume too, from De Silva's appeal to *Amoris Laetitia* and other Church documents in making the case for an openness to LGBTQ+ staff and students, to Sullivan's reference to scripture in promoting LGBTQ+ student voice: 'I have come that you may have life and have it to the full.' (John 10:10). I draw attention to this, not to suggest that theological resources should not be engaged with in future research on queer thriving in Catholic education (in my earlier chapter I argue that queer theologies offer much food for thought), but rather to emphasise the need to spell out the *educational* basis for committing to queer thriving. In this sense, it would be worthwhile for the Catholic education research community to provide educational rationales for queer thriving, and not only theological ones, and to think about the relationship between theology and education in light of this. This is important, not only in terms of safeguarding Catholic education from being reduced to a merely theological project (Whittle's work [2014] complicates this idea), but also in defending this work against attacks from conservative commentators and critics both within and beyond Catholic communities.

Wareham's work in this volume does this well in its appeal to educational goods, as does Kennedy's in its valorisation of fragile hermeneutical spaces in the context of interruptive pedagogical encounters.

Finally, what has been largely absent from this volume is any meaningful engagement with thinkers or resources from other Christian and wider religious communities. In previous work I have done on these themes, I have engaged with Jewish and Muslim queer theologies as well as Catholic and Christian ones (Henry, 2022a, 2022b). Future research on queer thriving in Catholic education would benefit from interfaith dialogue not only in terms of enriching the intellectual and spiritual life of Catholic education research, but also in terms of expanding the frames of reference that would otherwise contour research around diverse genders and sexualities. Indeed, diverse genders and sexualities are interpreted very differently across and within different religious traditions. In this way, it would be a loss to the Catholic education research community if it were to limit its encounters with these diversities to the boundaries imposed by the logics of natural law theory, the Magisterium, and/ or other Christian, westernized theological and philosophical constructions.

In this vein, engaging in this kind of approach also has the important effect of building solidary coalitions across difference. While it might be a cliché to say that we live in polarizing times, it is nonetheless true: what better way to open up the hearts and souls of others than to encounter them in solidarity across ethical and religious differences? Curating this kind of scholarly encounter is perhaps the most complex challenge facing Catholic education research on queer thriving. This is a challenge that cannot and should not be romanticised, but is nonetheless one worth pursuing if we are to render queer thriving a viable and life-affirming trajectory for Catholic education research in the years to come.

References

Althaus-Reid, M., & Isherwood, L. (Eds.). (2004). *The sexual theologian: Essays on sex, god and politics*. A&C Black.

Brecht, M. (2019). See–judge… act? The role of action in the anti-racist Catholic theological classroom. *Religious Education, 114*(3), 202–213.

Britzman, D. (1995). Is there a queer pedagogy? Or, stop reading straight. *Educational Theory, 45*(2), 151–165.

Cullen, P. (2011). *Daring to desire: Towards a feminist pedagogy of desire in Catholic theology* (Doctoral dissertation, St Mary's University College).

De Silva, V. (2023). In Whittle & Henry (Eds.), *Relationships and sexuality education (RSE) in Catholic post primary schools in Ireland: LGBT+* matters *in a Church that is learning to love*. Springer.

Eick, C. M., & Ryan, P. A. (2014). Principles of Catholic social teaching, critical pedagogy, and the theory of intersectionality: An integrated framework to examine the roles of social status in the formation of Catholic teachers. *Journal of Catholic Education, 18*(1), 26–61.

Henry, S. (2022). 'Why? And how?' Translating queer theologies of sex education. *Sex Education, 22*(1), 7–21.

Henry, S. (2022b). Pedagogies of dissent: Bridging the religion–LGBTQ divide. *Educational Theory*.

Henry, S. (2023). In Whittle & Henry (Eds.), *Queer thriving in Catholic education: The role of queer theologies*. Springer.

Jenkins, C. (2023). In Whittle & Henry (Eds.), *A transgender perspective on concerns about TGNB young people in Catholic schools*. Springer.

Keenan, H. B. (2017). Unscripting curriculum: Toward a critical trans pedagogy. *Harvard Educational Review, 87*(4), 538–556.

Kennedy, D. (2023). In Whittle & Henry (Eds.), *Encounters with LGBTQ+ lives in Catholic schools: A fragile hermeneutical space?—A response to Dr Seán Henry*. Springer.

Malatino, H. (2019). *Queer embodiment: Monstrosity, medical violence, and intersex experience*. University of Nebraska Press.

O'Farrell, C. (2023). In Whittle & Henry (Eds.), *A call to reimagine Catholic education and schooling—A response to Dr Seán Henry*. Springer.

Sullivan, G. (2023). In Whittle & Henry (Eds.), *On the journey to authentic inclusion: One school's experience of empowering student voice to mobilise positive change*. Springer.

Sweetman, B. (2023). What can the adult religious education and faith development project (AREFD) tell us about the research agenda in Catholic education in relation to LGBTQI+ matters? In Whittle & Henry (Eds.), *Relationships and sexuality education in Catholic Schools in Northern Ireland*. Springer.

Wareham, R. (2023). In Whittle & Henry (Eds.), *Faith-sensitive RSE and Catholic schooling: An educational goods approach*. Springer.

Whittle, S. (2014). *A theory of Catholic education*. Bloomsbury Publishing.

Whittle, S. (2023). In Whittle & Henry (Eds.), *Relationships and sexuality education in Catholic schools in Northern Ireland*. Springer.

Dr. Seán Henry is a Lecturer in Education at Edge Hill University. Prior to this, Seán worked as a Postdoctoral Researcher at the Research Centre on Inclusive and Equitable Cultures, Technological University Dublin (2021–2022), and as an Assistant Lecturer in Philosophy of Education at Maynooth University (2019–2021). He currently has a monograph in development entitled *Queer Thriving in Religious Schools*, which offers a queer theory of Jewish, Christian, and Muslim education, and is also in the process of co-editing a special issue on gender and adult education for the journal *Studies in the Education of Adults*. He has published around issues of sexuality, gender, religion, and education in several international, peer-reviewed journals including *Journal of Philosophy of Education*, *Sex Education*, *Educational Theory*, *Ethics and Education*, and *Cambridge Journal of Education*. He currently sits on the advisory board for the International Network of Philosophers of Education, as well as the editorial board for *Ethics and Education*. Throughout his career so far, Seán has contributed to a range of funded research projects. These include projects on: building equitable policy responses to the Covid-19 pandemic; crafting resources for responding educationally to so-called radicalisation and extremism in schools; and designing materials for integrating social justice concerns into higher education teaching. In addition to his research on religion, gender, and sexuality, Seán has started research on the queer pedagogical potential of comedy, and on theories of embodiment and intersectionality more broadly. Before starting his academic career, Seán qualified as a teacher of Religious Education and English.

Index

A
Adult faith development, 6, 113–116, 120
Adult religious education, 115
Agency, 4, 15, 22, 26–28, 30, 31, 36, 44, 46, 87, 91, 138
Althaus-Reid, M., 25–27, 149

B
Binary, 3, 7, 75, 77, 100–103, 107, 110, 148, 149

C
Catechism of the Catholic Church, 10, 36, 93, 125, 130
Catholic church, 4, 9, 59, 78, 110, 139
Catholic Education Service (CES), 2, 107, 109, 129, 134, 137, 139, 140
Cisnormativity, 9, 16, 149, 150
Complementarity, 11, 12, 14, 103
Congregation for Catholic Education, 9, 13, 14, 16, 38, 103, 110, 111
Cornwall, S., 23

E
Educational goods, 7, 124, 127–129, 132–134, 137–140, 148, 151
Educational Guidance in Human Love: Outlines for Sex Education, 13
Embodiment, 4, 8, 18, 25, 32, 95, 101, 152
England, 2, 99, 104, 107, 108, 123–125, 127–129, 133–135, 140
Erickson, J.J., 27
Evangelii Gaudium, 107, 110

F
Faith, 6, 27, 29, 57, 58, 60–62, 102, 105, 113–121, 123–126, 129, 133, 134, 138–140
Faith-based carve outs, 124, 125, 138
Faith-oriented, 6, 124, 126, 140, 148
Faith-sensitive, 6, 124, 139, 140
Familiaris Consortio, 11, 61

G
Gaudium et spes, 10, 11, 61, 78, 108, 110
Gay and lesbian theology, 24
Gender, 3, 4, 7–10, 12–15, 18, 21–23, 25, 28–30, 32, 37, 57, 59, 60, 62, 63, 78–80, 88, 89, 94, 100–110, 112, 114, 118–120, 128, 131, 133, 136, 138, 148, 150–152

H
Hermeneutics, 5, 24, 42
Heteronormativity, 2, 9, 22–30, 149, 150
Humanae vitae, 10, 11

I
Identity, 5, 9, 14, 23, 24, 26, 28–31, 35–38, 42, 43, 49–51, 60, 62, 65, 72, 73, 75, 79, 88, 91, 100–102, 105, 106, 108–110, 117–119, 126, 128, 130, 136, 139, 140, 147, 148
Inclusion, 1–3, 5, 7, 13, 35–37, 50–52, 64, 66, 71, 73–75, 77, 78, 80–82, 84, 88, 117, 147–149

Ireland, 2, 5, 6, 8, 35, 37, 40, 41, 59, 60, 62, 72, 73, 79, 85, 86, 113–116, 120, 122
Isherwood, L., 25, 149

L
Leadership, 8, 52, 69, 73, 90, 98, 110
LGBTQ+, 1–4, 6, 7, 12, 15, 16, 21, 22, 26–28, 30, 31, 35–39, 41, 43–46, 50–52, 82, 85, 97, 98, 125, 126, 128, 131–133, 135, 136, 138, 140, 147–150
Lundy Model of Participation, 5

M
Magisterium, 10–12, 14, 151
Malatino, H., 16, 149
Male and Female He Created Them: Toward a Path of Dialogue on the Question of Gender Theory in Education, 14
Martin, J., 16, 63

N
Normativity, 149, 150
Northern Ireland, 6, 8, 36, 50, 53, 85, 89, 97, 98, 115, 123, 148

P
Parental rights, 7, 123, 125, 126, 129, 134, 139, 148
Pastoral paradigm, 2, 3, 50
Pedagogy of interruption, 28, 42
Persona humana, 10, 11
Pope Francis, 2, 9, 36, 38, 58, 59, 62, 63, 65, 66, 78, 107, 110, 119

Q
Queer, 3, 4, 7, 15, 18, 21–28, 30, 32, 35, 36, 38, 46, 49, 50, 138, 148–150
Queer pedagogy, 8, 18, 32, 152
Queer theology, 3, 4, 16, 22–28, 30, 31, 35, 37, 51, 52, 138, 149–151

Queer theory, 24

R
Relationships and Sexuality Education, 5–8, 50, 57, 60–63, 65, 66, 85–98, 105, 107, 121, 123–140, 148
Religious education, 6, 8, 33, 39, 69, 71, 83, 87, 89, 90, 113–116, 121, 122, 131, 140, 152

S
Sensus fidei, 12, 15
Sex education, 13, 18, 25, 32, 94, 123, 125, 127, 130, 136, 152
Sexuality, 3–5, 7–10, 13, 15, 18, 21, 22, 25, 28–30, 32, 37, 50, 57, 59–63, 88, 91, 93, 97, 105, 109, 128, 131–133, 135, 137, 138, 140, 148, 150–152
Student voice, 5, 71, 72, 74, 75, 77, 80, 82

T
Taylor, C., 73
Thriving, 3, 21, 26, 30, 35, 42, 49
Tonstad, L.M., 25, 28
Trans, 1–3, 9, 12, 13, 16, 21, 24, 64, 99–101, 105, 112, 126, 135, 149
Transgender and Non-binary (TGNB), 6, 99, 100, 102–111
Trans pedagogy, 7, 148, 150

U
United Kingdom, 2, 8, 50, 52, 98, 105, 109, 110, 123, 124, 126–128, 133

V
Vulnerability, 4, 22, 26, 35, 50, 51, 109

W
Wales, 2, 63, 99, 107, 112, 123–127, 133–135, 137, 139, 140

Printed by Printforce, United Kingdom